DECEMBER 1994
WITH COMPLIMENTS
KEN GREENE

IN COBHAMS' COMPANY

Following page
Sir Alan Cobham

IN COBHAMS' COMPANY

Sixty Years of Flight Refuelling Limited

COLIN CRUDDAS

Cobham plc

This book is dedicated to all employees, past and present,
whose skills and dedication have made
Flight Refuelling Ltd a world-renowned company

First published in 1994 by Cobham plc
Brook Road, Wimborne, Dorset BH21 2BJ

Designed & produced by The Dovecote Press Ltd
Stanbridge, Wimborne, Dorset BH21 4JD

ISBN 0 9524488 0 7

Photoset in Palatino by
The Typesetting Bureau, Wimborne, Dorset
Printed and bound by Biddles Ltd
Guildford and Kings Lynn

Contents

Foreword

BY MARSHAL OF THE ROYAL AIR FORCE SIR MICHAEL BEETHAM, GCB, CBE, DFC, AFC, DL, FRAeS.

In the early days of aviation we were blessed with several great pioneering spirits who set out to explore the new frontiers. Some of them had entrepreneurial skills as well, and they founded the great Aviation Companies which established Britain in the forefront of this revolutionary new technology, producing a succession of world-beating aircraft.

They were all men of vision. Alan Cobham was one of them, but he was unique in that he also set his mind to solve the problem of extending aircraft range. His early experiments with aerial refuelling were exciting and imaginative. The Royal Air Force co-operated in these on a trials basis as did the civil authorities, but neither adopted the system operationally at the time. This was a pity for, with hindsight, it could have been used to great advantage in World War II and in particular to close the air gap over the mid-Atlantic in that vital battle against the U-boat. It was not until the 1950s that it was seen by the United States Air Force to give them the operational reach they were seeking, and they then adopted air-to-air refuelling in a big way.

The Royal Air Force picked up the ball soon after and I was privileged to command No. 214 Valiant Squadron which did the full in-Service development trials. Today in the Royal Air Force the Tanker Fleet is a tremendous 'force multiplier' and has proved its worth in the Falklands and Gulf Wars and in all our many other operations. Air-to-air refuelling has given us rapid deployment, longer endurance and extended range. It has truly transformed our combat capability.

This story however, is not simply about the art of refuelling in flight — for it embraces many of the highly innovative and diverse tasks undertaken by Flight Refuelling Limited during the past 60 years. It describes, for example, how the development of airborne fuel system equipment, accelerated by the introduction of pressure refuelling in the late Forties, played a key role in the Company's success. Much is seen to be owed too, to the work carried out by Cobham's team during the Berlin Airlift and, later, on the many hundreds of Meteor aircraft that passed through Tarrant Rushton's workshops for overhaul and major repair. Flight Refuelling Limited has also had a long association with remotely-piloted aircraft, ranging from the unmanned drone Meteor variants of the Fifties, to the Falconet high-speed target, and Phoenix battlefield surveillance air vehicle in quantity production at Wimborne today.

In Cobhams' Company traces vividly the progress of Flight Refuelling Limited, from its founding by Sir Alan Cobham in 1934 to its present position within Cobham plc, of which Michael Cobham is Chairman.

The book makes fascinating reading and I commend it to you.

Preface

BY MICHAEL COBHAM, CBE, MA (BARRISTER), FRAeS, CIMgt

1994 is not only the Diamond Jubilee of Flight Refuelling Limited, but it is also the centenary of the birth of the founder of the company – my father, Sir Alan Cobham.

It occurred to my colleagues and to me that this dual anniversary should be marked by something more permanent than a celebration, no matter how prestigious that event might be. Thus it was decided to produce a history of Flight Refuelling which would include a résumé of my father's career in aviation prior to his forming the company in 1934.

From 1934 to 1964 my father was Managing Director and from 1954 to 1969 Chairman of the Company. During those years Flight Refuelling acquired a distinct character which reflected my father's personal beliefs and strongly held opinions on management in general, and on industrial relations in particular. As well as being a truly outstanding leader of men, he was a man of extraordinary energy, enormous enthusiasm and of remarkable vision – a true pioneer aviator as well as a pioneer of the aircraft industry.

Since 1964 I have, as Managing Director and from 1969 as Chairman and until 1992 as Chief Executive, had the privilege and great good fortune to have been a member of the team which managed and directed Flight Refuelling, and subsequently created the FR Group. For me they have been interesting, frequently exciting and always rewarding years.

The writing of this book has entailed a vast amount of research in both my father's and in the Company's archives, and as no history of Flight Refuelling Ltd would be complete without a background description of its sister companies, a special section has been devoted to the evolution of the FR Group, now Cobham plc. I am grateful for this opportunity to thank and to congratulate my friend and colleague, Colin Cruddas, who, in the face of this very daunting task, has produced such a fascinating and readable account of the Company's first sixty years.

Acknowledgements

This book is the result of a great deal of close research — and the help and encouragement given by a large number of employees past and present, and other friends of the Company. To my regret, so many of the leading players who made Flight Refuelling Ltd. the fine Company it is today, have now finally left the stage, and we can only wonder at how affairs might have been recorded had their first hand accounts been available. Fortunately, the extensive documentation previously co-ordinated by the late Chris Farquharson-Roberts — much of it hitherto unpublished — has allowed most of the story to be linked together.

Sir Alan Cobham's exploits, reputation, and immense contribution to aviation, are common knowledge to older readers with aeronautical associations. Other personalities and subsequent events have however long since diluted the initial impact that he and other adventuring pioneers created in the period between the two major World Wars. Progress by its very nature isn't given to dwelling on the past, and the enormous influence exerted by Sir Alan in just about all aspects of the then brand new industry has inevitably become obscured. With a view therefore to giving the younger reader some appreciation of events leading up to the Company's formation, I have drawn extensively upon Sir Alan's autobiography *A Time to Fly* for the opening chapter, which sets the scene for the unfolding story.

I must give especial thanks to my 'core advisory team'; Percy Allison MBE, Ted Alsop BEM, Tony Ashley, Maurice Jenkins, Bob Leonard, Frank Russell, Ron Roberts, Graham Marriette, Dick Tanner MBE, and the late Pat Hornidge, for having given me such a clear insight into so many interesting and indeed historic events. I am deeply indebted to Mike Phipp of the RAeS Christchurch Branch, Graham Day of the MoD Air Historical Branch, and Graham Mottram — Curator of the Fleet Air Arm Museum, who never failed to provide me with information on the many occasions I turned to them. I would also express my gratitude for the anecdotes, log-books, inspection records, photographs and all round support given so freely by the following: John Annis, Trevor Armstrong, Frank Behennah, John Bond, Derek Bower, George Brown, Glyn Brown, Phil Brown, Colin Bruce, Dave Burriss, Arthur Chant, Robin Clark, Ken Coates, Air Marshal Sir John Curtiss, Dave Cutler, Alan Dedden, Sid Dennett, Simon Dickinson, Brian Edmondson, John Eyres, Dave Foulger, Phil Francis, Bill Free, Wilf Goddard, Mike Goodliffe OBE, Vince Gravenor, Sqn. Ldr. Tony Gunby, Ted Hall, Derek Harris, Ray Harris, Derek Henderson, Flt.Lt. Jim Hesketh, Mike Hooks, Frank Hudson, Adrian Jackson, Jock Kyle, Dave Langdon, Dennis Lewis MBE, Mary Lewis, Shirley Lockwood MBE (née Boniwell), Leon Maidment, Ron Marchant, Frank Marshall, John Medgett, Eric Miles, Geoff Millman, Brian Moore, George Moreton, Robert Odling, Graham Orchard, Eddie Ponsford, Mel Porter, Flt.Lt. Ted Querzani, John Reid, Ken Saltrick OBE, Derek Sheldrake, Dick Sherlock, Brian Sherry, Sqn. Ldr. Peter Singleton, Harry Smith, John Stephens, Dave Stevens, Phil Syms MBE, Mick Tanner, Freda Taylor, Ted Thickins, Roy Tier, Roy Trim, Peter Turner MBE, Air Chief Marshal Sir Neil Wheeler, Ken Wickenden, Don Williams, Keith Younge.

Two ladies deserve a very special mention, not only for the enormous patience they have shown in the production of this book — but also for the tact and skill they have exercised in keeping me headed in the right direction. My deep thanks therefore go to Michael Cobham's Executive Assistant, Diana Fuller, for having typed my frequently rewritten manuscripts, and to my wife Thelma, who, during so many late hours has co-edited and proof read every word of the text — fortunately without irreparable harm to our marriage!

My final thanks go to Michael Cobham for his time and recollections — and for his faith in entrusting me with a story that many authors far more experienced than myself would have relished the chance to write. I am delighted that he did.

COLIN CRUDDAS *Wimborne, 1994*

PART ONE

ONE

Prelude

Alan John Cobham first saw the light of day on 6th May 1894, at No.4 Hetley Terrace, (later changed to 78 Denman Road) Camberwell, and his early childhood was spent there until the family moved to Streatham some twelve years later. His father, Frederick Cobham, rather grandly referred to in those days as a 'Town Traveller', had married Lizzie Burrows, some ten years his junior, in 1888, and soon afterwards moved to London from the north.

Fred Cobham had already made his mark in the drapery trade before his son was born, but by the time the move to Streatham took place, fashions had changed and the Swiss embroidered skirts and petticoats every woman wore in quantity were being replaced by much simpler clothes. This inevitably had a significant impact on the Cobham business. Master Cobham however, not yet old enough to be involved in such serious matters, was already developing a passion for geography at the local council school which undoubtedly influenced his adventuresome nature in later years. Enrolled in 1904 into Wilson's Grammar School, he was the first to admit that he was never likely to join the sixth form high flyers who subsequently went to university, and so, aged fifteen he entered the world of business to start a three year apprenticeship at

Alan Cobham's father, Fred Cobham, and (below) his mother, Lizzie Cobham (née Burrows).

A 1909 cartoon from Punch, *whose caption read, 'The chief difficulty to be overcome in aviation is that of renewing supplies of petrol while in the air.' Alan Cobham claimed in later years that this cartoon did not influence his career!*

Master Cobham, already showing an independent spirit at eighteen months of age.

Hitchcock Williams, a large firm of wholesalers in St. Paul's Churchyard. Possessed of a forceful personality, young Cobham had five men working under him by the time he was seventeen, ensuring that orders sent in by the firm's travellers for various garments were despatched on time – all for four shillings a week!

Young Cobham's leisure time was largely taken up with tennis and cycling, but he gradually began to get involved with another hobby, one which foreshadowed his future since it was associated with a rudimentary form of aviation. Together with a friend he built large kites up to eight feet tall and flew them on Streatham Common. He took another step towards his destiny when on Good Friday 1910 he went to his first flying meeting at Brooklands, then the centre of aviation in England. He later recalled seeing one of the earliest aviation pioneers, Gustav Hamel, test his engine by attaching a butcher's spring balance between the tail of his aircraft and a stake driven into the ground, then revving to full power!

By the time he was eighteen, he had been encouraged by his father's cousin, Donald Birchley, to consider leaving Hitchcock Williams to embark on a farming career in Herefordshire. After a great deal of family opposition the determined young man got his way, but soon realised that there was all the difference in the world between working on a farm, and becoming a farmer. His father was experiencing serious business troubles by this time, and it became obvious that with no possibility of parental financial support, and no capacity to save from his meagre wage, a secure future on the land looked decidedly far off. So, it was back to the City, but after what he described as 'an age of barely endurable readjustment' working in the lingerie business, the enterprising Mr. Cobham began to make headway as a representative engaged in the West End. However this proved to be only a short interlude, as he became engulfed by the avalanche of patriotic fervour that overtook Britain upon the outbreak of war in 1914. A first attempt to join the Army came to nothing when he tried to enlist in the Honourable Artillery Company and was rejected. It took a chance conversation on top of a tram with a recruiting sergeant to point him in a different direction and the experience of looking after cattle and horses gained on the farm quickly secured him entry to the Army Veterinary Corps – the date was 14th August 1914!

After an initial indoctrination period at Aldershot, which turned out to be one of total administrative confusion, Private Cobham transferred to Woolwich where he was casually asked by a young Veterinary

Officer whether he would like to accompany him to France. He agreed at once, arriving there on 28th September, and beginning a life, as he put it, 'of much movement'.

Several weeks at the front line was followed by the best part of two years spent at establishments in France, which included the Convalescent Horse Depot, caring for horses that were sick or had been maimed in action. It was a harrowing period, but Cobham's practical skills quickly improved. After studying under Professor Raey Reynolds, the famous Irish veterinary surgeon, he became a qualified Staff Veterinary Sergeant. Veterinary Sergeants were still surprisingly scarce and on one occasion he found himself in sole charge of 1500 horses in various

Staff Veterinary Sergeant Cobham at the Convalescent Horse Centre, 1916.

Private Cobham after joining the Army Veterinary Corps in August 1914.

states of repair. Through his experiences he gained in confidence, and proved his capability to succeed in a world considerably rougher and tougher than any he had previously known.

After three years in France Staff Veterinary Sergeant Cobham began to think that his chances of surviving the war were looking increasingly good, but he also realised with concern that vitally important years had gone by which had left him educationally insecure, and clearly without positive career prospects. The use of motorized ground transport, and of course aircraft, was far more in evidence than when the conflict began, and he now began to consider how best to make his mark in what were clearly going to be growth areas, with aviation seeming particularly attractive. However, he was all too aware that the possibility of a transfer to the Royal Flying Corps was highly unlikely in view of the continuing need for 'horse doctors'.

At home for only his second short spell of leave in three years, Cobham was advised by his mother to discuss his thoughts with Mr. Grose, a neighbour who it turned out had an influential position in the Civil Service. Requested to attend the War Office, a surprised Sergeant Cobham was called upon by this gentleman to tell his story to a room full of assembled officers, and having done so, was even more amazed to find his request for a transfer to the Royal Flying Corps enthusiastically supported; what's more, everyone wished him the best of luck!

13

When the transfer order arrived at his unit, Sergeant Cobham had to endure the withering wrath of his Colonel who was, not unnaturally, very suspicious of the circumstances which had resulted in the arrival of such a top level directive. Cobham weathered the storm and, ruminating on how useful good neighbours can be, reported to the Cadet Depot of the Royal Flying Corps at Hastings. Young Cobham's course had now changed direction in a way that would soon have vital implications for him personally, and indeed the entire aviation world.

After his arrival at Hastings, he immediately found himself placed in rather a unique position. Although considered to be an 'old sweat' by the new cadet intake, the casual circumstances surrounding his Service introduction and move to France meant that he hadn't had so much as five minutes' formal parade ground training. The instructing staff were quite at a loss to know how to cope with a situation that involved an experienced NCO being shouted at, in no uncertain manner, in company with the basic recruits. It all worked out in due course without any serious problems, but life assumed a darker hue after his transfer to Denham for the start of a course in ground instruction. It became rapidly obvious that his lack of further education was going to present a distinct handicap when it came to keeping up in class work with many of the other cadets. Faced with this challenge and the underlying threat that failure would result in an ignominious return to his unit, Sergeant Cobham formed a fierce determination to succeed. Although the situation allowed little time away from his text books the aspiring pilot managed to take part in sporting and social activities, such as organising concerts, which went down so well that the Adjutant insisted that he took total charge of entertainments — which wasn't quite what he had intended! Eventually he successfully completed the ground instruction course in true tortoise and hare fashion, and this led to the commencement of flying instruction at Manston in Kent in early May 1918. By now, truly in his element, Cobham went solo on 1st June, and he later recalled that on that flight all doubts about the nature of his future career left him — a life in the air was unquestionably on the cards!

Progressing via a variety of training aircraft, such as the DH6, BE2c and the Avro 504K, Cadet Cobham rapidly ran up an impressive number of flying hours, but his embryonic career was nearly terminated when, after doing some particularly spectacular loops over Margate, it was found that the

Sir Alan (left) pictured in later years with his flying instructor, Lieutenant Holley.

engine bearer support lugs were bent through nearly 90° and the engine had been within an ace of falling out of the aircraft. Following the inevitable reprimand, a chastened and wiser cadet now became fully aware that flying clearly had its dangerous side, and he resolved that in future he would impress the local ladies in some other, less impulsive manner. Through a mixture of good luck and good management when faced with a succession of aerial mishaps, including engine and undercarriage failures (very common in those days) Sergeant Cobham was finally adjudged to be flying instructor material. It thus came about that on 17th August 1918, virtually four years to the day after his initial enlistment, he passed out as a proud Second Lieutenant, fully qualified flying instructor (see Footnote).

Alan Cobham's first task as a flying instructor was

Footnote: An interesting parallel may be drawn with the case of 'Chuck' Yeager, arguably the greatest test pilot of all, who after a magnificent combat record with the USAF in Europe during World War Two, found himself educationally underqualified following an invitation to attend the Test Pilots School at Wright Air Force Base. His lack of a formal college education led to stinging derision from certain classmates, and some high level intervention was necessary to ensure his successful graduation. Notwithstanding this, his inherent flying skills led him to become principal project pilot on the Bell X-1 research aircraft, and the first man to exceed the speed of sound in level flight on 14th October 1947.

to rehabilitate pilots who had recently crashed and needed to have their confidence restored. Yet again he found himself in a situation vis-a-vis his colleagues in which he was frequently mismatched in terms of rank and experience, as many of the pilots put into his care were senior both in rank and aerial combat flying time. Engine reliability still left a great deal to be desired and the inevitable failures required much stress to be put on 'dead stick' landings. Cobham had on many future occasions reason to be grateful for the experience he gained in teaching others how to get down safely into difficult landing areas under failure conditions. By this time the flying school had moved its operations to Narborough in Norfolk, and after a somewhat tortuous changeover period in terms of uniform and attitude, finally came to regard itself as no longer being part of the Royal Flying Corps, but of the fledgeling Royal Air Force.

In recounting the days he spent instructing student

Second Lieutenant Cobham, now an instructor in the Royal Flying Corps, 1918.

pilots, Alan Cobham painted a vivid picture of one particularly hair-raising flight. The student in question invariably managed to cut out his engine on landing, which required him to jump out and swing the propeller before getting back on board for another take off. It was his practice to shout 'Right' once back in the aircraft, whereupon the instructor negotiated the take off before handing over control. Having got airborne on this particular day and not having received any reply to comments he had made, Cobham turned around in the front cockpit to see, not a begoggled pupil sitting behind, but eight white knuckled fingers gripping the side of the cockpit. It transpired that the pupil had shouted 'Right' too soon and was hanging on for dear life outside the fuselage, several hundred feet above the ground. Cobham's mind worked quickly and by spiralling down with the aircraft banked over so that the intrepid novice was virtually lying on top of the fuselage, it was possible to ease the strain on his hands. Once the aircraft was safely down the pupil dropped off, was quickly onto his feet and, after apologies for having caused the emergency, was soon airborne again. Both instructor and student felt the subsequent drink in the Mess was fully justified!

Armistice Day was of course a cause for celebration, and all control and discipline was instantly put to one side. A Fighter Squadron from neighbouring Marham flew over and dropped several bombs consisting of bags of flour. This impudence was instantly reciprocated with a return mission by the Flying School instructors — only this time the bomb bags contained not flour, but soot! The conventional training pattern was however quickly re-established as there seemed a possibility that the new found peace might, after all, prove to be no more than a temporary truce. During this period the uncertainty of whether he would be allowed to stay in the RAF with a permanent commission, or failing this, be able to move into civil aviation was giving Cobham much cause for concern. Many job enquiries led only to either firm refusals or indecisive replies, but one thing was absolutely certain, there would be no going back to the lingerie business! So, in February 1919, as one droplet in the swirling tide of returning ex-servicemen, a newly re-instated Mr. Cobham strenuously redoubled his efforts, not simply to find a job, but a job in the air!

It was estimated that of the twenty-two thousand pilots about to be discharged from the RAF, perhaps one in a thousand would be fortunate enough to

Alan Cobham in the front cockpit of an Avro 504K belonging to Berkshire Aviation Co., 1919.

make the move into civil aviation. Cobham's relief can be imagined when he landed a job which entailed visiting several east coast resorts on behalf of the British Aerial Transport Company. The aim was to select an appropriate field near each town which could be used in order to provide pleasure flights. Disappointment soon followed however, for after only one month's employment the Company changed its plans leaving one very frustrated aviator with his feet again firmly on the ground.

After this faltering start came the breakthrough that launched the persevering Alan Cobham into the civil aviation fraternity. Following a lead in the Aerial Register and Gazette, he offered his services as second pilot to Fred and Jack Holmes who intended to set up in business giving local joy rides in the Berkshire area. A deal was struck, and with a total working capital of £900, most of it borrowed, an AVRO 504K, soon christened 'May Fly', was purchased from the Aircraft Disposal Company and the Berkshire Aviation Company was more or less ready to commence operations. Eventually, overcoming official concern about the guaranteed suitability of proposed landing grounds prior to their use, barnstorming and pleasure flights began

in earnest in May 1919, and 5000 passengers were carried in the remaining months of the year.

One of the major problems they faced was that of maintaining the aircraft and engine without encroaching on time that could be spent earning revenue. A typical illustration of how this was overcome was the occasion at Aylesbury when, by working through the night and in the open air, it was possible to undertake a top overhaul of the 110 hp Le Rhone rotary engine. An overhanging branch of an oak tree was used as a derrick in order to hoist the engine out, and the work was undertaken by the light of paraffin flares.

Inevitably there came the day of the first crash, again following an engine failure. This fortunately occurred in a field that required the insurance assessor to wade through a muddy stream if he intended to carry out a close up inspection of the damage. This he declined to do, but he agreed that from a distance the aircraft appeared to be a complete write off. The cash value of the aircraft was paid in full, a replacement aircraft immediately purchased, and business resumed with a minimum of disruption. By exercising ingenuity and improvisation the 'written off' aircraft was restored to flying condition within three weeks, and put into reserve as a spare.

The team soon came to regard itself as a branch of show business, often staying in theatrical 'digs' where their irregular and eccentric way of life seemed relatively normal. At Chesterfield, Alan Cobham made the acquaintance of one of the great comedians of the day, Will Fyffe, and this meeting was to have a momentous effect on his future. An example of the nomadic nature of the enterprise is illustrated by a spontaneous agreement reached whereby the team travelled up to Edinburgh and put in a joy ride and barnstorming show at Christmas — this in response to Will Fyffe's canny projection that Christmas was the only time the Scots could be persuaded to part with money!

As part of this northern itinerary the team travelled to Yorkshire where another touring revue, entitled 'Joy Bells', was appearing at the Middlesborough Theatre, featuring Miss Gladys Lloyd as its star. Within the space of three days Alan Cobham, having persuaded her to be taken on an introductory flight over the town followed by another at night, found himself travelling with her by train to the revue's next engagement at Newcastle. Never one to forsake an opportunity, the totally infatuated airman had secured the actress's promise to become his wife long before the train arrived at its destination. Although events were gathering pace, the business world is frequently a hard one, and for Alan Cobham 1920 proved to be as difficult and depressing as 1919 had seemed so promising. The Berkshire Aviation Company had decided to expand and run two touring shows simultaneously, but the old truism that people simply do not work as hard for an employer as they do for themselves, combined with appalling weather, quickly managed to drain cash and resources, and to dampen everyone's enthusiasm. Cobham had to withdraw his assets to offset debts and again found himself back on the starting line with only thirty shillings in his pocket. Casual jobs with a Birmingham engineering firm and at Shepperton film studios provided nothing really substantial and despite his earlier promises to himself, he drifted back into the Rag Trade for a time, selling ladies' dresses and ironically, he did quite well!

After the huge wartime expansion of men and machines, the virtually instant post war deflation created an enormous vacuum in aerial activity. Now and then major events such as the crossing of the

Miss Gladys Lloyd, who Alan Cobham married in 1922.

Atlantic by Alcock and Brown stimulated the public's interest and imagination, but by and large the country seemed to be more concerned with taking the time to catch its breath. After getting off to an impressive start, it now seemed as if aviation might never amount to much. Not for the first time Cobham reassured himself that there had to be a way forward in the aeronautical game. It was going to happen sooner or later and he had to be part of it — but how?

The answer it seemed arrived when, relying again on an influential personal contact, Alan Cobham joined the Aircraft Manufacturing Company. 'Airco' as it later became, had just decided to go in for aerial photography on a commercial basis, and Cobham now found himself, along with a newly engaged photographer called MacLennen, constituting a new branch called Airco Aerials. The kind of flying this entailed was very demanding. Low flying and steep turns combined with the vagaries of the English weather and lack of adequate navigational aids produced many frightening moments and forced landings.

The operation was deemed to be succesful as the

Part of the fleet of machines used by The De Havilland Aeroplane Hire Service

"AN AEROPLANE TO TAKE YOU ANYWHERE"

2/- PER MILE

A De Havilland Taxi-Plane

TO ALL TOURISTS AND BUSINESS MEN.

THIS service possesses a fleet of modern commercial Aeroplanes available at a moment's notice for the carriage of passengers or freight in safety and comfort at 90 m.p.h. to ANY DESTINATION in the British Isles or on the Continent. There are doubtless occasions when these high-speed transport facilities can be of the greatest service to you; either for the rapid transport of urgent freight, such as letters, samples or goods, or for the carriage of personnel travelling on important business. You are seriously recommended to consider the possibilities of this service as applied to your business.

The inclusive fare is only 2/- per mile, which when carrying three passengers, or 6 cwt. of freight, works out at only 8d. PER PASSENGER MILE, or 4d. per cwt. mile.

We have eliminated all "stunts" and make no attempt to create spectacular diversions. The success of the service depends solely on the amount of passengers and traffic safely transported, and the most scrupulous care is directed towards safety and reliability.

Travelling on an infinite variety of duties our machines covered over a quarter of a million miles in our first two years' operations.

We also undertake short pleasure flights, tours of any duration, week-end trips, instructional courses in flying, etc.

Enquiries are cordially invited.

THE DE HAVILLAND AEROPLANE HIRE SERVICE

STAG LANE AERODROME

(on the main Edgware Road, 7 miles from Marble Arch)

Telephone :
Kingsbury 160 & 161

EDGWARE - MIDDLESEX

Telegrams :
"Havilland, Edgware"

18

workload increased and customers, having received the exposed plates the next day, were invariably pleased and satisfied. It therefore came as yet another blow to both pocket and morale when 'Airco' went into liquidation. Alan Cobham almost managed to salvage the situation by approaching General Caddell, the Managing Director of Vickers, and persuading him to incorporate the aerial photography side of 'Airco' into his own company. However this proposal was too late and everything was sold to Aerofilms, the incumbents receiving instant notice. Aerofilms was founded in 1919 by F.L.Wills who had been a photographer with the Royal Flying Corps during World War One. Today, the Aerofilms library at Elstree houses more than half a million photographs dating from 1920 to the present day.

Despite the gloom, what seemed like yet another false dawn was to prove a blessing in disguise. With Airco going into liquidation, Geoffrey de Havilland who had joined it in 1914 as Chief Designer, elected to form his own company, the idea being to complement manufacture with the hiring out of aircraft, mainly to companies specializing in aerial photography. Whilst at 'Airco' Cobham had done a good deal of flying for Aerofilms, and had made a favourable impression. When de Havillands approached Aerofilms to undertake their flying requirements, they agreed on condition that they obtained the services of a pilot — Alan Cobham. Unaware of this, Cobham negotiated terms with de Havillands that would have been much more advantageous to himself had he known the strength of his hand.

1921 thus provided the prospect of relatively secure work at last, and the continual criss-crossing of the British Isles gave Cobham an intimate knowledge of the countryside and its landmarks, and, more importantly, potential emergency landing areas. Day to day maintenance of the aircraft was his own responsibility and when frequently away from de Havilland's Stag Lane headquarters for a month at a time, cleaning plugs and filters, stripping the carburettor, draining fuel tank sumps and checking all structural features, usually had to be done on an ad hoc basis. It was a common experience to have to picket down, service and cover up the aeroplane in the meadow of some reluctant farmer, possibly in the pouring rain, before setting off in search of lodgings, heavily burdened with cameras, photographic plates,

Left A typical de Havilland Aeroplane Hire Service advertisement of the early 1920s.

maps and personal baggage. Despite the obvious disadvantages it proved to be an exhilarating and varied life that began to pay handsomely as the role of the aeroplane within the commercial sphere expanded. Aerial photography, newspaper and cine film deliveries, and charter work for wealthy and prominent people all served to keep Cobham in the air, and not surprisingly competition for this trade grew fierce. At last Cobham sensed that the road ahead was relatively clear and that he could look forward to a solid career as a pilot.

It is interesting to note that whilst today the word 'pilot' is used without question to identify the person in charge of an aircraft, it was by no means a universally accepted term in 1921 — 'driver' was a description more often used. The matter was eventually resolved however, when the Royal Aero Club formed a committee to consider aviation insurance matters, and from this came the decision to opt for 'pilot'. Alan Cobham commented himself how strangely insufficient and unworthy it would have seemed had we at some time in the future had to refer to that 'gallant band of drivers of Fighter Command who saved the nation in 1940'. But that's another story!

It was during this period that Cobham made an indelible stamp on British aviation when he outlined the specification for what became the definitive 'light aeroplane'. This came about because, having flown the diminutive DH.53 Humming Bird, G-EBHX, powered by a 697 cc motor cycle engine, to Brussels for the 1923 Aero and Automobile Show, he was unable to fly it back against the prevailing head winds. After experiencing the humiliation of being overtaken by a slow moving freight train, Cobham had the tiny aircraft dismantled and shipped home. As a direct result of this, Geoffrey de Havilland asked Alan Cobham what he thought the ideal sporting aeroplane should be. He described an aircraft that would accommodate taking a girlfriend at least as far as Paris, at a reasonable cruising speed and with adequate space for weekend baggage. As a consequence the prototype 'DH.60 Moth' appeared within the year, a type which proved immensely popular and which led to a family of variants, which included the Gypsy, Puss, Hornet, Leopard, Fox, and of course the ubiquitous Tiger Moth used by the RAF virtually throughout World War Two for initial aircrew training. Perhaps the greatest step forward to popularize flying came about with the arrival of the Moth, a simple biplane fitted with an Airdisco

The de Havilland 53 Hummingbird in which Alan Cobham flew to the Brussels Aero and Automobile Exhibition in 1923.

Alan Cobham's recommendation to Geoffrey de Havilland resulted in the highly successful range of 'Moth' variants. The very first 'DH Moth' to be produced, powered by a Cirrus engine, is pictured here.

Kings Cup Air Race 1923. Alan Cobham, in the aircraft nearest the camera, and Geoffrey de Havilland warm up for the start of the Round Britain flight.

Cirrus engine, which was produced by cutting a V-type Renault engine in half. Hundreds of these engines were made available from the Aircraft Disposal Company, and thier low cost greatly assisted in allowing the Moth to be sold at one time for under £600.

1924 was certainly a notable year for Alan Cobham in other respects. Having been narrowly beaten in the Kings Cup Air Races of 1922 and 1923, it was now third time lucky. On this occasion he tried to steal a march on the other contestants by using a pressure system to increase the rate of refuelling. News of his novel scheme leaked out prior to the race however, causing the rules to be changed and thus cancelling out any advantage that he might have gained.

Alan Cobham's piloting career throughout the Twenties moved in an exhilarating sequence of stops and starts, but having married Gladys in 1922 the need for continuous employment was always uppermost. So much depended on being willing and able to respond to demands at a moment's notice, and attempting to plan ahead for any social activities was a risky business indeed. Cobham would point out much later however, that having to drop everything in order to respond so instantly was greatly assisted by having to observe only the minimum of formalities. He recalled that it was usually quite enough to be simply 'British' in order to have border

requirements such as passports, flight plans and load manifests waived, and he added that there was never any problem in cashing cheques drawn on London banks when overseas. Set against this informal background, his duties at de Havillands, in addition to the aerial charter and new delivery flights, now included test flying the latest designs.

It was also part of his job to carry photographers to wherever the big news stories were taking place, and organising special flights to ensure the Company's name was continually in the public eye. He made news by flying to Africa and back in record time, cheating a little he admits because although he landed at Tangiers, which is undoubtedly in Africa, most people at that time upon hearing the name of the Continent thought immediately of equatorial jungles many more thousands of miles further away!

Flying men were, at this time, relatively few in number, but most seemed to share two common characteristics — total devotion to their calling and chronic restlessness. Cobham's grand aerial tours with Lucien Sharpe, an extremely wealthy American determined to indulge his passion for European history and art (not to mention wine), had convinced him that the boundaries of aerial travel were largely in the imagination. Cobham rightly reasoned that if it was a question of rolling the frontiers back, then he was as well equipped to do so as anyone in experience and outlook. Armed with this philosophy he sought keenly an opportunity to extend his operations, and the farther afield the better!

In the immediate post-war period, much thought was given to the establishment of air routes that would link the Empire. However it was unclear whether the best form of transportation would be that of land based aeroplanes, flying boats or airships, and the Government was cautiously prepared to investigate each method. In fact the success of German passenger-carrying airships, flying between Europe and South America, encouraged air-minded officials to believe that regular air services westwards across the Atlantic, and eastwards to India, should be in place by 1929 at the latest. It was therefore with a view to establishing the viability of the route to India that the Air Minister, Lord Thompson, instructed the Director of Civil Aviation, Sir Sefton Brancker, to go there in 1924.

The initial idea was that he would proceed by sea but by raising money from within industry to cover the difference in costs, it was eventually possible for Brancker to charter an aircraft from de Havillands, with Alan Cobham as pilot. After all, in pursuing and advancing the cause of aviation, to travel by ship seemed hardly appropriate! So, in a de Havilland 50 bearing the registration G-EBFO — an aircraft that would become almost as famous and familiar as its pilot — Cobham and engineer Arthur Elliott, and Brancker, accompanied by an obscure Romanian general, took off on 10th

Sefton Brancker, Alan Cobham and Arthur Elliott, during their flight to India and Burma in 1924. Both Elliott and Brancker were later to die in separate bizarre circumstances.

G-EBFO and crew, all set for Cape Town.

November on what turned out to be an adventure-laden journey to India and Burma. The round trip lasted four months and, despite the odd forced landing which temporarily cooled his enthusiasm, Brancker was very impressed by the experience. He had originally intended to assess what facilities would be needed for mooring airships at Karachi, Delhi and Calcutta, but Cobham was convinced that as the flight progressed, Brancker's outlook changed and that he knew it would be aerodromes, not mooring masts, that would soon be required. With every possibility of speedy airliners appearing on the scene, the slower airships were clearly not going to win the race. It was to prove tragically ironic that, filled with these doubts, Brancker should die with most of the crew when the R101 airship crashed at Beauvais in October 1930 – attempting to fly to India!

That disaster however was still in the future, and the flight to Rangoon created sensational press headlines upon their return, although inevitably a sense of anti-climax set in after the flight. De Havillands were enjoying enormous success with the DH Moth, now being produced in quantity, but it became

apparent to Cobham that the de Havilland Hire Service had a limited future. He could see that with the advent of news picture transmission by cable and radio the necessity to transport this material by air from faraway places would soon no longer exist. 1924 also saw the formation of Imperial Airways out of Handley Page Transport, Instone Airlines and Daimler Airways, and although it became the biggest customer for de Havilland aircraft, the airline was showing increasing impatience with its major supplier competing for its passenger traffic in Europe.

All this led Cobham, whose ambition by now was to run his own airline, to consider the development of other world air routes. Africa, he thought, offered the greatest opportunities, and so immediately after the euphoria of the Rangoon flight had subsided, he set about organizing an exploratory flight to Cape Town. Enormous effort was required to secure adequate sponsorship before the flight eventually got underway on 15th November 1925. De Havillands again agreed to loan G-EBFO, now fully refurbished after its gruelling tour to India, and Armstrong Siddeley provided a 385 hp Jaguar III engine which would take care of the extra power

Cobham's pioneering flights invariably resulted in an ecstatic welcome from crowds such as this at Croydon following his return from Cape Town, March 1926.

required for 'hot and high' take-offs. The quartet of major sponsors was finally completed when Sir Charles Cheers Wakefield indicated he would donate the oil, and British Petroleum the petrol. Alan Cobham was again to be accompanied on the journey by his engineer, Arthur Elliott, and room was somehow found in the crowded cabin for a Gaumont cine cameraman, B.W.Emmott, and his bulky equipment.

Alan Cobham was all too aware that after the recent four month separation from his wife, it was going to put a severe strain on his marriage to be away for another extended period, especially as his first son Geoffrey had been born in July 1925. Gladys Cobham however, believed implicitly in what her husband was doing, and he was proud to the end of his days that at no time did she offer anything but loyal support and encouragement in all his ventures. Having thus firmly impressed her reassurances upon him, Cobham flew off, crossing southern Europe in order to pick up the Nile. At Athens however, Elliott discovered that the low compression pistons fitted to the Jaguar engine to accommodate lower octane fuel

were on the point of disintegration. In order to spare his sponsor any adverse publicity, Cobham tried to keep the real reason for a week's delay from the press. In the meantime, frantic activity at the Siddeley works in Coventry resulted in a replacement set of fourteen pistons being assembled, delivered by rail and steamer, and installed and tested within seven days. One journalist did however stumble on the truth, and created mischief by reporting in *The Evening News* that Cobham was 'as usual' putting out false reasons for the delay. Heated discussions between Sir John Siddeley and Lord Rothermere, the paper's owner, led to the journalist in question being sacked for carrying on a personal vendetta in the columns. Other than this, the flight attracted a favourable press and upon arrival in South Africa, Cobham and his crew were lionized from start to finish. It certainly did appear that the provision of a scheduled aerial link between Southern Africa and the mother country could become a viable proposition.

Spice was added to the return journey when the Master of the Union Castle liner, S.S. *Windsor Castle*, and Cobham agreed to race each other back to England. Both liner and aircraft left for Southampton and Stag Lane respectively on 26th February, with the loser committed to standing the winner a good lunch in London. After having had moments of serious danger in flying through torrential rain and dust storms extending to 12,000 ft. and which obliterated all ground reference points, Cobham did eventually triumph — beating his rival by two days. More importantly, his effort had shown that whilst the ocean liner was unbeatable with regard to elegance, space and comfort, speed could best be provided by passenger carrying aircraft (see Footnote).

It might be thought that following such a physically draining experience, Cobham would have been only too pleased to have relaxed and enjoyed the pleasures England invariably bestows on its returned travellers. Not a bit of it, for the day after his return on 13th March 1926, he was securing Geoffrey de Havilland's ongoing support for what would turn out to be his longest and most celebrated flight.

To fly to Australia and back had been a thought germinating in his mind for some time, the seed having been sown during a visit he made to the Department of Civil Aviation whilst preparing for the flight to South Africa. During discussions it had been suggested that in order to accelerate the Government's interest in civil aviation, Cobham might fly up the Thames, land opposite the Houses of Parliament and present a petition. This idea didn't arouse his enthusiasm, as all he could see resulting from such a scheme was a likely summons for endangering public safety and a few column inches in the papers, with no propaganda value at all. But, he thought, what if it were announced that Alan Cobham intended to fly from, say, Rochester (where his trusty G-EBFO would be fitted with floats) to the Houses of Parliament — by way of Australia! And so his brainwave rapidly turned once more into a frantic programme of coercing sponsorship, laying up spares at key locations en route, identifying suitable lakes, rivers, estuaries and harbours and arranging for moorings to be available. When one considers the effort to put all this in place, in addition to the

Footnote: FRL's Principal Contracts Officer Vince Gravenor tells today how, twenty-one years later, his father, Sqn. Ldr. H.N. Gravenor, flying an Auster light aircraft on a particularly gruelling trip, eclipsed Sir Alan's outbound time to the Cape.

An artist's flamboyant impression of the shooting incident that resulted in Arthur Elliott's death.

residual lecturing and writing activity that ensued from his flight to the Union, it is easy to imagine the physical and mental exhaustion he admitted to just prior to departure. Cobham was accompanied this time only by Arthur Elliott his engineer when he took off just after dawn on 30th June 1926. With the DH.50 looking strangely unfamiliar with its new sea boots in place of the undercarriage, they headed east over the fields of Kent into a lightening sky.

Cobham later recounted how the tension and emotional strain he felt at take off soon turned to a deep depression that he couldn't account for, nor shake off. With hindsight he often wondered whether this was a form of premonition of the tragedy that was shortly to occur. That truth is often stranger than fiction has long been established, but the fateful circumstances that overtook G-EBFO and its crew after leaving Baghdad were bizarre indeed. Flying down the Euphrates, Cobham found himself in a thickening sandstorm which necessitated him flying very low, but having gained a limited sight of the horizon, he was alarmed by a violent explosion in the cabin. Despite efforts to find out what had happened, there was little response from Elliott. Eventually the engineer managed to pass a message that he thought a petrol pipe had burst

Arthur Elliott's funeral at Basra. Alan Cobham is at the rear of the burial party.

Arthur Elliott's headstone. Note that 'Alan' is spelled incorrectly.

IN LOVING MEMORY
OF
ARTHUR BULLER ELLIOTT, A.M.I.Ae.E.
(SIR ALLAN COBHAM'S ENGINEER)
WHO DIED AT BASRA HOSPITAL,
JULY 6TH 1926,
WHILST FLYING FROM LONDON-AUSTRALIA
JUNE 30TH - OCT.1ST

THY WILL BE DONE.

Footnote: In 1957, Sir Alan received a letter from Mr. C. Littledale who had served in the Iraqi Police at that time, relating the following sequel. An Arab gazelle hunter had on several successive days had his quarry stampeded by low flying RAF patrols. He was just 'drawing a bead' on a gazelle when G-EBFO startled it, so he fired at the aircraft instead. Initially sentenced to death, he later had it commuted to seven years imprisonment.

but, more ominously, that he was bleeding profusely.

Cobham realised that he couldn't land and restart the engine single handed, and elected to press on as rapidly as possible to Basra, some one hundred miles distant. The searing heat in the cabin, coupled with severe injuries, must have created agonizing conditions for Arthur Elliott, who it later transpired had been shot by a local tribesman on the riverbank below. The bullet, having narrowly missed the floats, had entered the cabin, passing through a despatch box before fracturing a fuel line, and subsequently entering Elliott's left arm en route to both his lungs. The staff at the RAF hospital at Basra worked valiantly to save his life, but his injuries were too severe and tragically he died the following day, leaving Cobham totally devastated and with no heart to continue the flight. Arthur Elliott, although a civilian, was buried at Basra with full military honours and with eight RAF mechanics acting as pall bearers (see Footnote).

Despite the tragedy, Cobham came to realize that not only had he to fulfil his obligation to his sponsors back in England, but also a duty to uphold to his late flying companion. Cables of encouragement started to arrive from all quarters, including one from his wife, encouraging him to continue the flight, and when the RAF offered to provide Sergeant A. H. Ward as a replacement engineer he agreed to go on. The journey resumed on 13th July, and following arrival in Darwin on 5th August the floats were removed by crew members from HMS *Geranium* and stored for the return journey, and a wheeled undercarriage fitted for the cross country leg of the flight

Above *An alas rather poor quality photograph of the crowds that gathered following G-EBFO's arrival at Melbourne, 1926.*

Right *Cobham's dramatic arrival on the Thames, October 1926.*

to Melbourne. With Armstrong Siddeley engineer, C.H.Capel, who assisted Ward on the homeward run, Alan Cobham eventually arrived home on 1st October 1926, flying low up the Thames before settling his faithful aircraft gently on the river in front of the Houses of Parliament. Thus, with the eyes of the world upon him, and a crowd estimated at over a million thronging the embankments and Westminster Bridge, he brought the cause of civil aviation right up to the home of Government. As he wryly commented, "it couldn't have been done any other way because there's no room to land a wheeled aircraft on the terrace of the House".

By now, fame secured by a Knighthood for his epic flight, Sir Alan found himself in great demand to lecture to a seemingly endless list of organisations both in England and abroad, particularly America. Keen to visit the New World, Britain's aerial ambassador and Lady Cobham duly sailed on the S.S. *Homeric*, taking as deck cargo a de Havilland Moth for delivery to a purchaser in Washington. It was on this six week lecture tour that Sir Alan developed a reputation for being a witty story teller, and at one New York reception found that a theatrical agent,

Cobham in America in 1927, with DH Moth and a magnificent automobile loaned for his use.

convinced that he was a professional comedian, was determined to book him for a vaudeville tour.

Despite his genius for publicity, Cobham's own flying style could never be described as 'barnstorming'. On his own admission he was never particularly good at aerobatics, but he knew that his strength lay in his dead reckoning navigational skill, and being inherently capable of dealing with situations when a quick landing was required. In addition to this he always claimed that his organisational ability gave him a distinct advantage over many flying contemporaries who, although they may have proved to be more spectacular in the air, had little technical knowledge or business acumen, and had never managed to overcome the wartime principle of living purely for the moment. These characteristics were also frequently evident in aviators who operated on the barnstorming circuits in the USA, but occasionally they provided aerial thrills that turned out to have some serious potential for commercial development.

For example, Ormer Locklear, an ex-US Army Air Service pilot and an original wingwalker, had suggested that aerial refuelling could be used for a trans-continental service as early as 1919, but nothing came of the idea. (Sketchy references exist of aviators, even prior to World War I, having given serious thought to aerial refuelling, and it is possible that primitive attempts may actually have been made.) Thus amidst the death defying acts that were becoming commonplace at airshows, such as men hanging from aircraft literally by their teeth, and pilots stopping an engine in flight then (hopefully) hand cranking it to life, another stunt took place for the first time on 12th November 1921 that would have significant implications for Sir Alan's future. On that balmy day, with visibility unlimited, two red biplanes flew in close formation with one aircraft only six feet or so above the other, high over Signal Hill at Long Beach in California. Standing braced on the top wing of the lower aircraft, a Lincoln Standard, stuntman Wesley May waited with a 50lb. can of gasoline strapped to his back instead of a parachute. Grabbing the wing tip skid on the underside of the Curtiss JN-4's lower port wing, he swung his body pendulum fashion before finally managing to haul himself over the leading edge. He then proceeded to make his way along the wing until, with the can precariously balanced, he managed to transfer some petrol into the fuselage tank. The majority of it however was lost in the slip stream, and he became thoroughly drenched in the process. The 'Flying Tankerman', as he was billed, had nevertheless carried out the first recorded in-flight transfer of fuel in a display of incredible courage, or perhaps amazing foolhardiness! It was the first recorded step on a path that would eventually lead to the sophisticated aerial refuelling practices undertaken by today's tanker aircraft.

Soon after this, in 1923, serious endurance flights became a regular feature in the aviation calendar, but in most cases the participants were primarily concerned with becoming the latest entry in the Official Book of Records, rather than promoting technical development. By transferring fuel and other consumable necessities the flight times recorded became truly astounding over the next decade. For example in the 1923 attempt, 37 hrs. 15 mins. was achieved by a DH.4B supplied with fuel via a pipeline suspended from another DH.4B tanker. Encouraged by the progress being made in America, and following a proposal put forward by Boulton Paul's chief designer, J.D.North, at the 1923 International Air Congress, the Royal Aircraft Establishment (RAE) then began to underake experimental refuelling work at Farnborough. Rudimentary tests were also carried out in France at this time, and a French attempt on the refuelling endurance record in 1928, using DH.9 aircraft, raised the time aloft to 60 hrs. 7 mins. Back in the USA, also in 1928, a US Army Air Corp crew, headed by Major Carl Spatz (later Spaatz), in a much publicized flight to investigate running engines to the limits of endurance and the practical value of refuelling in flight, remained airborne for 150 hrs. 40 mins. in an Atlantic C-2A (American version of Fokker F-V11A/3m) refuelling in flight thirty-four times in the process. A final idea of the determination that accompanied refuelling flights may be drawn by considering the achievement of the Key brothers, who, in June 1935 and again in America, flew on and on for a total of 653 hours.

It was during Sir Alan's American tour in early 1927 that he met Charles Lindbergh for the first time. During their discussion it transpired that both had been approached by a wealthy man called Charles Levine, who, although himself a pilot of only limited ability, was desperately keen to fly the Atlantic — if only as a passenger. However it wasn't

An artist's impression of 'Flying Tankerman' Wesley May carrying out the first recorded aerial refuelling. The stunt took place at 3,500 ft. over Long Beach, California, on 12th November 1921. May was killed shortly afterwards in a freak parachute accident.

within Sir Alan's plans to contemplate such a flight and although Lindbergh was determined to do so, his clear intention was to undertake the first solo crossing — a flight he famously completed in 'The Spirit of St. Louis' only a few weeks later.

Gladys Cobham meanwhile had returned home some time ahead of Sir Alan, and on 22nd February 1927 she gave birth to a second son, Michael. In later chapters it will be seen that although Geoffrey preferred to follow his father's love of the land and pursue a farming career, Michael would develop a deep interest in aeronautical affairs and successfully build on the business foundations laid by his father.

At this time however, Sir Alan was still struggling to create and build up a business. His relationship with de Havillands had been strained for some time,

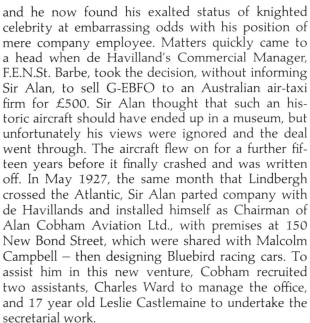

Above *New arrival Michael Cobham shows an early interest in aviation — brother Geoffrey is otherwise engaged.*

Right *Lady Cobham strikes a formidable pose alongside a de Havilland DH60 Moth in the 1920s.*

and he now found his exalted status of knighted celebrity at embarrassing odds with his position of mere company employee. Matters quickly came to a head when de Havilland's Commercial Manager, F.E.N.St. Barbe, took the decision, without informing Sir Alan, to sell G-EBFO to an Australian air-taxi firm for £500. Sir Alan thought that such an historic aircraft should have ended up in a museum, but unfortunately his views were ignored and the deal went through. The aircraft flew on for a further fifteen years before it finally crashed and was written off. In May 1927, the same month that Lindbergh crossed the Atlantic, Sir Alan parted company with de Havillands and installed himself as Chairman of Alan Cobham Aviation Ltd., with premises at 150 New Bond Street, which were shared with Malcolm Campbell — then designing Bluebird racing cars. To assist him in this new venture, Cobham recruited two assistants, Charles Ward to manage the office, and 17 year old Leslie Castlemaine to undertake the secretarial work.

It became immediately obvious that to further his airline ambitions, more practical demonstration flying would be necessary to secure the support of the various Colonial governments, and so within a month of the Company's formation, Cobham and Ward drew up a plan for a flying boat journey around the whole of the African continent. Unfortunately competition had now appeared in the form

of the North Sea Aerial and General Transport Company Ltd. operated by Captain Tony Gladstone and Robert Blackburn. However both parties eventually agreed that co-operation and not confrontation was the best way forward, and in April 1928 the two companies amalgamated and Cobham-Blackburn Airlines was born. In pressing ahead with the plans for the survey flight, Sir Alan got the Secretary of State for Air, Sir Samuel Hoare's permission to use a Short Singapore I flying boat, G-EBUP, that was surplus to Service requirements, and the ever dependable Lord Wakefield again agreed to supply the fuel and oil. Having enlisted Captain H. V. Worrall as co-pilot, along with two engineers and another Gaumont cameraman, Cobham's crew was almost complete. He knew though from his previous exploits that the physical demands of flying a heavy aircraft, coupled with the never ending social pressures, would leave little opportunity for administration work en route, and this, added to his concern that he had left his wife behind too often and for too long, made Cobham decide that Lady Cobham would admirably fill the role of Ship's Purser, and she readily agreed!

The successes and near disasters which attended the six month long return voyage that commenced in November 1927 are, along with details of all his long distance flights, vividly described in Sir Alan's memoirs, *A Time to Fly*, and do not require

Ready for departure to Africa 1927. Co-pilot H. V. Worrall appears to be doing all the work!

Just another hard day at the office. Sir Alan and Lady Cobham catch up with en route administration.

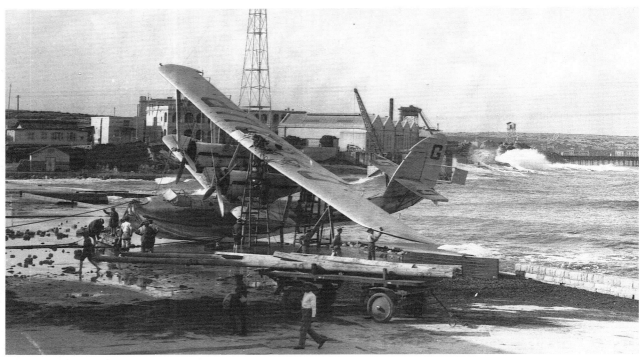

Continual storms in Malta caused severe damage to Cobham's Singapore flying boat.

The Ivory Coast. Two crew members caught by the camera assiduously attending to pre-flight planning details!

elaboration here. It is however, tempting to add that what should have been an overnight stay at Malta on the outward journey turned into a highly frustrating eight week delay due to continual storms which severely damaged the aircraft. Sir Alan commented later, presumably with tongue firmly in cheek, that when he finally took off he was escorted by three RAF aircraft whose pilots had orders to shoot him down if he showed any signs of returning!

On his eventual return to England, Sir Alan had two thoughts uppermost in his mind; firstly the need to consolidate Cobham-Blackburn Airline's presence in Africa, and secondly to capitalise on his fame by visiting all the major towns and cities in Great Britain. In undertaking the latter task his aim would be to persuade local officials to earmark suitable sites for development as municipal airports. Cobham had long since realised that he would face an uphill battle when his aviation schemes ran up against strong vested commercial interests. The Secretary of State for India, Lord Birkenhead, was particularly dismissive of any revolutionary ideas that threatened the status quo, pointing out that the turnaround time for cables to England was a mere seven weeks. So, despite the staunch efforts of a few air-minded politicians, like Sir Sefton Brancker, progress had to be hewn from a rock face of entrenched prejudice.

Politicians were not the only influential people to adopt negative views regarding air transport. In order to take advantage of the ticketing and reservation systems already in place, Sir Alan contacted firstly Lord Kilsant, Chairman of the Union Castle Line, then Lord Inchcape, Chairman of the P and O Company, to enquire whether they would consider setting up aviation sections within their shipping operations. These approaches were distinctly unsuccessful and to Cobham's dismay, patronizingly rejected as little more than an amusing diversion. Sir Alan knew that such rejections stemmed from a total lack of imagination on the part of those who had traditionally enjoyed a highly privileged and relaxed position in the social order. But a strong undercurrent of change was beginning to make itself felt, and Imperial Airways now began to raise its sights beyond Europe. In chasing the opportunities that Africa readily presented, Sir Alan had earlier been given Sir Sefton Brancker's personal assurance that the government backed airline only intended to operate across Europe, as far as Cairo. The rest of the world's air routes would be left to private enterprise to develop.

Short Singapore G-EBUP flying over Liverpool's Clock Tower during the Round Britain flight following Cobham's return from Africa, 1928.

It therefore came as a serious shock to Cobham and his colleagues when Imperial Airways announced that they intended to extend their operations to include Africa. Sir Eric Geddes and George Woods Humphrey, respectively Chairman and Managing Director of Imperial, had realised somewhat belatedly that a major revenue earning opportunity was about to be missed, and had put pressure on the government to exercise their rights to operate where they wished. Despite all the pioneering activity undertaken by the Cobham-Blackburn fliers, they lacked the muscle to dislodge the nationalised cuckoo that had now appeared in the nest, and Cobham-Blackburn Airways was offically wound up on 29th July 1930, the price received being £24,750 in cash, together with 25,000 ordinary £1 shares. Imperial Airways Africa Ltd.'s inaugural service flight between London and Mwanza subsequently took place on 28th February 1931.

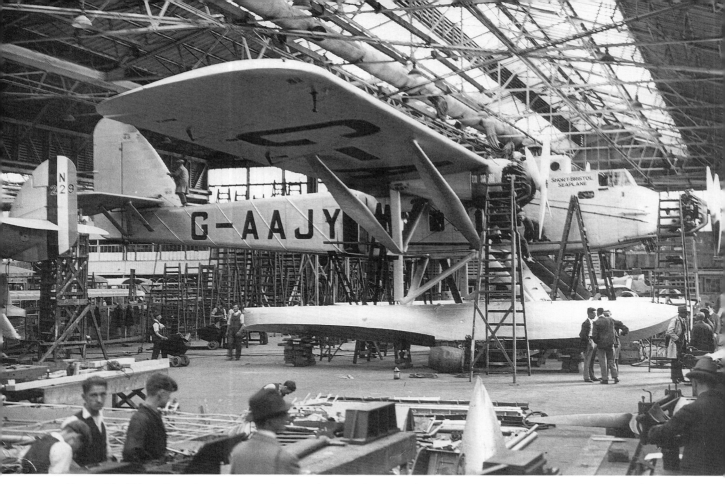

Above The Valetta G-AAJY, nearing completion at Shorts' Rochester Works, 1931. Below Imperial Airways pilot C. F. Wolley-Dod.

Notwithstanding his devastation at the shattering of his dream, 22nd July 1931 saw Sir Alan take off yet again on another exploration flight, this time to Lake Kivu in the Belgian Congo. The essential purpose of the flight was to undertake a five week aerial survey for the Air Ministry, but it was also an opportunity to evaluate the Short Valetta, a large brand new tri-motored seaplane that had been designed for this kind of route. Sir Alan soon found that its handling qualities both in the air and on water were greatly superior to the Singapore he had flown before. Despite having no serious vices, the aircraft and crew nearly came to harm during one flight when Cobham, against his better judgement, allowed a senior Imperial Airways pilot called Wolley-Dod to attempt to land the unfamiliar aircraft. Cobham noticed to his horror that Wolley-Dod had committed a novice's error in allowing airspeed to fall almost to the stalling limit, and rapidly had to push the nose down to regain a safe speed. On another less critical occasion it was found that the petrol containers brought overland by native bearers to Lake Kivu contained not fuel — but

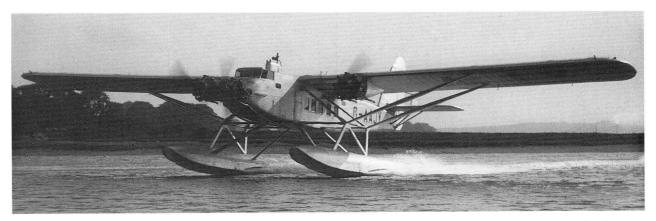

Above *Off to Lake Kivu in the Short Valetta.*

Below *The DH.61 'Youth of Britain', used by Sir Alan during his Municipal Aerodrome Scheme tour round Great Britain 1929.*

water. Apparently one native, having accidentally punctured a four gallon can, had emptied all the others in order to lighten the load, having reasoned that the liquid that had leaked from the damaged can was water, and that it would be a simple matter to refill the cans on arrival at Lake Kivu! Fortunately the local Shell Oil representative was able to replenish supplies before the aircraft arrived, and the 12,000 mile survey was completed in 128 flying hours without more serious mishaps.

As mentioned earlier, Sir Alan already had schemes in mind for developing civil aviation in Britain, and the first of these, which he termed the Municipal Aerodrome Scheme (MAS), got underway in May 1929. His idea was to try to persuade mayors and councillors of various towns and cities of the need to establish their own aerodromes — and barely concealed in each proposal was the suggestion that Sir Alan should be retained as an adviser. In this manner he intended to build up a business as an

England's 'youth and beauty' line up for pleasure flights sponsored by Sir Charles Wakefield (next to Lady Cobham). On this occasion, attention seems to be diverted from the familiar figure in the cockpit.

aviation consultant. With a DH.61, bought from de Havillands and christened 'Youth of Britain', Cobham and a small support team undertook a twenty-one week tour. The daily routine invariably consisted of the team's airborne arrival at the chosen town by mid-morning, followed by flights which allowed officials to appreciate their locality from the air. This was undertaken entirely at Cobham's own expense. Then it was the turn of schoolchildren, whose flights at ten shillings a head were paid for by the ever generous Lord Wakefield. In the afternoon and evening, seven minute flights were available to the paying public, and the tour rolled along in this manner very successfully. In all, some 10,000 schoolchildren and 40,000 other passengers gained their first experience in the air, and a handsome profit was generated. Cobham, as he had anticipated, received many commissions to advise on suitable sites, and airports such as Speke (Liverpool), Yeadon (Bradford) and Hurn (Bournemouth) can trace their origins to his recommendations.

There was however a poignant sequel to this tour. During the period when Cobham-Blackburn Airlines was locked in negotiations over African routes with Imperial Airways, it was decided that a special survey flight should be undertaken by a crew including

pilots from both airlines, and an Air Ministry representative. The 'Youth of Britain', having fulfilled its MAS mission was sold to Imperial Airways for this purpose and it was flown to Salisbury in Rhodesia by Sir Alan. He arrived there on 7th January 1930 and handed the aircraft over to Wolley-Dod, who it will be recalled had not found much favour with him after the close call in the Valetta. Their relationship was not improved when Wolley-Dod, on his post-delivery inspection, managed to find fault with almost every aspect of the aeroplane. Sir Alan had carried some 50,000 passengers and made perhaps 5000 landings in this aircraft during his Municipal Aerodrome tour, and the frustration and anger he felt when he heard that Wolley-Dod had crashed the aircraft immediately after his long delivery flight can well be imagined!

Sir Alan was kept busy carrying out surveys of potential aerodrome sites in the two year period after the MAS tour, but the slow progress civil aviation was making generally, was evident to all. Cobham felt that the country simply wasn't air minded, but this was hardly surprising since the great majority of people had rarely seen an aircraft, certainly not at close range, and the number of people who had actually flown was minute. Cobham decided that the only way to stimulate the government into more support would be through public opinion and pressure, and that the most direct way to achieve this would be to present a mandate containing a million signatures to the government – that should really get things moving! His first thought was to promote a National Aviation Day which would become a regular feature on the annual calendar, somewhat akin to Shrove Tuesday or Guy Fawkes Night. Aware that he couldn't be everywhere at once he modified his idea to one whereby each major town would have its own special air day, and so the National Aviation Day (NAD) organisation came into being in 1931.

Side by side with Sir Alan's own efforts to promote flying, technical developments were also gathering pace. Mention was made earlier of J.D.North's 1923 proposal for the refuelling of commercial aircraft in flight. Following this, only a very limited amount of practical work took place at the RAE, although water was transferred from one Bristol Fighter to another during trials in 1924. In 1930 however, and through the early Thirties, in-flight refuelling experiments were resumed at RAE with a view to exploring their serious application. These trials involved DH.9A, Vickers Virginia and Westland Wapiti aircraft, and required an observer in the receiver attempting to catch a weighted cable suspended from the tanker flying above, using the curved head of a walking stick. The first public demonstration of this was given at the 1931 Royal Air Force Display at Hendon.

It is important to introduce at this point the activities of Richard Atcherley, then a Flying Officer in the RAF. Well known for his air racing achievements,

A Vickers Virginia tanker refuels a Westland Wapiti using Sqn. Ldr. Atcherley's 'cross-over' method. The RAF demonstrated this technique at the 1931 Hendon Air Pageant.

As a flyer yourself you've liked it—Tell others
Alan J Cobham

The Airspeed Ferry. Sir Alan's initial order was placed in April 1931, just in time to save the Airspeed Company from bankruptcy.

he attended the American National Air Races in Chicago in 1930 and noted some of the refuelling endurance flights then taking place. Upon his return home and subsequent posting to the RAE in 1934 he developed a system of making contact whereby the tanker lowered a cable and crossed over a line trailed behind the receiver. After the observer in the receiver hauled in the tanker's cable, and an attached hose, fuel was allowed to flow. It was this work that was very shortly to be absorbed into that undertaken by Sir Alan as the Thirties progressed.

In 1931 however, Cobham's attention was concentrated on the air display tour, and to this end he recruited pilots and ground staff, and bought a fleet of more than a dozen aircraft ranging from gliders to autogyros, and an 18 seater Handley Page W.10. In his search for really suitable passenger carrying aircraft, Cobham came to the conclusion that there wasn't one on the market that met his ideal specification. Fate took a hand in matters again however, when, following the winding up of the airship programme in the wake of the R101 crash, two old friends of Cobham's from Airco and de Havilland days decided to form a company called Airspeed Ltd., to design and build small aircraft. Hessell Tiltman was to be the new firm's chief

designer, and Neville Shute Norway, the chief engineer. Following a Board disagreement in 1938 Norway, always a difficult character, was invited to leave Airspeed, and this he did to concentrate on writing. He subsequently achieved far greater fame as the novelist Neville Shute.

An approach was made to Sir Alan to join the Board of the new Company, and after a great deal of persuasion he agreed to become a member. Two years previously, Sir Alan had been in serious discussion with Short Bros. regarding an appointment as Sales Director, but this had come to nothing. Now, due to pressure of work and conflicting interests, Sir Alan was having to renounce other directorships with National Flying Services and Speedways Trust Ltd. In these circumstances he was aware that it hardly seemed consistent to be shedding responsibility on the one hand, while taking on more with the other. But, with the decision made, he announced his requirement for a ten seater miniature air liner at Airspeed Ltd.'s first board meeting on 17th April 1931.

Shortly afterwards the contract was signed and the Ferry, a three engined biplane, began to take shape in a disused bus garage in York. It arrived in time to join the NAD fleet in April 1932 and was christened 'Youth of Britain II'. A second Ferry was delivered a couple of weeks later and naturally became 'Youth of Britain III'. People were now appearing on Sir Alan's payroll who would rally round his banner for the rest of their working years. For example, Hugh Johnson, Percy Allison (invariably referred to as 'P.R.') and Charlie Craig are names that will constantly recur throughout this story, and it is fortunate that so many of their written thoughts and impressions have survived.

In addition to finding the right team and equipment, it was important to find a base from which to operate, and Cobham eventually settled on Ford aerodrome near Littlehampton in Sussex. By pure coincidence the owner of the hangars he rented was the Ford Motor Company! With Dallas Eskell as General Manager, the National Aviation Day tour got underway in 1932 and in that year, 168 towns and cities were visited throughout England, Wales and Scotland.

Percy Allison clearly recalled his interview for a temporary engineering post just prior to the start of the tour. He remembered Sir Alan as autocratic and felt totally overawed by his reputation and manner. Having been asked what he expected in the way of wages, Allison requested £7 for a seven day week, whereupon Sir Alan promptly refused — and offered him £6! It was also pointed out that although there was a canteen, employees were expected to pay for their own meals, whilst sleeping accommodation and toilet facilities would be largely a question of pot luck. Although Allison provided his own tent, and Sir Alan shared a caravan with Chief Pilot Johnson, up to eight people would sleep in the Handley Page W.10 every night. Despite this nomadic existence, Sir Alan would not tolerate anyone referring to the show as a 'circus', and the new employee quickly realised that his boss, always a man in a hurry, would have to be handled with care.

Operating in such difficult circumstances, patience and tempers frequently became frayed, but Allison found that although sacked more than once by Sir Alan both in the air and on the ground, things went on much the same. Sir Alan frequently needed to let off steam, and on one occasion made it clear in no uncertain manner that he considered the work Allison was doing in repairing the Airspeed Ferry's cracked exhaust pipes to be an unnecessary waste of time. After what might be described as a 'forthright exchange of views', Sir Alan stormed off and avoided Allison for days before common sense prevailed!

The stresses and strains of ensuring the tour's continuity did cause Sir Alan many problems, and few of the team escaped the rough edge of his tongue, often delivered within the amused earshot of the crowd. Percy Allison found it virtually impossible to give his full attention to maintenance work and to coping with crowd control and administration. He was constantly worried that passengers in their enthusiastic haste to rush forward and thank the pilot would be hit by the revolving propellers — and indeed this did happen, although fortunately without fatal results! Relationships improved only when the team's duties gradually became more automatic and individual responsibilities more clearly defined.

It became obvious as the tour progressed that time aircraft spent on the ground equated to lost revenue, so a routine was established whereby precisely 4½ gallons of fuel would be put into the Ferry, which allowed it to fly a couple of three minute circuits with simultaneous embarking and off-loading of passengers using opposite doors between flights. Allison suggested to Sir Alan that perhaps there was a case for refuelling in flight, but this met with an outright rejection. Two weeks later however, Sir Alan, having reconsidered the idea, thought it might be included in the display as a stunt item, but Percy Allison made it clear he thought it should be properly investigated, and at this point he somewhat forcibly reminded Sir Alan of his previously stated intention to join Imperial Airways after the tour finished. Cobham's reply was to invite him to stay on and look into this intriguing idea of refuelling in flight. This he did and it resulted in an association that, whilst incurring frequent confrontations, lasted until Allisons's retirement in 1969.

The 1932 display season, despite all the frustrations and two occasions involving public loss of life, proved that success was there for the taking — so much so in fact that two tours were scheduled for the following year. These were planned to operate in parallel, one being managed by Sir Alan and the other by Dallas Eskell. It was also arranged that between the 1932 and 1933 British tours, a winter programme would take place in South Africa, and this duly opened in Cape Town on 1st December 1932. For a variety of reasons, and despite the fact that the shows, as always,

The 'Flying Circus' comes to town in the early 1930s. A Handley Page Clive leads two Airspeed Ferrys, two DH Fox Moths, two DH Tiger Moths and a Cierva C19 autogyro.

An Avro 504, nearest camera, accompanies the Fox Moth and the HP Clive (later renamed 'Astra').

Pure nostalgia. The pilot is Flt. Lt. Hyland, and his aircraft is an Avro 504K. This picture, taken during an NAD visit to Gravesend, was used by the Ford Motor Co. as a publicity photograph for their products.

Eight year old Michael Cobham (nearest the camera) with brother Geoffrey, was required on occasions to fly with the National Air Display.

were immensely popular with the crowds, the tour was not a financial success, and Sir Alan's sense of disappointment and personal loss were compounded when he received a cable in February informing him of his father's death.

Back in England once more, Sir Alan continued providing his crazy flying, wing walking and parachuting displays throughout the summers of 1934 and 1935, during which time he furthered his work as adviser to many municipalities, and as Aerodrome and Air Routes Consultant to his old adversary, Imperial Airways. In 1934 the possibility of taking the itinerant air show to India was rejected after a fact-finding team, which included Lady Cobham, found the opportunities for success to be limited.

In addition to the loss of staff to the newly expanded Air Force Reserve, reduced takings eventually indicated a waning of public interest in the Displays, and this convinced Sir Alan that the double event planned for 1935 would have to be the last, and so it turned out. The Display was sold — without the right to use the Cobham name — to C.W.A.Scott who, with Tom Campbell Black, had won the Macpherson Robertson air race from Mildenhall to Melbourne in 1934.

Sixty years or so after the tours, Michael Cobham retains vivid memories of how, armed with his

41

father's advice to 'always walk in front of a horse, but behind an aeroplane', he was called occasionally to assist. It happened sometimes that after Geoffrey Tyson's aerobatic display, people would be slow to come forward for 'the flight of their lives'. However the sight of a young seven or eight year old boy, keen to be the first, and hailed over the loudspeakers as a good example of 'Britain's air minded youth', invariably did the trick. During W.W.II, it was estimated that some 60 per cent of the RAF's pilots received their flight baptism in Cobham's care, and over the subsequent years, Michael Cobham has been approached by countless people, including many high-ranking Service officers, who experienced their first flight during the NAD tours.

At this time Sir Alan was still doggedly determined to operate his own airline, despite the high failure rate of others who were being encouraged by the arrival of more reliable, better quality aircraft. A Service between the mainland and Jersey was already operating successfully, so Cobham — not to be outdone — and in addition to his duties as a member of the Board of the Portsmouth, Southsea and Isle of Wight Aviation Ltd., formed Cobham Air Routes Ltd. in May 1935. Using Airspeed Couriers, twin engined Envoys, and a tri-motored Westland Wessex, passengers were carried between London and Guernsey with intermediate stops at Portsmouth, Southampton and Bournemouth. The Wessex, G-ADEW, was specifically purchased to provide increased safety over the sea, but the aircraft was ill fated — crashing due south of Durleston Head whilst heading for Bournemouth in the early evening of 3rd July 1935. Captain Ogden, a long time colleague of Sir Alan, was drowned in the accident, but the only passenger, a Mr. Grainger, was picked up by the S.S. *Stanmore* after surviving in the water for one and a half hours. No distress signals were received from the aircraft, and the accident was never satisfactorily explained.

With hindsight it would appear that the Guernsey venture stood little chance of success from the start. Apart from the incident involving the Wessex, the volume of passenger traffic was never likely to be sufficient to cover operating costs and make a substantial profit, and Sir Alan's choice of L'Eree airfield as suitable for airline operations met with severe criticism. Wing Commander Measures, Superintendent of Railway Air Services Ltd., who was also considering providing an aerial link with

the mainland, issued a report in which he claimed that he had never seen such a small and unsuitable area for the regular landing of passenger-carrying aircraft. He added that that he was at a loss to understand how the Air Ministry could ever have granted even a restricted licence to operate from such a place.

When Cobham formed his Air Routes company he had also intended to extend services to the Scilly Isles and between Dublin, Liverpool and London, where again Railway Air Services was proving to be a competitive thorn in his side. These factors, coupled with a combination of Irish political and business difficulties, influenced him to sell his Air Routes interests to Captain G.P.Olley's Olley Air Services, which had the backing of Sir Hugo Cunliffe-Owen, then Chairman of British American Tobacco Ltd. Gordon Olley was an early Handley Page pilot who on his first flight to Paris had to make seventeen forced landings. After each descent he cleared a choked petrol feed by hand pumping, correctly estimating that despite the recurring problem, he could just clear the Channel. He

Captain Gordon Olley, who took over Cobham's Air Routes in the mid-1930s.

finished up at nightfall on a football pitch near Paris, and was preparing for his eighteenth and final take-off when he discovered that his passengers had vanished!

The sale of Air Routes is yet another indication of the restless urges and attitudes which drove Sir Alan and other aerial pioneers forward. Each phase of Cobham's life seemed to require a new beginning and, true to form, he was now ready to lengthen his stride and take on yet another challenge — the development of air-to-air refuelling and the birth of a legendary company.

TWO

The Founding Years

For some time, Sir Alan had been vexed by the fact that it took considerably more power to get an aircraft off the ground than it did to sustain it in flight. As will be seen, some highly innovative methods would be tried during later years to overcome this problem, including rocket and jet assisted take off, catapult launching and the Short-Mayo Composite Aircraft 'piggy-back' system which involved an aircraft being carried to a suitable height by a larger, more powerful one before being released to fly under its own power. Cobham however, had, both from his own tentative experiments and observations of other developments already mentioned, become convinced as early as 1932 that refuelling aircraft in flight offered the most practical solution. If an aircraft's fuel load on take off could be minimized, but 'topped up' once in flight, then the power requirement, and hence engine size, could be

reduced and the payload or range capability greatly increased. The opportunities this would provide for the advancement of both military and civil aviation seemed immense, and in considering how such a refuelling system could be most effectively implemented and demonstrated, the idea of another proving flight to Australia had taken shape — but this time it would be non-stop!

At his base in Sussex, Cobham's efforts became increasingly directed towards the development of a practical aerial refuelling installation, and some of the National Aviation Display (NAD) crews began to carry out flight tests during the winter months of 1932 and 1933 using the Handley Page W.10 as a tanker, and the DH.9a as a receiver. Two major problems immediately became obvious. Firstly, a hose trailed in the tanker's slipstream thrashed about rapidly and violently unless a sizeable weight was

The Short-Mayo Composite Aircraft was a novel attempt at obtaining maximum range.

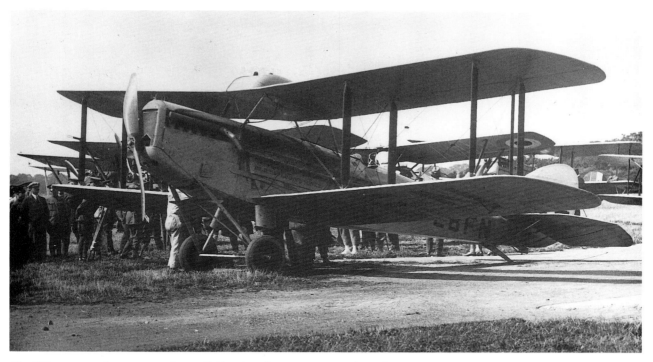

The DH.9a was used as a receiver during Cobham's early attempts at aerial refuelling.

attached. Secondly, the biplanes of the day, whilst reasonably suitable as tankers, were generally difficult and cumbersome to manoeuvre as receivers, and in view of the proposed flight to Australia the need for a custom-built demonstrator aircraft soon became apparent. Sir Alan discussed the situation with his colleagues at Airspeed and this resulted in a specification being drawn up for what became the Airspeed AS.5 Courier, and a price of £5,500 was settled upon. Design work commenced immediately following an unofficial agreement reached on 6th May 1932, and a sleek single engined low-wing monoplane, the first to be produced in quantity in Great Britain with a retractable undercarriage, emerged from Airspeed's premises only twelve months later.

With his unique aeroplane firmly on order, and refuelling equipment being installed and tested at Ford, Sir Alan decided to try to obtain the Air Ministry's co-operation in providing facilities en route to Australia. At this time Sir Hugh Dowding (later Lord Dowding) was the Air Member for Supply and Organization (A.M.S.O.) and, as such, was receptive to Cobham's suggestions. He was equally aware of how a successful demonstration might influence official thinking and assist the eventual extension of the RAF's operational capabilities. However, he warned against the undertaking of too ambitious and expensive a flight at this stage and proposed India as a more realistic destination. In supporting Sir Alan's plans, Dowding arranged for the RAF to supply fuel in the air from converted Vickers Victoria and Valencia bombers at Aboukir and Basra. Cobham in turn agreed to send out Ogden and Allison to do the conversion work, and to refuel the Courier using the NAD Handley Page W.10s, the first operation being scheduled for just after take-off over the Isle of Wight, and the second over Malta. Whilst these arrangements were taking shape Cobham was as usual, busily engaged on several other fronts; as a prime example we need look no further than the serious consideration he gave to joining Sir Malcolm Campbell on an expedition to the Kalahari Desert in a search for gold — a scheme which ultimately came to nothing.

In the meantime, after completing its Certificate of Airworthiness trials programme at the Martlesham Heath Test Establishment, Courier G-ABXN was finally delivered to Ford, and with an old colleague, Sqn. Ldr. Bill Helmore, newly recruited as co-pilot for the trip to India, Cobham began an intensive

Geoffrey Tyson, who flew with the NAD team during the 1930s, pictured with Sir Alan at the Paris Air Exhibition, 1967.

series of air tests behind the W.10 tanker. Also taking part in these trials, along with tanker pilots Bembridge and Johnson, was Geoffrey Tyson who much later in his career would be renowned for his memorable demonstrations of the majestic Saunders Roe Princess flying boat at the air displays held at Farnborough in the Fifties. He provides the following entertaining description of this early work:

"Making the original contact with the tanker involved a certain amount of juggling in the Courier both for the pilot and the refuellee — mostly for the pilot. He could make or mar the operation. But the refuellee had to be hardy; appropriately dressed, he stood with the upper half of his body exposed to the slipstream with a walking stick in his hand ready to catch whatever came his way. From the belly of the W.10 tanker was trailed a heavy picture cord and on it a small football filled with lead shot. I say 'small' for it wasn't a man-size ball, it was the kind one gives small boys at Christmas when they're not old enough to stub their toes on the big ones. Small diameter cord ensured low drag as did the high solidity of the ball, so all in all a fairly steep angle of trail was obtained — a kind of quarter elliptical arc. The Courier was a single engined aircraft so there were two ways of bringing football to walking stick,

either get the ball over the port wing-tip about 6 ft. above and shunt left or, line up directly behind, bring it over the top of the propeller and then pull up slightly. I preferred the latter way because it is easier to fly accurately looking straight ahead than with a crick in the neck and eyeballs off-centre; one then seems to get an extra dimension involved though in fact there isn't.

With practice, and stable air conditions, it wasn't too bad a method to bring the ball over the prop disc; one could drop it on the cabin roof about a foot above the eyes and then roll it back. But in bumps it was a different matter, the bowed line would change shape, always at the critical moment when you were about to run the prop underneath; magically the football would belie its appearance of a child's toy and become a lethal weapon. If one was trying the wing approach method it would thud on to the wing; if the direct approach was chosen it would suddenly run down the propeller disc a bare foot or two in front of it causing an involuntary jerking back of the throttle to get out of the danger zone. Then all over again the tedious cat-and-mouse approach. Above, the tanker pilot would be getting tired of trying to fly to plus or minus six inches of his allotted height and mutter 'Why the hell doesn't he get a move on?' In the Courier it was 'Why the hell doesn't he keep still?' Plainly the solid object had to be replaced by something less likely to do damage – particularly to the propeller.

After a flight of near misses one day we returned for our customary round-the-table chat. Something was needed that would disintegrate on touching the prop – a container of water for instance. From one of those present, whose mind was obviously not wholly on his business, came a brilliant suggestion and a car was sent down town post haste. Unfortunately the specimens had a factor of less than 1.0 for the purpose that we needed them, but the idea was good and within a week Dunlops produced some strong rubber bags. Thereafter we headed for the dangling spheroids with gay abandon, having just done a couple of test bursts to prove our theories."

Sir Alan made vivid mention too of one dramatic trial flight when in turbulent weather, the cord carrying the weight became entangled in the Courier's port aileron hinge, causing him to spin precariously out of control. He managed to free the obstructed line with very little altitude to spare directly over Chichester Cathedral, and both he and Helmore would recount for many a day how they were convinced their last hour had come. Percy Allison also recalled a weighted cable becoming trapped in the rudder gap of a DH.9a piloted by Bill Helmore. Again the snagged cable caused a dangerous spin and matters were not helped when, having finally landed, Sir Alan wanted to know in his invariably colourful way what they thought they had been doing. Helmore pointed out in no uncertain manner that the situation had been caused by Sir Alan moving position once having trailed the hose – and added just what he could do with his blasted refuelling! Allison further commented that "standing half in and half out of an open cockpit without a parachute and in a cold howling gale was bad enough, but with a sizeable lead weight also attacking you from different directions – we must have been mad to do it for the money we got paid".

And so with all preparations finally in place and temperamental differences resolved, Cobham and Helmore took off from Portsmouth early on 22nd

Bill Helmore and Sir Alan before their attempt to fly non-stop to India.

Handley Page W10 G-E BMM refuels Cobham's Airspeed Courier during the attempted record flight to India in 1934. The Handley Page broke up in mid-air and crashed, killing all on board, after refuelling the Courier on 22nd September 1934.

September 1934 for Karachi. Both pilots intended to take two hour turns at the controls during what was expected to be nearly a two day flight. The first two refuelling operations were successfully carried out in calm weather, fuel being passed at a rate of 18 gallons a minute, but, after setting course for the Aboukir refuelling point, Sir Alan found to his horror and dismay that movement of the throttle produced no engine response whatsoever, and with power slowly decreasing he immediately turned back for Malta. In providing less drag, the retractable under-carriage greatly assisted in prolonging a shallow glide, and with the propeller barely turning, Cobham managed to literally scrape in for a belly landing at Halfar aerodrome. RAF personnel were soon on the scene and an inspection quickly revealed a split pin

lying in the lower cowling! Closer investigation showed that this penny item which should have locked a cotter pin holding the throttle linkage together, had never in fact been fitted, and that the cotter-pin had simply worked loose.

There was worse to come. After his emergency landing, Cobham was handed a cablegram by the RAF Commanding Officer which read: 'IF POSSIBLE ASK COBHAM COMMUNICATE WHITEHALL 7707 GIVING AUTHORITATIVE DETAILS FOR PRESS. INFORM HIM M.M. CRASHED FOUR KILLED — GLADYS COBHAM'. Termination of the record attempt had been bad enough, but the realization that G-EBMM, 'Youth of New Zealand', the W.10 tanker that had carried out the first refuelling, had come to grief two miles north east of

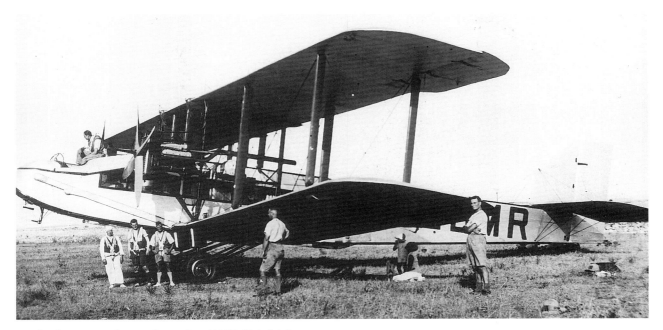

Hugh Johnson (in cockpit) and HP W.10 G-EBMR in Malta.

Halton on its return flight, rendered 22nd September a very black day indeed.

Although the mission had ended in tragedy and failure, Sir Alan was keen to point out to the authorities that the reasons for this had nothing to do with what he had been trying to prove. But the associations were too great, official interest in aerial refuelling suffered severely that day, and it would be nearly a decade before it was fully revived. Perverse as ever when faced with an official rebuff, Sir Alan was determined that the time and money already spent on refuelling development should not be wasted, and that work should continue. His belief in the advantages that had yet to be exploited became so strong that on 29th October 1934, the Articles of Association of his new specialist company were completed, and the name chosen – Flight Refuelling Limited – left no doubt about the business he intended to pursue!

After the 1935 NAD tours had finished, and all the equipment and aircraft, except for an Avro Tutor and a black Monospar, had been sold off, the only members of staff remaining apart from Sir Alan and his secretary, Miss Cameron, were Hugh Johnson, Percy Allison, Charlie Craig and Chris Tonge – who served as storeman, telephone operator and general clerk-cum-accountant, before eventually rising to become the Company's Financial Director. Geoffrey Tyson

had also left to join A.V.Roe as a test pilot. It was from this dedicated little band that Hugh Johnson officially became the first employee of Flight Refuelling Ltd. (FRL), but the others had all been transferred from the NAD payroll by the end of the year. Cobham was now faced with an uphill fight to impress the merits of airborne refuelling upon the Service and Airline establishments. He first approached Imperial Airways, who at that time were showing great interest in the Short-Mayo Composite aircraft scheme, about the possibility of using flight refuelling on the Empire and projected transatlantic routes. His powers of persuasion did not let him down, and Woods-Humphrey and his General Manager, Colonel Burchall, agreed to enter into partnership with Cobham – but with a 60 per cent stake in the new Company!

Further persuasion at high level resulted in 1936 in the Air Ministry supplying two obsolete Vickers Virginias, J 7711 and K 2668 for trials work, and it was a proud and enthusiastic team that motored down to Hawkinge in Kent to take delivery. This auspicious start nearly came to grief when Cobham, attempting to take off in the first aircraft, failed to release the brakes, and almost tipped the machine onto its nose. Percy Allison later revealed how disaster threatened again during the lumbering take-off run. The Virginia was fitted with an unusual

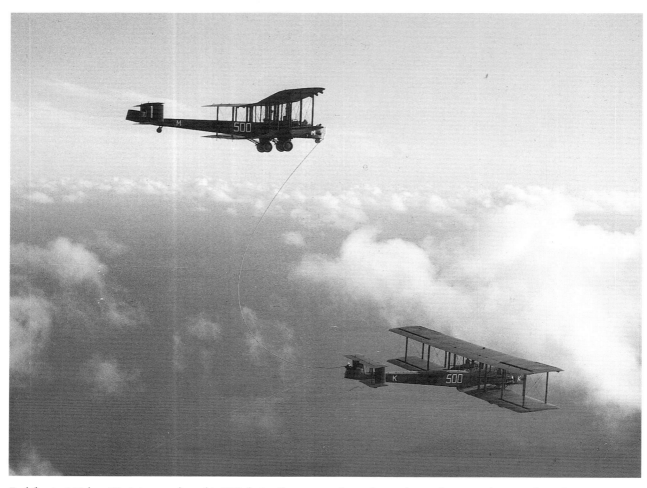

Fuel flowing! Vickers Virginias were loaned to FRL during the 1930s and served as tankers and receivers during early trials.

throttle control common to both engines which required movement to left or right to give individual engine power settings. This took a while to get used to, and co-pilot Allison noted that some fancy throttle work would be required if they were going to avoid hangars and the administration block looming directly ahead. With both of Allison's hands locked over Cobham's and in conflict over the power settings, the aircraft somehow managed to get safely airborne. Following the joint sighs of relief, Cobham, voice raised against the wind, made it abundantly clear that it was his job to 'fly the bloody aeroplane – it was Allison's to look after everything else!' Taking full advantage of the flight, Cobham and Johnson undertook formation practice all the way to Ford and business had commenced in earnest.

The first demonstration, carried out before Dowding, still employed the technique that required an operator, usually Percy Allison, located in the nose gunner's position to hook in the water bag and cord with a walking stick. Trials were also undertaken with both aircraft tied together, nose to tail, to see what would happen if for some reason it became impossible to separate in flight. Despite both pilots trying to pull each other out of the sky, fears proved groundless, and according to Johnson there was always a sufficient margin of control to get back into a straight and level position.

In an attempt to increase the rate of fuel flow to the receiver, it was decided to provide the Virginia with a rudimentary windmill driven pumping system. To undertake this work A.B.Dennistoun was persuaded to leave Blackburn Aircraft Ltd. thus becoming FRL's first bona fide designer. Unfortunately the pump and gear box mounted on top of the fuselage was heavy and cumbersome and did not provide any noticeable improvement in flow performance. The Company's cash flow position was a continual problem and this was directly reflected in the test flights, which rarely exceeded fifteen minutes. Contact between tanker and receiver was made almost before the aircraft had cleared the airfield boundary hedge, and after completion of a simple circuit at 3000 ft. over Bognor Pier and Littlehampton, it was always a frantic effort on the part of the operators to haul in the ropes and hoses before landing.

To ease this problem and to overcome the difficulty of pulling in heavy unwieldy hoses by hand in flight, Percy Allison fitted up a wooden reeling device in the nose of the Virginia receiver. Another line of development involved the attachment of long poles which extended forward from the receiver aircraft and were intended to guide the trailing cables toward the operator in the nose. Called the 'Horns Method' it was adjudged to be dangerous by both Johnson and Tyson, who had recently rejoined the team, and soon abandoned. Whilst working with the two Virginias a limited amount of work was also undertaken to try out the Atcherley 'crossed line' or 'Inter-Air' method as it was more formally referred to. As this meant invoking Atcherley's patents, Cobham realized that he was incurring some commercial risk and so, making full use of his personal contacts

in the Air Ministry, he asked for the opportunity to officially 'prove the practicability' of the Atcherley System.

By now FRL was considered to be expert in the refuelling field, and a development contract was placed with the Company in 1937 to evaluate and improve both the Cobham and Atcherley methods. In order to do this, all the RAE test data and equipment, along with a Boulton Paul Overstrand receiver, J 9970 and a Vickers Type 19/27 tanker, J9131 were transferred to Ford. Flight trials soon showed that hazardous disadvantages were inherent in the Atcherley method. Firstly, it was easy for the tanker pilot to lose sight of the other aircraft when crossing over into position to engage the receiver's streamed line and grapnel — thus increasing the risk of collision. Secondly, the system employed a heavy drogue which, when trailed, hauled in the refuelling hose via a system of pulleys. Because of the high drag forces acting on the drogue, it was impossible to retrieve it and it had to be guillotined free once the operation was complete. Not only was this wasteful in terms of lost equipment, it was illegal as only water or sand were permitted to be jettisoned from an aircraft over land, except in the case of genuine emergency.

Following on from this work, Sir Alan managed to

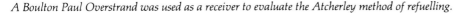

A Boulton Paul Overstrand was used as a receiver to evaluate the Atcherley method of refuelling.

A Fairey Hendon was allocated to FRL for flight refuelling development in the late 1930s.

A Handley Page Heyford was also used at Ford for aerial refuelling.

get a Fairey Hendon K 1695 and a Handley Page Heyford K 5184 allocated for further flight testing, and by now there was quite a fleet of aircraft at FRL's disposal with both hangars full. It was customary for each flight to be followed by an intense de-briefing session around a blackboard which often produced innovative development suggestions and improvements. On one such occasion, Hugh Johnson and Percy Allison came up with a scheme described as "a saucer like arrangement in the tail of the receiver and a form of nozzle that could be pulled into the saucer". Such an arrangement also required a reversal of the aircraft positions that had been tried so far, with the receiver flying in front of the tanker.

Johnson later wrote in an aide memoire how he assisted Allison to cast a large block of aluminium, full of nails and other impurities, in a Wakefield oil drum, and how this was used to produce the first receiver coupling. Allison went a stage further and refined the coupling to include a hydraulically operated lever and roller locking device which gripped the nozzle in a fluid tight engagement. This was a major improvement on the trigger operated nozzle used so far. Equipment had to be acquired in order to do this work and Allison and Johnson went off to London's East End to purchase a lathe and pillar drill from a second hand tool dealer. This profligate spending meant that celebration of the purchase was limited to half a pint of beer each, with no accompanying lunch!

Fred Wilkinson, FRL's first machinist, came to Ford from Rolls-Royce at this time, and Baldwins of Bognor sent Bill Tadd to wire up a building which served first as the machine shop and later as a combined machine shop and drawing office. Sir Alan was so impressed with Tadd's energy and enthusiasm he offered him a job on the spot, which he readily accepted. Ron Illesley, Harry Smith and others, who would become key figures, were also employed at this time, and Ron Woods recalls that in deciding to join FRL rather than Carter Patterson in 1937, he became the Company's first apprentice, working alongside Wilkinson.

The high expectations that attended the arrival of the Hendon and Heyford aircraft were short lived as both exhibited flight characteristics that rendered them totally useless as tankers. In the case of the Heyford, its flying performance could hardly have been improved when Geoffrey Tyson, taxiing out for take-off one morning, damaged a lower wing tip on some railings. He later explained that he had been distracted by Sir Alan's horse, 'Caractacus', which was tethered to the railings, and hadn't noticed any damage until he landed at Farnborough.

'Caractacus' provided much amusement for the engineering design staff, who lived in a converted ex-cow shed on the airfield. Bets were frequently placed on the time of Sir Alan's arrival from Middleton as it was known that the horse shied at certain gates, and his assorted modes of transport were also the subject of much speculation, varying as they did between horse and car in any given week!

The search for suitable trials aircraft continued in the wake of the disappointing Hendon and Heyford, and in response to Cobham's pleas an Armstrong Whitworth 23, K 3585, and a Handley Page 51, J 9833, (forerunners of the Whitley and Harrow bombers respectively) were provided on loan from the Air Ministry. It was with these aircraft that significant progress began to be made in the latter part of 1937. During its early flights it was discovered that the AW.23 tanker created a large bow wave which pushed the water bag out of the operator's reach, and this led to the use of a new form of contact called the 'Wing Tip' method. This required the tanker's wing leading edge outboard of the propeller disc to contact the weighted line trailed by the receiver. Having done this, the aircraft was turned away in a manner which caused the cable to

Sir Alan and 'Caractacus'.

The Armstrong Whitworth AW.23 (forerunner of the Whitley bomber) used as a tanker-receiver.

The Handley Page HP.51 also used in mid-1930s trials.

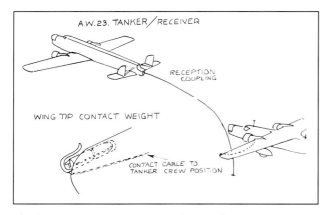

Sketch from a contemporary report showing the 'Wing Tip' method of contact.

run towards the wing tip and into a latched hook. This movement pulled the hook out of its housing, and because it was attached to the hose on a reel inside the fuselage, contact was automatically secured between the two aircraft. As contact speeds increased the water bag was replaced by a 15lb ball of lead, and steel cables were used instead of rope. Although not designed for formation flying, and possessed of spongy lateral control, the AW.23 became the preferred aircraft for use in the tanker role, and it contrasted favourably with the HP.51 which had an alarming tendency to dive and hunt on the landing approach. This was so predictable that Johnson's crew members were trained to run up and down the fuselage to counteract the pitching movement, seemingly with success!

The way the Company had progressed since its formation a year earlier suggested that it would probably soon become a tanker supply service. Imperial Airways foresaw that with this probability, it might be appropriate to withdraw its interest, and in June 1937 sold its major shareholding to Shell, with Sir John Salmond replacing S.A.Dismore of Imperial Airways as Chairman, but Sir Alan continuing as Managing Director.

Cobham's other widespread activities had not abated in the slightest, and when at this time it was proposed to form a new company in Australia, called the Airplane Construction Development Pty. Ltd., he was nominated to sit on the Board. The initial intention was to import complete Airspeed aircraft into the country, and subsequently to fabricate and assemble the Oxford trainer, but Australian aircraft production, after much confusion and acrimonious governmental debate, eventually

concentrated on other types and the plans were shelved.

The closing months of 1937 and the period leading up to April 1938, saw preparations in hand for equipping Imperial Airway's Short 'C' Class flying boat 'Cambria' with airborne refuelling equipment, and the ad hoc design efforts of Sir Alan, Johnson and Allison were now overtaken by trained designers, such as Edward Tripp, Marcus Langley, Harry Smith and Peter Procter. Further significant work carried out about this time included the fuel distribution and management system designed for the 'Cambria' by Tripp, and a treatise prepared by Langley which addressed the technical requirements for an aircraft designed from the outset as a tanker. Langley was a very capable engineer who, prior to joining Sir Alan, had been Chief Designer of the British Aircraft Manufacturing Company which was in the process of being absorbed into the General Aircraft Company.

The first proving and airworthiness flights involving 'Cambria' and the AW.23 were carried out over Rochester and Felixstowe, the aircraft being flown by Shorts' test pilots John Lankester Parker and 'Pincher' Martin, and FRL's stalwarts Johnson and Tyson. Following this, repeated and equally satisfactory tests were carried out during January 1938 over the Solent with Captain A. S. Wilcockson of Imperial Airways flying 'Cambria'. Seventeen flights were carried out, many in extremely bad weather, 'Cambria' being forced on occasions to fly at no more than 75 feet above the water in order that the AW.23 tanker might remain below the cloud level. Frequent combinations of blinding rain, reduced visibility — sometimes to half a mile — and extremely bumpy conditions, required flying skills of a high order to maintain contact and pass the maximum amount of fuel — but it was successfully achieved. So successfully in fact that FRL issued a guarantee of "service in any part of the world to deliver 1000 gallons of fuel in ten minutes, at speeds with existing equipment ranging from 110 to 125 mph." This led to an agreement with Imperial Airways to operate a series of air refuelling transatlantic crossings the following year, for which purpose two Empire S.30 boats, 'Cabot' and 'Caribou', were structurally modified to allow an increase in all up weight from 46,000 to 53,000 lbs. FRL's new commitment meant that more aircraft were required and Hugh Johnson visited Ternhill four times to collect brand new Handley Page Harrow aircraft. Two were registered

in March 1939 as G-AFRG and G-AFRH, but, by waiting a few days, the third was appropriately registered G-AFRL. The AW.23 was also allocated the civil registration G-AFRX at the same time.

The proposed trials involved eight return crossings, the first commencing on 5th August 1939. The starting point for the westbound journeys was to be Foynes, a village on the south bank of the River Shannon, and a few miles south west of Rineanna, where FRL would be basing one of the Harrow tankers. Another Harrow was retained at Ford for general development work and to act as a reserve for the aircraft at Rineanna. Two other Harrows were to be despatched to Gander in Newfoundland to refuel the flying boats prior to their eastbound crossings.

Conscious of the fact that the methods used for making contact were anything but foolproof, experiments continued at Ford. Attempts were made to improve the 'Wing Tip' method, and a set of 'horns', now called the 'Cobham-Tripp' method, were fitted to a Harrow for evaluation, despite the earlier reservations expressed by Johnson and Tyson. The real break-through came however, when Cobham had the idea of firing a throwing line from the tanker, in a

The fuel jettison system fitted to 'C' Class flying boats was designed by FRL. This machine was destroyed in Norway during a Luftwaffe attack, 1940.

A close-up of the drum unit and hose nozzle installed in a Harrow tanker.

similar fashion to that employed by coastguards on cliffs when ships were stranded on the rocks below. So, to prove the principle, Sir Alan and Hugh Johnson visited the lighthouse station at Selsey Bill and borrowed a Greener gun which had been originally designed in 1880, and even used by the cavalry!

Eventually a gun was obtained from the BSA Company which was capable of firing a 15 inch steel rod with a grapnel on the end, taking with it 300 feet of 5 cwt. steel cable. It was now going to be a simple matter to fly alongside the receiver, a few feet below it and fire the line across the receiver's weighted sinker line — or so it was thought! The first time this was tried in the air Charlie Craig was given the honour of standing up in the rear turret of one of the corrosion ridden Virginias. Holding the gun to his shoulder, he pulled the trigger, and was nearly thrown overboard by the recoil! Nevertheless every

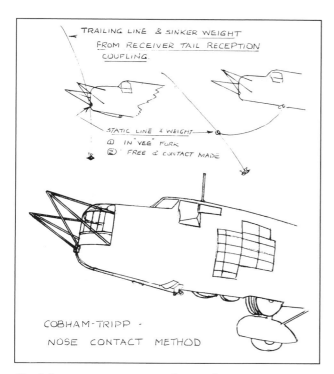

Sketch from contemporary report showing the 'Horns or Cobham-Tripp' method of contact.

Charlie Craig (left) and Percy Allison working on a Harrow tanker in the late 1930s.

Forty years later – Allison (left) and Craig with Michael Cobham in 1979.

one was encouraged by the fact that by aiming forward, the line would travel in a horizontal plane before it started to descend.

The flying side of the operation was now certainly more straightforward, but mechanical problems still plagued the trials. Firing steel cables across rope-covered cables did not always result in them sliding down until the grapnels enmeshed. As soon as the crossing cables touched the sinker line they frequently seared through the rope covering and remained firmly in the grooves, and if the tanker pilot pulled away hoping that the projectile would cling to the receiver cables by its grapnel, it would invariably whip clear as it was pulled across. Eventually, by baring the lower 50 feet of the receiver's sinker line, and by careful positioning of the tanker, the 'Ejector' or 'Looped Hose' method of contact became a practical reality – just in time for the North Atlantic trials (see Appendix I). Development of the equipment went on in parallel with training of the Imperial Airways crews right up to the commencement of trials, and long after Hugh Johnson, along with a small team, had sailed for Canada in the spring to set up FRL's refuelling base at Gander in Newfoundland.

Following their arrival in Canada, Johnson experienced immense difficulties in getting personnel and two Harrow aircraft, G-AFRG and G-AFRM, transported to Newfoundland. After unshipping at Quebec on 24th April 1939, frozen river conditions delayed the aircraft being ferried, firstly to Montreal

Above *Sir Alan Cobham (right) and Hugh Johnson who flew in the National Air Display team, and later led FRL's tanker team in Newfoundland.*

Opposite page *A fine study of a Harrow tanker in contact with 'Cabot', over Southampton docks, 1939.*

Below *Bound for Newfoundland! One of two Harrow tankers on board the SS Beaverford, prior to transatlantic trials, 1939.*

and then to Fairchild Flying Field. The availability of special cranes for finally unloading the aircraft was also hindered by a mountain of red tape, and it was even necessary for the FRL team to locate suitable timbers before a special ramp could be built which enabled the aircarft to be hauled up to the edge of the airfield. Working in the open, the aircraft were finally assembled, tested and flown to Newfoundland by mid-May. Even then trouble was never far away. Flt. Lt. Atkinson, recruited in England just prior to the team's departure to share the piloting duties with Johnson, had to return to Montreal when a washer in a fuel tank perished and caused over one hundred gallons of fuel to discharge into the fuselage. It was with great discomfort that Atkinson managed to return to Quebec, with petrol fumes nearly choking him and his crew.

Some idea of the primitive conditions facing Johnson once he arrived at Hatties Camp in Newfoundland can be gained from the fact that the construction of an office and stores had to be carried out from scratch, with both pilots' wives assisting in the setting up of a stock records system. Living accommodation was extremely scarce and the travelling distances such, that leaving his rented rooms in the early hours in a hired boat, and arriving back often as late as 10.30 p.m., was the only way initially to overcome the problem. The Johnsons

found this situation untenable and after a short while took up residence for the next three months in a railway box-car, hired from the Newfoundland Railway Company. The domestic arrangements were unhappy to say the least, and with the other team members living in small shacks with a communal bath-house and cook-house, morale was at times decidedly low. But a job had to be done and to the credit of all concerned, when the trials finally got underway, all the flights, apart from the first eastbound return, were refuelled from either the Hatties Camp base at Gander, or from Rineanna, and usually involved the transfer of some 950 gallons of fuel over a fifteen minute period.

For the inaugural service on the 5th August, Mr. de Valera, the Prime Minister of Eire, visited Foynes, the take-off point for the flying boats, and was keen to see an actual refuelling take place. 'Caribou's' pilot, J.C.Kelly-Rogers, had intended to take off and continue heading west on a steady course, but it was now necessary to rendezvous with Tyson's Harrow in the immediate area in order to provide an impressive flypast. This required smooth handling and timing if 'Caribou' was going to gain full benefit from the added fuel reserves. Kelly-Rogers lifted off the Shannon and met up with Tyson as planned, contact was made on the turn and the fuel cocks opened as the aircraft came in towards Foynes. However, at 125 mph, the minimum safe speed for refuelling 'Caribou', it required virtually full throttle for the Harrow to fly straight and level; on the turn it was possible to keep pace only if half a dozen other conditions were met. This time they were not and with throttles wide open, Tyson started dropping back, just enough to drag the hose nozzle out of the reception coupling. Although the automatic nozzle valves closed, enough fuel escaped to create a fountain of spray which to the onlookers must have looked like a disaster. Standing beside Mr. de Valera on the Foynes jetty, Sir Alan had an agonizing time, but for the last mile of the run up, Tyson managed to get the Harrow's nose down sufficiently to gain some extra speed and allow the men operating 'Caribou's' winch to pull the nozzle home again. The final passage over the official gathering was later reported as sedate with everything apparently well under control!

Whilst the preparations for the transatlantic venture had made large demands on FRL's manpower and materials, other projects had required the organisation's attention during the period leading up to the outbreak of war, and Hesell Tiltman was brought in on a regular consulting basis to assist the overstretched designers. For instance, the interest of the Air Staff in the possibility of refuelling bombers in early 1938, led FRL to undertake a thorough investigation into the effect of refuelling on their performance, particularly range and load-carrying capacity. Specifications were drawn up and performance figures calculated for several hypothetical bombers in order to compare them with standard service aircraft. The first proposal was presented to Gp. Capt. Saundby on 19th October 1938, and referred to the FR.5 which with a crew of five or six had a projected cruising speed of 300 mph, and a range of 2540 miles when carrying a military load of 4120 lbs. However, the Group Captain was looking for a smaller and faster machine that would carry no armament, and which would depend for its defence on its higher speed. From this redirection came another proposed design, the FR.7 — this time with a two-man crew and a top speed of 377 mph at 13,500 ft. (see Appendix II). The range, with a bomb load of 2000 lbs., was predicted to be 2,900 miles. Although Saundby's requirements are quoted directly from an FRL development report for the 1938 period, they appear to be inconsistent with the Ministry's lack of interest in the proposal for a high performance aircraft submitted by de Havilland. This was soon to become the highly successful Mosquito, which only gained acceptance into service through the perseverance of Air Vice Marshal Sir Wilfred Freeman — the aircraft being initially referred to as 'Freeman's folly'!

Both the FR.5 and FR.7 were to have used the Harrow as a tanker, taking on board nearly 1000 gallons of fuel. These projects were under the Ministry's consideration for some time, but they eventually suggested that rather than resort to specifications and designs of this sort, it would be in the general interest to concentrate on modifying the designs of some of the more modern bombers then in course of construction, and to suggest how they might be adapted for flight refuelling. Exactly one year after the first submission to Saundby, FRL received an Air Ministry letter formally requesting them to present a case for refuelling Service aircraft with particular reference to the Short Stirling, the RAF's first modern heavy bomber. The resulting study culminated in a proposal submitted in June 1939, and which included a recommendation for the bomber taking off at night in formation with,

Proposals to convert the Fairey Swordfish into a tanker were not pursued.

and connected to a tanker. Following an immediate refuelling, the tanker would land and repeat the exercise with another aircraft. This suggestion was made on the assumpton that only small numbers of bombers would be involved in raids, and that a 'one to one' arrangement was therefore both practical and manageable. It would however have been totally impossible to have applied such a scheme to the increasingly large numbers of aircraft employed as the war progressed. It is of interest to note that in addition to the Harrow tanker, Marcus Langley also gave serious consideration to using the beautifully streamlined D.H.Albatross airliner in the tanker role. Despite all this early activity, the Air Ministry did not express any further interest in flight refuelling until much later in the war.

The case for refuelling Fleet Air Arm aircraft had also been given some serious attention during the immediate pre-war period. It had long been realized that ship-launched aircraft could never match their shore based counterparts in any aspect of performance, being restricted by the length of take off run from a carrier deck, physical dimensions dictated by lower deck stowage, and the extra structural weight carried to provide the ruggedness required for deck landings. If some way could be found to overcome these handicaps, the military effectiveness of the Fleet Air Arm would be greatly increased, and refuelling in flight was offered by Sir Alan as a likely

solution. In order to gain a first hand understanding of the problems, FRL sent a designer to sea in HMS Ark Royal in June 1939, to discuss possible ways of installing equipment in Fairey Swordfish and Albacore aircraft. A scheme was subsequently prepared which included a cylindrical fuel tank of 120 gallon capacity being carried in the torpedo crutches under the fuselage, and the hose drum and winch located in the redundant navigator's cockpit. The Swordfish tanker would carry a refuelling operator in place of the air gunner in the rear cockpit, and the hose would be trailed through a hatchway. Cobham requested that two Swordfish aircraft be sent to Ford for experimental work, but they never materialized, and it was not until the early 1960s that FRL's equipment was first fitted to the Royal Navy's aircraft.

The possibility of providing a regular flight-refuelled service across the Atlantic had not escaped the notice of other carriers, and discussions took place between FRL and Air France during 1939. The intention was to equip Farman 2234 aircraft with refuelling equipment, enabling them to undertake a mail service, and to provide Latécoère 631 flying boats with similar equipment for long distance passenger flights. As will be seen, world events would soon thwart these plans and nearly claim two key FRL individuals in the process. Back on the home front Sir Alan was engaged in a lengthy

French Elegance — an Air France Latécoère 631 flying boat at rest in the Solent. FRL's aerial refuelling proposals were shelved when France was invaded in 1940.

correspondence battle with the Admiralty regarding the continuance of FRL's tenancy at Ford, which had now become a naval air station. In March 1939, Cobham had been informed that he would be permitted to remain in occupation of hangars and workshops on the west side of the aerodrome at the same rent of £100 per month, with the proviso that the arrangement could be terminated immediately should an emergency arise. This uneasy situation persisted throughout the summer months and as a safeguard Sir Alan took out a lease on two dilapidated hangars which were being used as brick kilns adjacent to what was known as the Southern hangar. In strenuous attempts to defend FRL's need to stay at Ford, he wrote many letters to the Admiralty emphasizing the upheaval and expense that would attend moving elsewhere — always assuming there was suitable alternative accommodation available.

He also put forward various compromise schemes to the Admiralty whereby hangar space could be shared, with FRL in addition to its normal work undertaking storage, overhaul and maintenance work on the FAA's aircraft. Harold Wilson, the Machine Shop Foreman, summed up the prevailing mood in a letter to Sir Alan many years later, in which he commented — 'In an atmosphere of complete engulfment, work was a challenge rather than a chore. 1939 had seen domestic harmony at last and the real integration of everyone into a team which in turn became a family. Friendships too had blossomed outside of working hours, and the associations made with the local villagers had resulted in very happy times.'

Time was running out however, and with the official hammer poised to strike, Cobham and his team were faced with the prospect of picking up the pieces and starting elsewhere.

THREE

War Clouds

It was while FRL was operating at Rineanna that war broke out in September 1939, but for many months very little happened to upset home front activities. After FRL's working party returned from Ireland, the existing development programme continued and a strong possibility even existed of extending the transatlantic service over the winter period, using the larger and more powerful 'G' Class boats. It was proposed to fly them from Poole via Lisbon, the Azores and Bermuda to New York, a more southerly route aimed at avoiding the more extreme weather conditions. Cobham made many enquiries about obtaining 'Maia' (the carrier half of the Short-Mayo Composite) and a Saunders Roe Lerwick for conversion into flying boat tankers for this operation, but despite the usual early flush of official encouragement and enthusiasm, this option, along with a proposed in flight refuelled service via Marseilles to Egypt, and a suggested repeat of the Foynes — Botwood service in the summer of 1940, was not pursued. In the meantime further training took place of flying boat crews who, following the merging of Imperial and British Airlines, now wore the uniform of the newly created British Overseas Airways Corporation. It was obvious to Cobham that the flight refuelling and jettison systems demonstrated so ably on the 'C' Class boats had a comparable military application, and in addition to his unrelenting lobbying for use of the equipment on bomber and Fleet Air Arm aircraft, he made a strong representation for its inclusion in the Short Sunderland, used by the RAF's Coastal Command for convoy escort and ocean patrol duties. Had the Short Sunderland been given this capability, it would have possessed sufficient range to cover the notorious mid-Atlantic area, and the loss of vital ships, men, and equipment in the Battle of the Atlantic might well have been reduced significantly. Regrettably, this suggestion simply became the latest to enter the official maze, never to re-appear.

As part of the continuing development programme, Geoffrey Tyson and George Errington took a Harrow and the AW.23 to Boscombe Down in February 1940 to carry out a series of night flying experiments. The original intention was to start refuelling on fully moonlit nights and work progressively towards total darkness. Only two flights actually took place however, during which, methods of illuminating the receiver aircraft and formating techniques were investigated, but the results were sufficiently encouraging to show that night refuelling operations could become a practical proposition. During the same month, tests were also undertaken with the same aircraft taking off in contact. The first time this was tried the Harrow tanker experienced an engine problem which caused it to swing off the runway before the pilot brought it to rest. The AW.23 however continued its take off carrying with it the light 3 cwt. cable which ran out through rollers on the tanker's fuselage and wing tip. No damage was done, and the incident served to demonstrate that a predicted design failure case could be successfully met. A second attempt was carried out which was entirely trouble free, and the concern felt that the connecting line might snag on runway surface irregularities was overcome when the cable was seen to rise clear within a few yards of the start of the take off run.

Throughout the period prior to the sudden German breakthrough into the Low Countries and France, Sir Alan and others had visited the Air France Trans-Atlantique base at Bordeaux to discuss the installation of refuelling equipment in two Farman 2234 mail carriers. It was the intention that the first Farman, to be fitted out as a receiver, would arrive at Ford on 18th May 1940, and crew training would then take place before the French commenced transatlantic operations on June 1st 1940. However, it later transpired that the aircraft were solely intended to fly the French government to South America, via the Azores.

In working towards this goal, Percy Allison and Harry Smith flew to Paris in May for final discussions at the Farman plants at Billancourt and Bordeaux.

The Farman 2234 Transatlantic Mail Carrier.

By now however, the Germans had outflanked the Maginot Line and a return trip to Paris was looking decidedly risky. When an empty Imperial Airways Lockheed 12 airliner suddenly arrived at Bordeaux on its way to London, Smith enquired if they could 'hitch' a ride home, but the captain, unwilling to flout orders, refused – but wished him 'good luck'! Back in Paris, they found the British Embassy deserted, but Thomas Cook's representative suggested sailing from Le Havre. They eventually arrived there to find an air raid in progress, but were relieved to spot a blue RNVR flag on the far side of the harbour. Fortunately the Navy proved to be more accommodating than Imperial Airways, and after an all night wait for some fifty priests travelling from Switzerland, the vintage craft, aided according to Smith by copious prayers, finally left for England. In recalling this incident, Harry Smith added that the crew chief in charge of the Farmans was later shot by French resistance fighters for having delivered the refuelling equipment into German hands!

Throughout the latter part of 1939, Sir Alan had been conducting a lengthy correspondence battle with the Admiralty defending his need to remain at Ford, and pointing out how it would directly benefit the Admiralty if the Company was to undertake the storage, maintenance and repair of Fleet Air Arm aircraft. Considerable money had already been spent on the renovation of hangars and when considered along with Cobham's experienced team of pilots, designers and other skilled personnel, it all added up to being a valuable national asset. Matters came to a head when an Admiralty team headed by the Fifth Sea Lord, arrived unexpectedly at Ford and carried out a close inspection of everything in sight. Following in their wake, Sir Alan was astounded to hear the view expressed that as everything appeared to be in good order, and as no problems attached to extending the

runway, the Navy would be pleased to take complete and immediate control of the airfield. FRL would therefore have its facilities requisitioned forthwith, and be expected to find other premises!

While Cobham regarded this decision as typical 'high handed, audacious, bureacratic behaviour', he found it difficult to counter the rider added by the Admiralty that Ford lay easily within the enemy's radius of action and was therefore vulnerable to air attack. Faced with no choice, Cobham sent out people in all directions tasked with finding an alternative factory or site. By this time it was becoming extremely difficult to obtain permits to carry out experimental flying and coupled with the seeming official indifference to airborne refuelling, the need for an airfield was receding fast. Call up demands for the Armed Services were also depleting the staff, and although the FRL Board seriously considered closing down the organisation for the duration, the shareholders decided that things should be kept going for at least a little while longer. Marcus Langley had fortuitously been spending much worthwhile time and effort cultivating a working relationship with the RAE at Farnborough, and it was this that was soon to provide the Company with a life line to survival.

It was under the long shadow cast by this depressing situation that Sir Alan and Lady Cobham travelled to Stroud in Gloucestershire to check out a possible alternative site recommended by Geoffrey Tyson. It proved, like all the others inspected so far, to be totally inadequate, and it was with dismay that the Cobhams decided to call off the search for the day. Almost as an afterthought they decided that being relatively close to Malvern they would use the visit to make a social call on Sir Alan's cousin, Francis Birchley. Just prior to their departure on the following day, Cobham met an old friend who, upon hearing of his difficulties, suggested he made a bid for the Morgan Motor Works lying half empty close by. A quick look convinced Cobham that he had indeed found a promising solution and after reaching an agreement with the Morgan family the Cobham organisation transferred itself from Sussex to Worcestershire. Now reduced to a working staff of sixteen, plus wives and families in certain cases, the move was achieved within a week, leaving only a skeleton staff to clean up and generally keep an eye on the Harrows and the AW.23 still in the hangars, pending disposal. Two weeks after the main move had been completed, the Admiralty's prediction regarding Ford's vulnerability to attack came true. In addition to Ford, a bomber force concentrated on targets along the south coast, including Thorney Island, Gosport and the radar station at Poling, and the Ju.87 'Stukas' created serious damage on that bright sunny Sunday afternoon in June. Once the bombs had started to fall on FRL's hangars, Dockeray, one of the retaining staff, rode off as fast as he could on his bicycle, but not fast enough to avoid his rear tyre being punctured by a piece of shrapnel. This minor incident was tragically eclipsed however the following Sunday, when the raiders reappeared and Dockeray was fatally wounded during the attack. The Harrows and the AW.23, which ironically were due to be flown away the following day, were badly damaged in the raids, and this put a definite full stop to FRL's flying activities for the foreseeable future.

When it became known that FRL was going to leave Ford, a good deal of cynical and resentful comment circulated in the village. Despite the generally good relations that had previously existed, such were the tensions and suspicions engendered by the prospect of imminent invasion, that it was thought by some that Sir Alan had prior knowledge of what was going to happen, and that he was in fact an enemy agent. The air attack, coming so soon after the move, only served to fuel the speculation, and with the subsequent gossip campaign gaining in strength, Cobham received many harsh and opinionated letters. Tiresome and idiotic as the affair later seemed, it stung Cobham into sending a strong letter to the secretary of the Middleton-on-Sea Sports Club condemning such foolish behaviour!

At this point, a thought should be spared for Hugh Johnson and his team still beleaguered in Newfoundland. When they had sailed in the spring of 1939, it was with the expectation that they would be facing a three month stay. Now, over a year later, the Company and the country's fortunes had changed dramatically, and transporting civilians back to England was far from being a simple matter. After the flying boat trials were completed there was, as already stated, the strong possibility of another service being provided in 1940. As a bridging exercise, Imperial Airways requested FRL to conduct a winter programme which included evaluations of landings and take offs in snow and slush conditions and a calibration of the airport's instrumentation. Johnson was also asked to try and establish a meteorological contract with the Canadian government. In addition to this, as part of Langley's having obtained sub-contracted work from Farnborough, FRL were now beginning to investigate the thermal de-icing of aircraft wings, and it was looking likely that a specially equipped Fairey Battle or Bristol Blenheim would have to be sent to Newfoundland for cold weather trials.

However, the general uncertainty of the situation, the remoteness of the base with its unremitting poor weather, and the long turn round in receiving spares, clothing, money and mail, were all beginning to take their toll on morale and motivation, and the cable traffic between Gander and Ford took on a personal and icy edge. It appeared to Johnson that as far as the people at Ford were concerned, it was a question of 'out of sight, out of mind', and that their frozen existence was of little concern. To Sir Alan, Johnson's complaints seemed to be totally unmindful of the fact that there was a war on and that the entire future of the Company was threatened. Eventually this acrimony receded and events were brought into focus when Sir Alan sent a rational letter to Johnson in mid-July 1940 in which he commented that, in addition to Tyson leaving to join Shorts at Rochester as a test pilot, all the other flying personnel had also departed, and indeed should Johnson return there could be no guarantee of work as a pilot. Upon hearing this, Johnson still on the RAF reserve list, joined the Royal Canadian Air Force and became a flying instructor, whilst Atkinson secured a more envious posting to flying boat duties.

The mention of flying boats brings to mind the sad fate suffered at about this time by the two 'C' Class flying boats, 'Cabot' and 'Caribou', which had been used on the Atlantic service. Commandeered to assist in the evacuation of troops from Norway in May 1940, both aircraft were raked by machine gunfire during air attacks, and sank at their moorings in the fjord at Harstad.

FRL now had a home at Malvern, albeit one in which the various offices and stores were marked out in chalk on the floor, as spare materials for luxury items such as partitions simply were not available. This turn of events meant that FRL, far from becoming the centre of a world wide tanker supply service as envisioned by Shell and Sir Alan, had now become a small concern totally devoted to research and development. Fortunately Shell was still prepared to support the Company and to provide a loan account on the condition that it continued to be well managed. FRL's new association with Farnborough required close collaboration with the Directorate of Technical Development (DTD) at Millbank, and this soon led to the award of more direct contract work for the Ministry of Aircraft Production (MAP). At first it was possible to meet the need for increased floor area by taking over extra bays in the Morgan Motor Works, but when Standard Motors also laid claim to part of the space available, new buildings, financed by the MAP Capital Assistance Scheme, had to be erected in an adjacent field.

One of the earliest tasks undertaken at Malvern was an investigation into methods of wing de-icing in conjunction with RAE at Farnborough. Icing had become a problem in need of an urgent solution when it was estimated that two thirds of the forty aircraft lost on one particular raid by Bomber Command had succumbed to icing conditions. To carry out this work however, required not only an aircraft, but an aerodrome, and so the wheel had turned full circle again! Fortunately Sir Alan was able to summon the assistance of Group Captain Smyth-Piggott, whom he had known for many years and who now commanded the RAF Station at nearby Pershore, along with its satellite base at Defford, and an agreement was reached whereby FRL could use Defford for its preliminary work. No sooner had this comfortable arrangement been made however, when the fortunes of war turned things around yet again.

In 1941 a small force of British commandos carried out a daring raid on the Normandy coast at Bruneval, and returned with secret radar components and two prisoners. It was then reasoned that as the raid had been so successful, it would be a natural temptation for the Germans to mount a retaliatory raid on the Telecommunications Research Establishment (TRE) then located at Worth Matravers overlooking Swanage Bay. Orders were therefore issued for the station to be moved to Malvern, and in taking over Malvern College, they almost succeeded in also getting FRL evicted from the Morgan

The Fairey Battle was used to evaluate wing de-icing systems using engine exhaust gas.

A Wellington Mk.1C of No.149 Squadron — one of several equipped with wing de-icing systems by FRL.

The Ministry of Aircraft Production loaned a Whitley bomber to assist in the wing de-icing test programme.

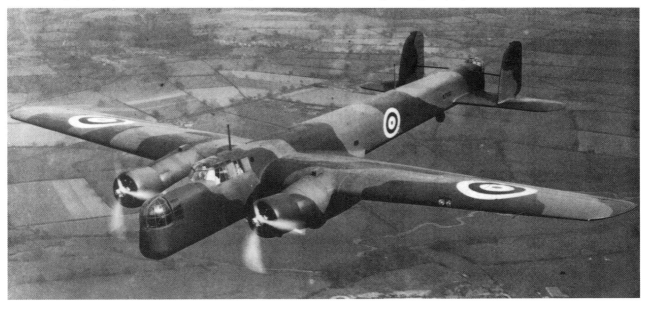

Motor Works. They certainly managed to take over Defford which meant, not for the first time in his life, that Sir Alan had to seek accommodation elsewhere. Fortunately this problem was quickly resolved and with Air Ministry assistance three hangars were constructed at Staverton, some twenty-three miles away.

Following the initial jostling for space FRL developed a close working relationship with its new neighbour, and all of TRE's prototype installations, in various test aircraft including the revolutionary H2S scanning radar, were undertaken in the Staverton flight sheds.. Now that the joint use of an airfield had become available, discussions commenced with the MAP regarding the equipping of an Avro Manchester so that it could receive fuel from a Harrow tanker, but from a veritable whirlpool of discussions, in flight refuelling advanced no further, and efforts were concentrated on other experimental work. A Fairey Battle was fitted with steel leading edges which were extensions of the engine exhaust pipes, and during late 1941 and early 1942 twelve Wellington bombers from Nos. 115 and 214 Squadrons were equipped with a Dunlop system which ejected a depressed freezing point fluid over the wing leading edges, which had also to be armoured in order to fend off barrage balloon cables. The method employed on the Wellingtons was subsequently regarded as unsatisfactory, and further meetings with Kelvin Spencer (later Sir Kelvin Spencer) at the MAP and Bob Graham at RAE resulted in a Whitley bomber arriving at Staverton for more trials.

FRL encountered many difficulties in attempting to produce an acceptable de-icing system, for inevitably the straight transfer of exhaust gases into leading edge ducts resulted in engine performance problems. After much trial and error it was found that a more scientific approach, which incorporated a proper heat exchanger, produced better results but the unwelcome corrosion introduced by leaded fuel still created difficulties, as witnessed one day when the Chief Pilot, C.D.Barnard, leaned on the Whitley's weakened leading edge device, causing it to fall off. It was this research however that eventually led to satisfactory systems being fitted to the Bomber Command Squadrons of Lancasters and Halifaxes, and, much later in the war to the Lancaster's successor, the Avro Lincoln.

Whilst this work proceeded, the knowledge that Sir Alan had gained during the pre-war years regarding possible sites for airfields was suddenly called upon. By 1941, aircraft were being turned out of the factories at a rate which far exceeded the RAF's ability to co-opt them into the Squadrons. Consequently it became necessary to find dispersal areas where they could be stored temporarily, and safe from bombing attack. Lord Beaverbrook, the Canadian firebrand in charge of the MAP, remembering Cobham's pre-war activities, called him to a meeting at Thames House. Although, as Sir Alan recalled, it would have been a simple matter to arrange the meeting over the telephone, Beaverbrook, eccentric as ever, sent half a dozen reporters off with the simple brief – "Find Cobham!" It was with some surprise therefore that he was accosted whilst having breakfast at the Royal Aero Club and told of the Minister's immediate demand. The meeting in Beaverbrook's palatial office was short and to the point. Beaverbrook, having outlined his requirements, summarized them by saying "Cobham, God bless you – go ahead and find the landing grounds, I am on the run. Goodbye!". Cobham's first thoughts were that the RAF had already combed the whole of Britain when Lord Trenchard formed a

special committee for a similar purpose; and that surely those findings would serve as a basis for his exercise. It was quickly pointed out, however, that Beaverbrook would not tolerate any connection with the Air Force – he did not want them infiltrating his organisation and did not wish to seek their help – an incredible disassociation in view of the desperate need for Service and industrial co-operation!

Unwilling to accept such a ridiculous constraint, Cobham secretly arranged for nine ex-Battle of Britain pilots to be allocated to the search. With a young and able surveyor attached to the team, a meticulous exercise was carried out over the whole country, starting on the west coast and working eastwards, but with his penchant for hitting trouble when dealing with officialdom, Cobham soon found it. It had been agreed that as the search progressed, the team's findings would be assessed by a special committee – unfortunately chaired in this instance by a man who knew nothing about flying or its attendant problems. Largely because the RAF had already earmarked the best sites for operational use, it proved to be a difficult job to find other areas that were sufficiently flat, clear of approach hazards, and accessible. Nevertheless, many proposals were put forward – only to be constantly rejected by the obdurate Chairman.

Frustrated and dispirited, Cobham made it clear to Beaverbrook that there was little more he could do and that he would be much better employed back at Malvern. This led two days later, to an uproarious meeting of all parties during which the Chairman attempted to prove that Cobham was completely incapable of carrying out the work. Sir Alan was called upon to defend his credibility which he did with great vigour, before finally describing the Chairman as an 'incompetent bumptious ass' and walking out. It eventually transpired that enough perfectly acceptable sites were later used as recommended, principally in Worcestershire and Gloucestershire, and honour was restored! It has since been revealed that Cobham's search for airfields coincided with a similar exercise in which Station Commanders throughout the RAF were instructed to find at least one area (even sections of roads if necessary) close to each main base that could be used as Emergency Landing Grounds. The fact that Sir Alan was not called upon to offer his assistance in this exercise can almost certainly be attributed to Beaverbrook's paranoid attitude towards the RAF!

In 1941 the delivery of bombs to Germany was, to say the least, an inexact science, bedevilled by a shortage of accurate navigational aids, crews lacking long range night flying experience and unreliable aircraft. It is amusing therefore to note with hindsight, a conversation held in mid-1941 in which Noel Pemberton-Billing, the eccentric founder of the Supermarine Aviation Company, outlined to Cobham a scheme for solving the problem. His idea was to form a civil aviation company that would buy up all the old airliners, convert them into bombers, and to quote the Air Force so much per ton load for delivery of bombs to the target. It seems he had already been quoted favourable insurance rates and in addition to his intention to pay high salaries to the crews, he had estimated that the chances of their being shot down were 'not too great'. Sir Alan elected not to help in promoting the idea! (see Footnote).

By 1942 the Company's activities were spread over numerous operational aircraft, and along with the wing de-icing systems, included the development of irreversible flying controls on a Blenheim, heated windscreens, self sealing fuel tanks and engine exhaust flame damping. The need to reduce the glare created by exhaust flames arose because night fighter pilots, such as John Cunningham, had complained that it affected their night vision. The RAF's night bomber force also felt particularly vulnerable when, in addition to radar vectoring, an enemy night fighter had the bonus of homing onto a set of glowing exhaust stubs. FRL set out to investigate the problem with the aid of Professor Norrish, Professor of Physical Chemistry at Cambridge University, who explained that he already had a highly secret fluid called 'Xylene' which would extinguish the flames, and all he needed was an injection system to force it into the exhaust manifold. The success of the system was dependent on the correct amount of fluid being metered, and after a series of tests using an engine in Rotol's wind tunnel, a valve

size was arrived at which did the job. Naturally everyone was curious to know what the special fluid was, and it was almost an anti-climax when it was discovered that it was 100 octane fuel — exactly the same as that used by the aircraft, and it simply made the mixture in the manifold too rich to burn!

As the work increased, the housing of staff and the provision of canteens at Malvern and Staverton became a problem. Sir Alan had therefore good reason to be grateful to a Mrs. Carter Bowles, who in addition to turning her house into a guest house for FRL staff, also ran the Company's canteen at Staverton. Realising that it was a favourite trick in the Works to create a diversion during which cakes and rolls would rapidly disappear from her trolley, she armed herself with a long ebony stick and became very adept at rapping an offender's knuckles, causing much hilarity all round.

It was during 1942 that Ted Thickins and Mike Goodliffe joined the Company. Thickins, an electrician with the RAF, was seconded for an initial six months' spell as a draughtsman, after which the situation was periodically reviewed and the position renewed, until one day notice came for his return to the Service. Harry Smith however, insisted that he ignore the summons and carry on with the Company, and this he did, despite his concern at being forcibly removed as a deserter, for a further forty-two years, before retiring as Technical Services Manager in 1983.

Starting as a draughtsman at Malvern which provided the organisation's administrative, production and design headquarters, he soon transferred to Staverton which, in addition to housing the flying operations, also possessed a small drawing office, run by Mr. Cornthwaite. Thickins recalled that in addition to the friendly rivalry which existed between the two design teams, eighty hour working weeks with no paid overtime were commonplace. He also added that with so much secret work being carried out, it was difficult to know what was going on outside one's own project!

Mike Goodliffe, who would eventually become the Company's Technical Director, was sent to FRL from London Transport as a design draughtsman and thus met his future wife, Kay Howard, who, having transferred from Gloster Aircraft, was also employed in the drawing office. Not surprisingly the increase in staff brought with it occasional personnel problems, and Cobham was particularly irked when a Mr. Fletcher decided to appoint himself shop steward,

Footnote: Pemberton-Billing was an extremely colourful character and original thinker, who produced some highly innovative aircraft. He temporarily suspended his interest in aviation to enter politics, but Sir Geoffrey de Havilland, in his autobiography, *Sky Fever*, tells how this ambition was terminated when, after seeming to take leave of his senses, he was forcibly ejected, kicking and screaming from the House of Commons. He returned to aeronautical matters, and his fertile imagination gave rise to a stream of radical projects, but none ever flew!

and immediately set out to cause trouble. FRL's wages and working conditions were generally considered to be as good as wartime conditions would allow, but Fletcher became a distinct menace, sowing seeds of discontent and causing disruption whenever possible. Despite appeals to his Union and the Ministry of Labour, it seemed that little could be done to remove him, and it was with great annoyance that, despite managing to bar his entry to the site, Sir Alan still had to pay his wages through the main gate. This frustrating state of affairs was only brought to an end when he was found to be in possession of stolen tarpaulin sheeting, and duly convicted.

At this time, FRL was given the task of finding out how a fireproof tank would stand up to machine gun fire, and two Halifax wings were delivered, fitted with the tanks and mounted in a supporting rig ready for the trials. Sir Alan recounted how, motoring from Malvern to Cheltenham one day just prior to the trials he became stuck in a long line of traffic behind a slow moving low loader being escorted by policemen on motorcycles. Finally the low loader stopped to allow the accumulated traffic to pass, and when Cobham drew alongside he was astonished to see his Chief Stressman, J.J.Gerritson, seated inside the cab. After Cobham pulled into the lay-by and enquired what he was doing on the lorry, Gerritson explained that he was escorting the tower for mounting the machine gun — a vast steel structure some 25 ft. high with a 6 ft. square platform at the top, and a 20 ft. square base, weighing several tons, safely through to Staverton. Cobham was appalled to find that such a structure, to mount a single machine gun, had been constructed without his knowledge, but realised that he couldn't very well argue about it at the roadside, and the journey continued. However, once at Staverton, he really exploded and demanded an explanation of the circumstances surrounding the production of such a monstrosity. John Davies, the Station Manager, then caused him to have total apoplexy by inviting him to view the foundations. Cobham simply couldn't believe it when he saw four concrete blocks, each a cubic yard, buried in the ground, and four others to be located 50 ft. or so away from the corners. The intention was to attach 50 ton steadying cables from the top of the tower to picket rings sunk into the blocks. Cobham instantly dismissed all the builders still working on the final installation and despairingly agreed simply to locate the tower on the four inner

William Oke Manning was a highly inventive designer who joined FRL in 1942. He died in 1958.

support blocks. There was no need to secure it further because, as Sir Alan observed, a 500 mph wind wouldn't have shifted it. Although Mr. Gerritson left soon afterwards, the Company's engineering capability was enhanced by the arrival of W.O. Manning from RAE Farnborough. Manning was a highly inventive designer who had taught himself to fly prior to the First World War, later becoming Chief Designer of the Coventry Ordnance Works (Aviation Division) and also the English Electric Co. Ltd. upon its formation in 1918.

FRL's work for Farnborough and the MAP became increasingly varied as the war months went by. Spot welding was in its infancy at the time, and for quite a time there were only three spot welding plants in the country, one each at Westlands, Vickers and FRL. Having been requested to embark on an investigation into welding techniques, the arrival of the new equipment was eagerly awaited. Its delivery however was not without incident! FRL's driver was a local jolly type, who enjoyed a good sing-song as he rattled his way down the country lanes, and this trip was no exception. However, after negotiating one particularly sharp bend, he decided that, although the truck seemed to be running better and felt lighter than before, a quick check might be in order, and to his dismay discovered that the large heavy piece of equipment, which he had thought unnecessary to tie down, was no longer in evidence. Retracing his steps he found that his precious load, after having gone through a hedge, had landed in the middle of a heap of fresh manure. This must have cushioned the shock of impact, because the spot welder was found to work perfectly on its eventual arrival at Malvern.

Another important area of work that FRL engaged in was the standardization of materials. At the request of MAP's K.T.Spencer, a broad investigation was undertaken into the strengths of various materials used in aircraft construction. It had been a long running concern that different design organisations used widely varying safety factors for the same materials and this eventually led to aircraft and equipment being overweight in some cases, and understrength in others. Now the opportunity presented itself to determine consistent criteria for the industry's design teams. Sheet metal, bar, tube and casting samples were sent off to the universities and larger companies with the necessary testing apparatus, and the results were co-ordinated in a monumental report, which led to every aircraft design organisation having an FRL Standards Book as a basic reference work within its technical library.

How to get fighter aircraft to Malta was a desperate problem facing the Service Chiefs in 1942. With its defence force reduced to three Gladiator biplanes, the chances of holding out against sustained air attack looked slim, and yet it was crucially important to prevent the island becoming a vital staging link in the chain supplying Rommel's Afrika Corps. No single engined fighter possessed the range to fly to Malta, and a concept that involved bombers air-towing fighters was passed to Cobham for consideration. The idea was soon expanded to cover the possibility of bomber squadrons towing escorting fighters to the target area, whereupon they would have enough fuel to return to base under their own power. On the clear understanding that development of a practical system would not interfere with the de-icing investigations, Cobham's team started work on what was referred to as the SB.22 contract.

The method adopted was to attach the two arms of a Y-shaped towing bridle to support lugs on each wing of the fighter, thus providing propeller clearance, and to connect the single cable to a wooden framework in the bomber's rear turret. Tests

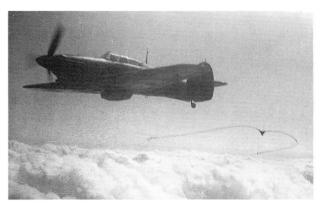

Off the leash! A Hurricane used in fighter towing trials jettisons the towing cable in this rare wartime photograph.

Sketch from a contemporary report showing a Wellington taking off with a Hurricane in tow.

under the co-ordinating control of Mike Inskip were carried out with a Wellington tug and either a Spitfire or Hurricane in tow, and naturally the development flying period produced its fair share of incidents. Steel cables, being inflexible, caused the tow to proceed in a series of jerks, whilst nylon rope went to the other extreme and catapulting occurred. Hemp rope was finally found to offer the best compromise. The wooden framework was a device which obviated the need for a winch in the tug, and the rope was secured with twine at each point of its contact with the frame work. After both the bomber and fighter had taken off virtually side by side, with the tow rope held by a special release clip, the fighter would gradually fall behind the bomber, but still remain flying under its own power. At this stage the rope would be released from the clip allowing the load on the tow rope to transfer to the light twine securing the rope to the framework. The twine fixings broke in sequence thus allowing the rope to deploy in an orderly manner, and once the rope was fully trailed, the fighter's engine was shut down. The main problem encountered was re-starting the cold engine after a long tow, and this required jacketed immersion heaters being fitted around the engine to avoid oil overcooling. Sir Alan honestly admitted at the time that this was a job in which his technical staff had not covered themselves with glory, as it was later discovered that the towing loads had been greatly overestimated, and, as a result, much time and effort was wasted in needlessly modifying the front spars of the fighters, when it had only been necessary to make a hole in the leading edge fabric and put a simple clip round the spar!

This resumption of flight test work had come at a time when Sir Alan had only one pilot, C.D.Barnard, on his staff. Barnard had been a colleague of Sir Alan's at the de Havilland Aeroplane Hire Service and had joined FRL in 1942, when the RAF cut back the numbers of aircraft and pilots engaged solely for transporting senior personnel from six hundred to one hundred. With an urgent need for extra aircrew, Cobham had to submit to the MAP a list of pilots employed by Gloster Aircraft and Rotol Airscrews who, based also at Staverton, could be called upon to assist with test work. Three pilots who became closely associated with the towing experiments were Rotol's 'Ginger' Hall (later killed flight testing contra-rotating propellers), Brian Greensted and Denis Dickson, who subsequently recorded this abbreviated account of the trials period:

"At our first meeting, Cobham propounded the reasons for the experiment, and his enthusiasm led to us being suitably impressed, although sceptical that a practical solution could be achieved. A great deal of work had already been done in towing gliders which invariably possessed an extremely low wing loading which allowed them to become airborne rapidly and able to climb above the turbulence caused by the towing aircraft's propellers. A fighter aircraft with its much higher wing loading would not be able to leave the ground until much the same time as the tug and was therefore at greater risk. We foresaw the possibility of the fighter being turned completely over and striking the ground upside down, but to convince the indomitable Cobham, tests had to be done which almost achieved this result. At last came the day when theory was put to the test. Taking off together with Greensted in the Hurricane, we arrived at 2500 ft. and I gave the signal for him to release the clip holding the towing bridle at a point under

the fuselage. He in turn signalled that I could release the 700 ft. of hemp rope. By inching back on his throttle, the rope became fully deployed and eventually the 'V' part of the bridle appeared in front of his wings. He then closed the throttle completely and experienced the enormous thrill of being pulled along by the Wellington at a reduced but acceptable speed. After both aircraft landed at Staverton, the irrepressible Cobham hurried to congratulate Greensted, but forgetting to unhitch the leg straps of his parachute, fell heavily and lay imprisoned on his back with arms and legs waving in the air like a beetle. Midst much laughter, we helped the great man to his feet and repaired to the office to discuss developments. As the programme progressed, Air Marshal F. J. Linnell, who was in charge of Aircraft Research and Development, witnessed a demonstration and whilst declaring himself satisfied with our efforts, still wished to see other test pilots fly the fighter. Sir Alan, fearing that his scheme might not be put to practical use, invited his friend Jeffrey Quill, Vickers-Supermarines' Chief Test Pilot, to try his hand. Quill, having arrived by Spitfire, listened nonchalantly to the briefing. Shortly afterwards we were in the air and he was attempting to place his aircraft in tow. Unfortunately he misjudged the speed at which he should have withdrawn the fighter with the result that the heavy rope snapped like a piece of cotton. His spirits dampened a little by the set back, Sir Alan next invited Gp. Capt. Wilson, Chief Test Pilot of the RAE at Farnborough, to demonstrate — once and for all — the simplicity of this "Towing Business". With his inevitable cigarette burning in a long holder, the Group Captain listened carefully to the briefing instructions. 'Seems feasible, old boy' he said to Cobham, and without further delay all concerned clambered into their respective aircraft and took off. 'Willie' took the Hurricane back into the towing position without incident. Regrettably however, he stationed the fighter too high above the Wellington, pulling the bomber's tail upwards. Both aircraft went into a steady dive towards the ground. With only 200-300 ft. of height left, I had begun to despair that Wilson would appreciate my dilemma and I was about to order the tow rope to be cut with an axe. Had this been necessary it would almost certainly have killed Wilson. At the last moment however Wilson decided that something was amiss and released himself, allowing both aircraft to climb to safety. Sir Alan, reluctant to accept this extra setback to his hopes, invited one

Gp. Capt. 'Willie' Wilson, Chief Test Pilot at RAE, Farnborough, had a narrow escape during towed-fighter exercises.

put to practical use, but one side benefit Cobham achieved was that he gained dual instruction on the Wellington and went aloft to complete a solo circuit. Considering that he had not flown any kind of aircraft for several years, and that it was a far more sophisticated aeroplane than he had previously known , it wasn't a bad effort for a fifty year old!''

Sir Alan however, wasn't the only Cobham to fly in the Wellington. Michael, then a sixteen year old boy keen for adventure, flew on two or three of the test flights as part of the ''heaving'' crew. He remembers clearly today a flight during which the failure of a fuel transfer valve caused one engine to stop, at which point the Hurricane pilot started up and overflew the Wellington before releasing the tow line slightly late and causing a spectacular backlash in the rope. The usual technique was to jettison the tow line near the Staverton flight sheds, but on this occasion it remained firmly attached, causing damage to some Nissen huts and bringing down telephone wires.

Charles Barnard too, nearly came to grief when, piloting a Spitfire, the tow rope broke and whipped back to foul the propeller before wrapping itself round the cockpit and flying controls. Fortunately he managed to put this tangled mess down on Thame aerodrome in the Cotswolds, only to have a car arrive alongside and a young officer inform him that he had landed on the wrong runway! Mike Goodliffe remembers that having landed the Wellington alongside, and viewed the damage, all concerned ''went to the pictures in the afternoon!''

Thame aerodrome also featured in other towing tests undertaken by FRL using a Boulton Paul Defiant and a Slingsby glider. A series of experimental flights was undertaken to see whether the Defiant, fitted with a hook, could engage a cable stretched between two posts and snatch the stationary glider into the air. This it did, but although this particular combination of tug and glider was not put into operational use, snatch take offs were employed by the Americans later in the war in the Far East. Goodliffe recalls too, a requirement to re-design the hand operated traversing system of the rearward firing gun fitted to the Vultee Vengeance dive bomber. An aircraft was delivered from the Cunliffe-Owen works in Southampton to Staverton where power traversing equipment was installed. Unfortunately it was not considered that the interrupter gear provided sufficient protection for the fin, and when maximum traverse was selected the gun pulled

more pilot, George Errington, Chief Test Pilot of Airspeeds, and a man who probably had more experience of towed flight than anyone else alive. Cobham commented 'If George can't do it first try — I'll give up'. Errington, very aware of the implications of failure, turned in a faultless performance, and with great glee, Cobham reported to the Air Marshal that a 'strange pilot' had mastered the technique at the first attempt. Linnell however, after considering the reports of the three illustrious pilots, finally decided that the operation was beyond the ability of the average Squadron pilot, and called a halt to the tests, which had lasted twelve months. We were all saddened that our toil and trouble would not be the ammunition belt completely out of its tank, whereupon it wrapped itself around the tailplane. The installation was not proceeded with!

In 1942 the Americans, still smarting from the attack on Pearl Harbour, were desperately keen to mount a retaliatory raid on the Japanese mainland. Accordingly in March, the British Air Ministry was requested to send a representative to an air refuelling conference at Wright Field in Dayton, Ohio. The Air Ministry informed Washington that Hugh Johnson was serving with the RCAF somewhere in Canada, and that the best approach would be for them to contact the authorities in Ottawa in order to secure Johnson's attendance. This resulted in him attending a ten day long series of meetings during which he lectured to the Commanding General and his advisers on the looped hose system used during the Atlantic service in 1939. The Canadians meanwhile had taken over the two Harrows that FRL had used at Gander, but there was now no sign of the refuelling equipment that had once been fitted. Johnson however, thought that the equipment fitted to the UK-based Harrows could still be readily located and made available for use by the Americans.

Arrangements were quickly made for Johnson to fly to England, and this he did in a B-24 Liberator bomber, perched on the unyielding spout of an oxygen bottle for five solid hours. The reunion with Cobham led to a request for Marcus Langley and Percy Allison to return with Johnson to the US. Ministry permission was given for Langley to go overseas for two weeks only, but Allison was granted a stay for an indefinite period. Before their final departure, all three travellers spent three uncomfortable nights sleeping on the floor at the Royal Bath Hotel in Bournemouth before journeying from Poole to Shannon in a 'Golden Hind' flying boat. Having sat on duck boards in the hull throughout the flight, it was with some relief that they transferred to the luxurious comfort provided in the Pan American Boeing 314 Clipper for the crossing to Baltimore. Following the eventual arrival of the ex-Harrow equipment, Johnson was named Project Controller in charge of preparing a B-24 Liberator as a tanker, and a B-17 Flying Fortress as a receiver. Attached to General Putt's staff, he was also assigned the unofficial title of "The Expert in the Dangling of Ropes in the Air"! Allison supervised the installation work which was done by Pennsylvania Airlines at Washington National Airport. The aim was to enable a B-24 to fly over 1000 miles

A B-24 Liberator tanker fuels a B-17 Fortress during wartime trials in the USA, 1943.

alongside a B-17 carrying a full war load, then to transfer sufficient fuel for the B-17 to fly a total of 5,800 miles, whilst allowing the B-24 to return to base.

The trials began at Eglin Field in April 1943 with Captain Fred Bretcher nominated as the project pilot for the tanker. Johnson took over the instruction of the crew on flying procedures, and Allison assumed responsiblity for the installation and operation of the equipment and operator training. One particular flight in the B-24 gave Percy Allison the worst moment of his life, when, flying over Lake Erie, he suddenly realised that fire had broken out near the refuelling operator's compartment. Due to some oversight during the structural conversion, the compartment floor had been extended over the fire extinguisher, rendering it totally useless, and apart from telling the trainee operator to inform the pilot that 'he would keep an eye on things', there was little he could do. Allison remarked later that he could never understand how, with the aircraft reeking of 100 octane fuel, there had not been the biggest bang in creation, but amazingly they survived, and the Liberator landed safely at Wright Field. The tests which took place over seven weeks, were part of the Americans' policy of trying out all the various methods of increasing range, and then putting them on the shelf pending their eventual use. In this case, the retaliatory raid on Japan which initiated the refuelling requirement, was undertaken by a carrier-borne force of B-25 Mitchells led by Lt. Col. J. H. Doolittle, and a more ambitious scheme to equip large bomber groups was turned down because of the time required to train crews, convert aircraft, and also the advent of the new long range B-29 bomber.

It might be thought that Cobham was uniquely unfortunate in getting so close to having his system adopted, only to have it passed over repeatedly — but as the war progressed, other methods were also evaluated both in the USA and Germany which similarly met with limited success. In 1944 for example, a system was tried, again using a Liberator tanker, which required a P-38 Lightning fighter fitted with a fuselage mounted device to make contact with a towed fuel tank. The results were unsatisfactory. Another method attempted involved the Cornelius XFG-1, an expendable pilotless glider which, whilst being towed through the air would theoretically pump 700 gallons of fuel to the towing aircraft. On completion, the combination fuel hose and towing cable was to be jettisoned along with the glider. Two models were built for test purposes, the first of which crashed, killing the pilot, and the trials were discontinued.

1944 also saw the Luftwaffe experimenting with a Heinkel III tanker and it was also proposed to equip a variant of the massive six engined Junkers Ju.390 as a tanker for refuelling Ju.290 reconnaisance bombers out over the Atlantic. Official interest and development ceased however as the war fronts contracted and moved closer to Germany.

Whilst the mighty allied war effort geared up for the final onslaught, serious attention was also given by the Americans and the British to the shape and structure of post war civil aviation. In the USA the Air Transport Command (ATC) had been formed which, in addition to operating its own aircraft, exercised virtual control over all the US airlines, and this was seen as a major threat by air minded parties on this side of the Atlantic. Of necessity, and in order to support the ever increasing spread of armed forces, the ATC had developed a global network of routes and maintenance facilities, but the prospect of this infrastructure being handed over to American civil operators as a going concern after the war ended was a major headache for the British. It was even suggested that the ATC should be made a joint United Nations Command in which the United States and Britain would take principal roles, but with the Americans lodged so firmly in control, it was never likely that they would accept a shared interest.

Cobham, along with other air leaders, was also disturbed to note that as part of the American aim to dominate world civil aviation, a powerful group of industrialists was proposing to build a chain of seadromes across the Atlantic. It was intended that each of these massive floating islands would weigh some 64,000 tons and have a large stabilized landing deck 70 ft. above the sea. With these stations located at intervals of 800 miles, it would then have been possible for aircraft to cross the ocean in a series of short hops, which required taking on board relatively little fuel and hence allowing more freight or passengers to be carried. This concept was not new. A British inventor, F.G.Creed, had previously submitted a similar plan to the Admiralty in 1935, but it was rejected on the grounds that such structures would be indefensible in times of war. In 1941 however, interest was renewed and tests even carried out at the National Physical Laboratory when it was thought that they could provide bases for air cover and help reduce shipping losses. As British building resources were taxed to the limit, it was decided to obtain quotations for construction from the USA, but when faced with a new demand to supply vast amounts of materials to Russia, the Admiralty reconsidered the matter and finally rejected it.

Sir Alan now saw that not only would a colossal enterprise of this nature cancel out the need for refuelling aircraft in flight, but by its sheer size the venture would constitute an international monopoly that would swallow up the rest of the world's airlines. With large numbers of big American transport aircraft already plying the main trade routes, and with no comparable British aircraft with large load carrying capacity either in service or even on the drawing board, the future looked bleak. Despite the total commitment to the production of wartime needs, the British government, in time honoured fashion, set up a committee to combat the problem. Under the Chairmanship of Lord Brabazon, it produced a a set of recommendations which outlined Britain's post war civil aviation policy, and the types of aircraft required to implement it. Whilst an exceptional success could eventually be claimed in the Viscount, the findings also resulted in two aircraft being built which, though mightily impressive in size and appearance, were commercially doomed from the very start.

The specifications for the Bristol Brabazon and the Saunders-Roe Princess resulted from thinking still linked to the pre-war Empire routes and the associated need to provide space and comfort for only a privileged minority of travellers. Consequently, these aircraft were immediately obsolete in terms of performance and payload, a fact heavily underlined by the rising tide of four engined Douglas DC-4s, Lockheed Constellations and (a little later) the Boeing Stratocruisers now starting to appear in the skies over Britain. The Ministry however, faced with all its immediate problems, still considered It prudent to request a report from FRL which addressed the economics and possibilities afforded by refuelling civil aircraft in flight (see Appendix III).

As concern grew over Britain's post war prospects, Cobham was invited to attend a series of high level meetings at which politicians, along with airline and industry heads, explored ways forward in line with the Brabazon Committee's findings. When asked for his views, he stated in typically forthright manner that he believed a state run monopoly, such as BOAC, was inherently undesirable, and bound to stifle enterprise, initiative and competition. He was equally forthright in stating that influential figures from the shipping and railway sectors should not, under any circumstances, be allowed to infiltrate the aircraft business. Past experience told him that the interests of different transportation sectors simply did not mix, and that the future of aviation would best be served by a hard core of young, technically-competent people drawn from the various armed forces if necessary. As he fully expected, these views aroused strong reactions from the mandarins in Whitehall, and top executives in BOAC, and the ensuing arguments revealed just how deeply divided the opinions were.

With this recognition of future problems however went the more immediate need to win the war, and this meant ceaseless attention to weapon development. FRL continued to undertake a wide variety of contracted tasks on behalf of the MAP, and one Wellington was equipped with a radar array for use in detonating magnetic mines, and another with a device constructed on the lines of a honeycombed radiator into which were loaded tubes of plastic explosive, linked together like sausages. The aim was to fly low over the Normandy invasion beaches just prior to the troops landing, and drop the 'line charges' as they were called, onto mined areas. After a predetermined time the charges exploded and caused the surrounding land mines to detonate as well. To prevent the explosive tubes landing in an untidy heap, however, various methods were tried, including the attachment of small parachutes and grapnels, and, most effectively a sack of metal chain.

Having spent weeks perfecting the system, FRL was informed that there was insufficient time to make up the charges in the quantities required for D-Day, and flails mounted on armoured tractors were eventually used. In 1944 the company was also contracted to install methyl bromide and nitrogen fire extinguishing systems on Lancaster, Halifax and Stirling aircraft, design a radio installation for Oxford trainers and to fit stores winching equipment into Bristol Beaufort torpedo bombers. The thermal de-icing and hot air windscreen tests were also progressing well, so well in fact that a net weight saving was achieved on the Handley Page Halifax after it was fitted with wing and tailplane de-icing systems. This resulted from FRL's redesign of certain basic structure in order to accommodate the new parts, but the changes introduced, despite the weight improvements, were not well received by 'H.P.' and his design staff!

A Halifax also featured in another major exercise undertaken by the Company over a fifteen month period which commenced in mid-1945. This was work carried out in partnership with Shell Oil to determine the effect of leaded fuel on aircraft engines under all conditions. For this purpose, a Mk.III aircraft, MNA 684, fitted with Bristol Hercules engines, was made available for flight trials. Christened 'The Knocker, for obvious reasons, it had the distinction of carrying two very notable passengers when Lt. General Doolittle and Group Captain Douglas Bader, both senior executives with Shell, visited Staverton in September 1946.

During the period leading up to D-Day, many Spitfires flew in for fitment of the Mark II Gyro Gun Sight, and another task undertaken was the installation of new engines into a number of Lockheed Lodestar transports belonging to the Royal Norwegian Air Force.

So it was that with the works humming along at full capacity, Sir Alan, along with Marcus Langley, was summoned in late February 1944 to a large meeting in a Downing Street government building. After the representatives from Rolls-Royce, A.V.Roe and FRL, along with RAF and Ministry officials had been sworn to secrecy, a Group Captain explained that it was their intention that a British Very Long Range bomber force would assist the US air fleets in attacking Japan. Although to achieve the long range required the Air Staff had considered using existing Lancasters carrying reduced bombloads and later variants of the Lancaster which were eventually

'The Knocker', used by FRL and the Shell Co. for fuel development tests, is shown here at Khartoum, 1945.

developed into the Lincoln Mk.1 and 11, it was announced, to Cobham's undisguised astonishment, that it was going to be achieved by means of in-flight refuelling. The proposed plan was to convert 600 Lancasters to tankers and 600 Lincolns to receivers, and operate from bases 1500 miles away from the target, in Burma or mainland China. Following the issue of many analytical reports and being well aware of all the representations made by Sir Alan over the years, the Air Staff had finally found an application for Cobham's system - he could barely believe it!

The war in Europe was expected to be over by the time the operation took place, and therefore all the equipment had to be ready for the instant diversion of aircraft and personnel to the Far East in early 1945. The A.V.Roe representatives, after agreeing that the project was technically feasible, said that they considered the delivery dates impossible. Despite this, everyone was told to find a way round the difficulties and report the following week with an

implementation plan for their part in the operation. Cobham recalled that Langley's excitement was such that his driving during the return journey became distinctly dangerous, and after some twenty miles they decided to telephone Harry Smith and share the news that FRL was back in the in-flight refuelling business. Suddenly it seemed that Cobham could do no wrong, and every avenue of assistance was opened up. FRL discovered that it had priority over virtually everyone and literally hundreds of subcontract companies in the Midlands were told to drop what they were doing and accept FRL's work. Even so it was a problem finding enough firms with the right kind of resource and experience, and the Company's management was put to a severe test. To assist the programme it was even made possible for Hugh Johnson to resign his duties with the RCAF and return to England, whereupon Cobham, with great relief, put him in control of the enormous task of subcontract co-ordination.

The overwhelming size of the operation was soon

apparent, and more staff, money and premises had to be found - quickly! It was thought originally that one sizeable airfield would suffice, and RAF St. Athan in South Wales was made available, but in order to cope with the constant flow of aircraft arrivals, conversions and general preparation for despatch to the Far East, two further airfields were deemed necessary, and thus Rhoose and Llandow were put at Cobham's disposal. A school for training the large numbers of aircrew was set up at Staverton, and there also appeared on the airfield a feature which became known as 'Allison's Tower'. Because the refuelling system was dependent on gravity feed, it was essential for flow tests to be carried out in a condition simulating the distance separating the tanker and receiver aircraft. Accordingly a small tank was mounted on top of a rickety scaffolding structure over eighty feet in height, and piping led to another tank on the ground. When the time came to undertake the tests there was only one man who could face the journey up eight ten-foot ladders lashed to the rig. Several, including Sir Alan tried, but all became nervous at the halfway point and had to climb down, and it was left to the indomitable Allison to show the way!

As designers of the Lancaster and Lincoln, overall project responsibility rested with A.V.Roe, but following approval of the installation schemes, they took no further part in the manufacture or assembly of equipment. Under what became a very straight forward arrangement, FRL's 'money man', Chris Tonge, sent up sheets of accounts which were invariably paid on the spot. If FRL needed more working capital the bank had been instructed to make it available immediately, and Cobham reflected that never before or since had red tape been so easy to avoid than when the operation code named 'Tiger Force' got underway.

The organisation was constantly having to adapt to cope with changing circumstances. By the end of 1944, Ted Thickins was engaged on more practical test work under the Chief Technician, Carr Young, and Hawker Aircraft's ex-Chief Draughtsman, Percival, had now taken over Marcus Langley's work following his retirement. C.D.Barnard had also left the Company owing to ill health, and Sqn. Ldr. Fisher now flew Sir Alan in a Percival Q.6 communications aircraft. Tom Marks and John Oliver were also seconded from the RAF to assist with the intensive flight development programme, and it was at this time, in December 1944, that Michael Cobham left the London School of Economics and joined the Company as Hugh Johnson's personal assistant.

One day in the spring of 1945 Sir Alan received a telephone call from 'Tiger Force' H.Q. at Bushey to inform him that Air Marshal Sir Hugh Lloyd requested his presence on secret business at 11.30 a.m. the following day. On his arrival, Cobham was conducted down numerous corridors to the Air Marshall's office, cordially welcomed and introduced to several other officers. Fully expecting to be asked to report on progress, he was unprepared for the blow which followed. The Americans had captured an island, complete with airfield, only 400 miles from Japan, and as this was now available for use by the RAF, in-flight refuelling would no longer be required. The new official directive was to complete the sets of equipment already started but to cancel as much as possible!

Later that evening, Sir Alan discussed the decision with Lady Cobham, who drew the philosophical conclusion that it had to be regarded in the light of an improved situation that heralded a shortening of the war. Sir Alan knew she was right, but also realised the huge disappointment yet to be absorbed by the workforce at not seeing their efforts bearing fruit. Johnson masterminded the redirection of parts and materials, and after two weeks everything had been transferred from St. Athan to Staverton. Several cubes of sheet material, eight feet high on a six feet square base, a pile of refuelling hoses some twenty feet high, plus endless racks of castings, tubes, bars and chains etc., took up a large floor area in a hangar-that had to be made environmentally suitable under the terms of a Ministry storage contract.

Coincident with the cancellation of the 'Tiger Force' contract, it came as an added surprise to Johnson when Michael Cobham announced that his extended deferment was shortly due to expire, and that he would soon be leaving to join the Royal Navy!

It is of interest to note that, despite the original intention to equip the Lancasters and Lincolns for use in the Far East, the results of refuelling trials carried out by the Bomber Development Unit at Feltwell during 1945 showed that operational problems would certainly have occurred. Squadron pilots received no instruction regarding close formating techniques during their standard flying training, and successful refuelling had been shown to be highly dependent on the tanker aircraft maintaining a specific optimum position relative to the receiver.

A mixed bag of Service and civilian flight test personnel flew in the Company's Lancasters; including Ted Thickins (front row extreme right), Joe Sword (directly above Thickins), Ron Roberts (back row extreme right), John Palmer (white overalls) and Tom Marks (on Palmer's right).

Unless this could be maintained, retaining sight of the lower aircraft, especially through the heavily framed Lancaster cockpit, would have proved a difficult business, even in good conditions.

Two Lancasters had been supplied by the Ministry to carry out the flight trials with the 'looped hose' system. One, ND 648, was fitted out as a receiver, and the other, PB 972, was equipped as a tanker with cargo tanks and a hose drum unit. Both aircraft were operated from late 1944 as standard service aircraft before being eventually purchased by the Company in 1949 and transferred to the civil register as G-33-1 and G-33-2. Ted Thickins flew regularly from November 1944 onwards and recalled how, when it came to firing the Greener gun, the order had to be changed from 'Fire', to 'Shoot' to avoid giving the impression to Flying Control that the aircraft was about to descend in flames.

On one occasion, when measuring hose drag loads with a large 9000 lb. spring balance, the test equipment separated from its mountings and disappeared overboard, and the pilot experienced feelings not far short of panic when he thought the test operator had gone with it. Thickins also described a particularly terrifying moment he experienced when setting up a large cumbersome camera by the crew exit door to photograph the other formating Lancaster. A sudden lurch by the tanker caught him whilst unsecured, and he came perilously close to making a spectacular if unscheduled departure! Portable oxygen equipment too was non-existent, and Thickins usual procedure at altitude was to take a deep breath before running down to the next oxygen connection. This proved to be a risky business at 30,000 ft. – higher than Mount Everest – and more than once he had to be dragged to the oxygen connection by another crew member.

Thickins described the closing months of 1945 as a time of change in the flying ranks. Flt. Lt. Oliver who, though on detachment from the RAF, had acted as Chief Test Pilot, rejoined civilian life and was replaced by John Palmer, a very experienced ex-Rotol pilot.

The war years began and ended with FRL optimistically engaged in flight refuelling projects that were not to be fulfilled. In between, the Company had moved, tenuously at first and then with growing confidence, into a work sector entirely devoted to research and development, an area which in wartime especially was bound to include many projects destined to be stillborn. Cobham however, had in his time, experienced a good deal of disappointment and refused to bow to it. In taking stock, he noted with satisfaction that his organisation now consisted of a larger more experienced team. As 1946 approached he was as strongly convinced as ever that the opportunity to provide an international tanking service was just around the corner.

FOUR

Post-war Overture

By the end of 1945 the immediate demands of war on the Company had begun to fade, although much effort continued to be put into the thermal de-icing and fuel detonation projects. Sir Alan was well aware that renewed efforts would have to be made in all directions to sell the concept of refuelling in flight, and the economic advantages it offered. To assist him with the theoretical analysis work, he engaged Cecil Latimer-Needham from A.V.Roe, who, after conducting a thorough study of all the airline long-haul routes, produced a detailed report which also included Company design proposals for aircraft capable of long range operation. Armed with this data and a demonstration film made with the assistance of TRE at Malvern, Cobham began another intensive campaign to secure the interest of anyone prepared to listen in the various Ministry and Service Departments. The Air Ministry and the RAF's Bomber, Fighter, Transport and Coastal Commands, along with the Ministry of Civil Aviation, were all targets for voluminous correspondence, and continual invitations to witness flying demonstrations.

As might be expected however, things did not always go to plan. During a demonstration flight for the benefit of Lord Winster, the new Minister for Civil Aviation, Tom Marks overshot the runway during landing, leaving the undercarriage embedded in a ditch, and the rest of the aircraft wrapped around a concrete pill box. Curiously enough John Oliver did the same thing the following week after landing in the opposite direction, and Cobham found himself with Lancasters DV 163 and ND 623 out of action at both ends of the runway. At this point, on 10th December 1945, Ron Roberts arrived at Staverton for the start of what was to be forty-one years' service, and the sight of Marks's crashed Lancaster was hardly a confidence inspiring introduction to the Company! He added wryly that his career was nearly cut short for an entirely different reason when, only a week later, whilst working on top of a Lancaster wing, he accidentally dropped a large spanner which came perilously close to denting Sir Alan's head.

Convinced that someone had deliberately aimed it and therefore warranted immediate dismissal, Cobham's humour was severely stretched. Fortunately, it was not evident from which direction the missile had suddenly appeared and Roberts took the only action he could, which was to slide back over the leading edge and remain pressed flat, out of sight, until the danger had passed. Roberts had good cause to remember Lancaster wings, for, in addition to this incident where one shielded him from Sir Alan's wrath, he was not so fortunate just over a year later when, working on a wing slippery with ice, he fell and broke his leg. The ensuing complications meant that he was unable to resume his flying duties, and he then formed a Technical Records section which controlled the documentation required by the

Ron Roberts.

Air Registration Board following the transference of aircraft onto the Civil Register.

It was at this time that Cobham discovered that Lord Beaverbrook was still in a position to exert his immense authority. Summoned again to his presence, this time he was presented with a rough plan showing how the east end of London had been destroyed by bombing. Beaverbrook explained that far from rebuilding it, it was his intention to turn it into a large aerodrome complex. Impatient to proceed with the scheme, he instructed Sir Alan to visit the area and return with more detailed plans the following week. Cobham commandeered a taxi and spent a day exploring the proposed site which included the Isle of Dogs, Kennington and Barking. Working through the night he sketched in possible runway locations, but when it became apparent that huge disruption to the existing road and rail systems would be caused, the whole plan seemed highly questionable. Furthermore, in order to take advantage of the prevailing winds it would have meant that on departure every aircraft would have had to fly over the Houses of Parliament at a height of some 300 feet! Cobham returned three days later and tried to explain the obvious shortcomings of the plan to Beaverbrook as tactfully as he could. Showing no appreciation of all the trouble taken he simply growled and grumbled, and said that he intended to keep the drawings as he was confident that the scheme would go ahead. As it became clear that neither expenses nor thanks were in the offing, Sir Alan withdrew, reflecting that things hadn't changed much since their last encounter and his overall impressions of 'The Beaver' remained unchanged.

After the war ended, it became apparent that the Morgan family intended to start up business once again, and naturally expected to re-acquire their property at Malvern. It was an ironic touch therefore that, when faced with the uprooting of his organisation, the Air Ministry suggested to Cobham that Ford might once more become the home for FRL's operations. Hugh Johnson spearheaded the staff migration when he set off to find suitable office accommodation. His efforts resulted in the acquisition of a lease on St. Nicholas, an erstwhile preparatory school in nearby Littlehampton, and soon after work started on what would later be referred to as Site 'A'. This became the factory area and was situated a mile away to the north east of Ford aerodrome. It will be recalled that the bombing of the airfield in 1940 had demolished FRL's original

hangars, and these still lay in piles of rubble. The only accommodation that still remained was two small buildings, one of which had been the pre-war machine shop. It was September 1946 before the move to Ford was finally completed, and with limited resources and winter approaching, it was evident that rehabilitation was going to be difficult — especially for those working on unprotected aircraft in what would become one of the worst winters on record.

During all this upheaval, Sir Alan and his team were totally absorbed in trying to secure a future for the Company by selling 'flight refuelling', but early in 1946 another business opportunity presented itself. When faced with the attraction of becoming involved with airline operations, Cobham had, as his earlier endeavours have shown, rarely been able to resist 'waggling his own wings'. So, when Captain Ashley, one of his former pilots from the NAD tours approached him with a glowing proposition concerning aerial charter work, his interest was immediately awakened. Ashley explained that the potential for such work in Egypt, Africa and the Middle East was enormous, and that there were literally thousands of people employed by the oil companies needing repatriation after several years spent abroad during the war. Furthermore, Ashley had secured an undertaking from BOAC that, should he be able to form a proper company, they would be prepared to act as agents and offer the support of its ground organisation.

Faced with such an attractive prospect, Cobham produced a surprise of his own. In the early Thirties he had favoured the name 'Skyways' for his operations, but had found himself pre-empted by a small firm based in Norfolk. In 1936 however, his diligent solicitor, William Morris, had noted that the company was no longer operating and that Cobham could purchase the deeds and title for a very small sum if he so wished. This is how, ten years later, he was able to present an aptly-named and already-registered company to his co-venturers, who by now included Ashley's ex-commanding officer and Chairman of BOAC, Brigadier General A. C. Critchley.

The venture proceeded smoothly enough, with two brand new Avro Yorks being purchased for £60,000 each, and more aircraft were soon added as business flourished. When Cobham first negotiated with Sir Charles Lidbury, Chairman of the Westminster Bank, for a loan to buy the Yorks, he was asked by Sir Charles if he knew with whom he

One of the Avro Yorks originally purchased by Skyways.

The only surviving, if poor quality, photograph of the Company's fleet of Lancasters at Ford, 1946.

was going into partnership. Sir Alan replied that he knew Ashley well enough, and that although he had felt that between them they carried enough experience and prestige to float such a company, it was at Ashley's insistence that he agreed to Critchley's joining as a co-director. The reason for Lidbury's thinly veiled enquiry became clear as operations developed, and Cobham, after years of operating on a financial shoestring, was appalled at Critchley's openly declared 'policy of extravagance' – a policy which quickly outweighed any dubious contributions he may have made to the running of the company. Matters came to a head when Ashley and Critchley approached Sir Alan and suggested that more cash would have to be injected to meet operating costs. Sir Alan was advised that when the Articles of Association had been revised his solicitor had included a clause which stated that financial policy could only be directed by a body that represented 75 per cent of the shareholders. Ashley and Critchley

only accounted for 66 per cent, and could not enforce what was seen to be a move to oust Sir Alan, once his usefulness in the initial setting up had been served. After only several months he sold his interest in Skyways, and watched as over the next five or six years an enterprise which had started off with such promise, simply collapsed due to greed and mismanagement.

During 1946 the gun turrets and all other surplus military equipment were removed from the Company's six Lancasters, four of which were then accorded the civil registrations G-AHJT to G-AHJW, and stripped of their drab camouflage paint by using 'OFFKWIK' – a particularly messy 'degunking' fluid which induced severe stinging and irritation whenever it came into contact with bare skin. Arthur Watts had good cause to recall the exercise, for having unsuspectingly slithered about on a wet top wing surface, clad only in thin overalls which soon became saturated, he found out just how painful

The SBAC Exhibition at Radlett, September 1946. FRL's two Lancasters, G-AHJU and G-AHJT, can be seen in the front row.

life could be! Despite the personal discomforts incurred, the transformation of the aircraft to a natural aluminium finish was most impressive. It was only possible to prepare the tanker G-AHJU, in this manner in time for the first post-war SBAC Show held at Radlett in September 1946. A second aircraft, receiver G-AHJT, still in wartime livery but sporting cream registration letters, also attended the Show but naturally couldn't offer serious visual competition to its gleaming stablemate.

Cobham's team of pilots gradually increased over this period when Morrison, 'Pop' Taylor, Jeffrey, Large and others arrived. So too did an ex-trans-atlantic ferry pilot called David Prowse who was an exceptional character in every way. Perhaps best described as 'larger than life', Prowse was physically impressive, charming, wayward, and given to raising hell whenever he felt like it, which turned out to be often! Although highly regarded by colleagues for his undoubted flying skills, he was an extremely difficult man to contain and his general outlook on

life was more in keeping with that of sea-faring buccaneers from a previous age. Set against this background, one can sympathize with Ron Roberts who, during the Radlett Show, heard a request over the public address system for FRL's Lancasters to be moved to a different location. The problem was that the aircrew members were in no fit state to move themselves, let alone the aircraft, a situation that would not have pleased Sir Alan had he known!

During Roberts's wartime flying career as a flight engineer with the Air Transport Auxiliary, he had become familiar with the handling requirements of many different types of aircraft — experience which on this occasion fortunately allowed him to salvage what would otherwise have been a rather embarrassing event. It was, he said, nerve racking in light of the limited clearances to taxi the Lancasters past the other aircraft, which included some very expensive new prototypes. The fact that he was not licensed to do so would, had it been known, certainly have raised a furore, but fortunately the problems were overcome, and official censure avoided.

Following what turned out to be a highly impressive debut at Radlett, the Company was invited to give a demonstration soon afterwards at the Paris Aero Show. The static display was held in the Grand Palais, off the Champs Elysees, and it was proposed to fly both tanker and receiver in refuelling configuration over the Arc de Triomphe and down towards the Place de la Concorde. Cobham was concerned that the scheme sounded too ambitious and was surprised when the French authorities gave permission. As the time approached for the flight, he began to express real concern as the early December weather clamped down, and he, along with Lady Cobham and Hugh Johnson, could only see halfway up the Champs Elysees as the drizzle increased and obscured their view. Undeterred by the appalling conditions and a cloud base of less than two hundred feet, Prowse flying the tanker and Jeffery the receiver, took off from Le Bourget and, arriving to the minute, thundered down the Champs Elysees at just above tree top height, with the refuelling hose looped below the trees! Cobham declared that he had never seen anything more terrifying in his life, and was amazed and relieved to find that instead of receiving an official reprimand, everyone concerned had been thrilled by the display.

During the 1940s the BBC presented a radio programme entitled 'In Town Tonight' in which personalities were interviewed, ostensibly as they just happened to be passing through London. The interviews were of course pre-arranged, and usually included the celebrity being asked which person he or she would like to speak to at that given moment. Sir Alan, having been invited onto the programme in 1946, was soon asked the inevitable question and replied that as his Company was carrying out refuelling trials near Malvern at that very moment, he was keen to know how the tests were progressing. It was therefore an impressive piece of opportunism when the voice of the BBC's commentator, Charles Gardner, came over clear and strong to say that everything was going well, three contacts having been made and fuel passed at 130 gallons per minute. It was fortunate that only the previous day the BBC had been visiting Worcestershire to broadcast a county cricket match and the recording van and apparatus were still in position close to Malvern. This had facilitated reception of Gardner's message by means of the aircraft's trailing aerial and allowed

its relay over a landline to Broadcasting House. The listening public thought it was great stuff!

As part of Sir Alan's bombardment aimed at selling flight refuelling, approaches were made to the three major British airlines. British European Airways operated the franchise for Europe, British Overseas Airways Corporation's interests covered other parts of the world outside Europe, and British South American Airways had been formed to develop air routes across the South Atlantic to South America and the West Indies. Lord Runciman was appointed Chairman of BSAA, and Air Vice Marshal Don Bennett, who had set up the Pathfinder Force in Bomber Command, was its new Managing Director.

At the outset, Sir Alan met with little enthusiasm for his ideas, largely because each organisation was preoccupied with overcoming the more immediate problems of peacetime re-adjustment. Any further potential complications were distinctly unwelcome. Fortunately FRL's founder was a man of formidable persistence who believed that turmoil only served to provide opportunities for those willing to grasp them. His tenacity paid off and a visit to the Director of Air Navigation produced a welcome result when it was decided that £100,000 would be made available for further development. Under the watchful eye of a special Executive Operational Panel, it was planned to carry out a series of flights during the winter of 1946-47 wherein FRL's Lancaster tankers would rendezvous over the Channel with Bennett's aircraft equipped as receivers. Apart from establishing the viability of providing a tanker service, it was also intended that by carrying out some of the trials at night and in all weathers, the BSAA crews would gain valuable experience and training for the proposed long hauls over the South Atlantic. It therefore became a routine procedure for the airliner to take off from Heathrow with an FRL operator on board, to a schedule of pre-determined dates and times, receive from the tanker some one thousand gallons of fuel and return to base. For the first time in flight refuelling operations, a radar system codenamed REBECCA/EUREKA was used to assist the aircraft to converge accurately upon each other. With a range now extended from ninety to one hundred and twenty miles, this version was a significant improvement on that originally developed by TRE at Malvern for use by the Airborne forces. This successful adaptation was largely due to Sqn. Ldr. Brian Cape who had recently joined the Company to investigate radar interception techniques

FRL's instructor, Reginald Crompton-Holgate, holding court before a high level Ministry delegation.

'Star Leopard' which formed part of BSAA's fleet of Tudors. This type of aircraft was later considered for tanker duties with the Comet as a receiver.

and to provide an electronic capability within the technical organisation. Officially referred to as the Channel Trials, they consisted of a total of forty-three flights, twenty-six being by day, and seventeen by night, and what was known as the 'Johnnie and Titch' canteen played no small part in maintaining morale when crews returned to Ford after a late and bumpy trip. The 'Black Dog' at nearby Yapton also contributed in no small measure to aircrew well being, and, with all telephone calls being automatically transferred there, it was regarded as the unofficial crew room for Captain Prowse and his immediate associates!

The training of personnel for the Channel Trials and also the presence of representatives of the Bomber Development Unit at Feltwell necessitated the formation of a school for pilots where they received instruction from Tom Marks. The need to teach others about the equipment and its operation had however now become a sizeable requirement and led to the arrival of Reginald Crompton-Holgate, an ex-Rolls-Royce instructor. Sir Alan was always keen to enter the Lecture Room and would sit quietly at the back, noting with satisfaction the style and technique with which his new lecturer would spellbind a roomful of Air Marshals or company Chairmen!

Much theoretical work was done at this time trying to convince the airlines, A.V.Roe and the Ministry of Civil Aviation of the enormous advantages which a flight refuelling capability would confer on the Avro Tudor Mk.II. Latimer-Needham's

analysis showed that it would be able to fly non-stop from London to New York with forty-two passengers. Whilst all concerned expressed support, Cobham – despite his Company having undertaken the preliminary design work – simply could not get anyone to offer an aircraft for a trial installation, even when he undertook to supply all the equipment on a private venture basis. Discussions dragged on however until the Tudor met its eventual demise following the unexplained loss of BSAA's 'Star Tiger' in January 1948, and 'Star Ariel' just a year later, both over the South Atlantic. Although the Tudor had shown much early promise when it first entered commercial service in September 1947, accidents and its total rejection by BOAC resulted in the type being completely withdrawn from regular passenger use less than eighteen months later.

FRL conducted several design studies for airliners capable of crossing the Atlantic if refuelled in flight (see Appendix III). Latimer-Needham also produced other reports which showed that the Handley Page Hermes and Halton (the civil version of the Halifax) along with the Avro York would be contenders for transatlantic operation if they could be refuelled in the air. Unfortunately, although the makers invariably agreed with the findings, the provision of an aircraft for trials always proved to be a stumbling block. In addition to the possiblities of transatlantic operation, a particularly strong case was also made to Air Marshal Sir Ralph Cochrane, the new head of RAF Transport Command, for Yorks to be refuelled in flight over Malta, allowing them to carry troops non-stop to Egypt and beyond. But again, as in the other cases, existing demands always seemed to dominate and override the provision of an aircraft for evaluation. There was little else that Cobham could do to put pressure on the policy makers. The breakthrough always seemed to be imminent, and with approaches being made on so many fronts, and with the results of the Channel Trials there for all to see, it had now become a case of 'wait and see' regarding a military application. Disappointingly Coastal Command cancelled a contract for the equipping of ten Vickers Armstrong Warwicks as receivers, after the design work and a mock up had been completed. This decision was made after it was decided to re-equip the meteorological squadron with Halifax Mk.VI aircraft. FRL was then requested to instal receiver apparatus in ten such aircraft, and to fit three Lancaster Mk.III's as tankers. Only one Halifax, RG 389, and one Lancaster, SW 338, had equipment fitted and a single test flight was carried out before that contract too was cancelled in December 1946.

A good deal of other design and flight test development work was in progress however on improved couplings, tank pressurization and venting systems, night lighting and oil flow behaviour under negative 'G' conditions for the Fairey Spearfish and Percival Prentice aircraft. The continuing materials research programme and the increasing interest in fuel system components also ensured a varied level of activity within the Company. Maintaining a healthy cash flow however, never ceased to be a problem, and FRL's ebullient salesman, Peter Procter, described how at one particularly low point in 1946

FRL's sales chief, Peter Procter, headed the drive to sell pressure refuelling equipment.

he managed, along with Sid Ebel of Handley Page, to convince the Ministry to approve the installation of pressure fuelling equipment in the new Hastings transport aircraft. With the coffers running low, he returned from another long meeting at Handley Page to arrive late at the firm's dance at the Beach Hotel in Littlehampton. With a bottle of champagne in one hand and an order for £23,000 of equipment in the other, Procter mounted the platform, halted the band and announced that it was the best sale of component equipment the Company had ever had — and certainly it provided a timely financial relief! Encouraging though this was, there were still no signs that the corner had been turned, and as 1946 drew to a close with the staff level down to forty-eight, the question on everyone's lips was — 'What next?'

FIVE

Across the Big Divide

One day in early 1947 Sir Alan was at the Ministry of Civil Aviation discussing the results of the Channel Trials, when Jack Eaton, then Deputy Director of Aircraft Requirements, asked him what he saw as the next phase of development. Fortunately there was still a good deal of money left over from the original trials' allocation of £100,000, and he was quick to point out that a sequence of return flights across the

Southern Atlantic, from London to Bermuda, would be the next logical step. He added that such a programme would involve refuelling operations using tankers based in the Azores.

The suggestion was soon approved and a contract awarded for eleven flights in each direction between Heathrow and Kindley Field. The cost was estimated to be £20,000 and after the exercise was completed

FRL's Lancasters using the 'looped hose' system during South Atlantic trials. Tanker G-AHJW was later destroyed in a fatal crash during Berlin Airlift operations.

it was gratifying to note that this projection had been absolutely accurate.

Sir Alan and Hugh Johnson then visited Lisbon and were given permission to use the airfield constructed by the Americans during the war on Santa Maria, the southernmost island in the Azores group. Following this, an FRL team and two Lancaster tankers, G-AHJW and G-AHJU, were despatched, along with a chartered Avro York heavily loaded with spares and a Jeep for providing local transport. Johnson, chosen once again to head the team, added to his bizarre list of uncomfortable aerial journeys by sitting in the Jeep for the whole trip, as there was simply no other space available! In total, twenty two members of FRL were stationed in the Azores for a two and a half month period which, whilst generally providing perfect weather, also included unwelcome periods of persistent fog and torrential rain which played havoc with the radio communications equipment. Prowse and Jeffrey were the resident tanker pilots, although as the trials progressed, the opportunity was taken to train other pilots such as Taylor, Large, Hanbury and Roly Beaumont in tanking techniques. BSAA crews were appointed to fly two other Company Lancasters, G-AHJV and G-AHJT, equipped as receivers. After the Channel Trials it had been tentatively suggested that the airline's 'Stargirl' stewardesses might be asked to take on the refuelling operator's duties in addition to their normal work, but the idea was not pursued. A rather less glamorous alternative was instead provided when FRL's Ray Harris and Bob Chalk were seconded to BSAA, taking it in turns on round trips!

The tanker delivery flights from Ford to the Azores were not without incident, for not a single word was heard from either aircraft from take off to landing – some nine hours later. Their silent passage proved to be particularly worrying for technicians Ted Thickins and Peter McGregor who, though totally unfamiliar with weight and balance calculations, had been made responsible for loading the aircraft. Concern was also expressed at the Overseas Air Traffic Control Centres at Gloucester and Prestwick, as normal operating procedures required them to transmit their positions every half hour. It later turned out that a last minute decision has been taken to replace the electrical generators normally fitted on the Lancaster with another type that did not require the associated bulky test gear. It had been understood that the new items were tested

FRL's Mary Lewis, who worked alongside BSAA's Stargirls at Heathrow Airport for the inaugural flight to Bermuda.

and approved, but the ferry flights had dramatically proved otherwise, and standard items were soon refitted.

On 28th May 1947 a team of BSAA 'Stargirls', along with FRL's Mary Lewis, resplendent in wine coloured uniform, accorded Don Bennett and his companions a spirited farewell as they went aboard G-AHJV for the first outbound trip to Bermuda (see Footnote). Flying with Bennett were Sir Alan and Latimer-Needham, who found it a far from luxurious experience – the only concession to comfort being the provision of some extra cushions! Thus equipped, the crew then took off on a three thousand five hundred mile journey that could take up to twenty hours flying time depending on the prevailing headwinds. The main point of the flight

Footnote: One of the 'Stargirls' later married to become Mrs. Branson, and she continued her services to aviation by producing Richard, the founder of the Virgin group of companies.

89

was of course, to demonstrate the ease with which a long range interception could be made with the tanker, and this was achieved, according to plan, eight hours later. Soon after refuelling however, a malfunction occurred in the electrical system supplying the cockpit lighting and the radar equipment, and in order to conserve electrical power, Bennett ordered all lights on the flight deck to be extinguished. Tension increased further when the radio too, soon became silent, and Sir Alan later described how, faced with several more long hours flying in the eerie darkness, Bermuda seemed a very long way off! Fortunately the cloud-free starlit night allowed Bennett to exercise his renowned navigational skills, and using a sextant he took regular astro fixes to confirm the aircraft's position.

After some further eight hours' flying, knowing that survival depended on his dead reckoning abilities, Bennett announced that Bermuda, a relatively tiny dot in the western Atlantic, should be some ninety miles ahead, and that the island's lights should soon become visible. Apprehension grew when the lights failed to appear, but upon arriving over Bermuda's estimated position it became apparent that the whole area was covered by a low bank of cloud. Unable to contact the airport by radio, and with barely enough battery power left to drive the fuel pumps, it required a firm act of faith to embark upon the blind descent, and it was an enormous relief when at two hundred feet the clouds

Sir Alan Cobham and Air Vice Marshal D. C. T. Bennett just prior to the first non-stop flight to Bermuda, 1947.

En-route to Bermuda.

finally thinned, to reveal what appeared to be every light on the island shining in welcome. After three low circuits of the airfield to assess runway directions and likely obstacles, Bennett made a perfect landing – just twenty hours after leaving Heathrow!

After two days of so called rest, G-AHJV left on an uneventful return flight, refuelling again as planned off the Azores, before arriving at Heathrow to a triumphant press reception. Bennett thought that the remainder of the flights would provide excellent further training for his crews, and seven different pilots subsequently took part in the programme, engaging with the tankers on a routine basis. Cobham immediately returned to Ford, determined to root out the cause of the total generator failure which had marred the operation, and which could have caused disaster had not a pilot of Bennett's calibre been on board. After a strong lecture to all concerned, enquiries revealed that the ground engineers had placed total reliance on Government surplus items which carried labels declaring them to be tested and serviceable. From that point onward, every critical item was subjected to rigorous in-house testing, no matter what the label stated.

Following the arrival at Santa Maria of personnel, aircraft and equipment, Hugh Johnson was faced with the old problems inherent in setting up and administering a tanker base in a short period of time. Perhaps not surprisingly, the sudden release from the constraints of austere post-war England proved too tempting for some, and with the gregarious Prowse naturally assuming the role of head coach, bar activities soon came to be regarded as part of the team's organized games! The initial novelty rapidly wore off, and with everyone settling into their specialist roles, good working relationships quickly emerged. When Sir Alan visited the base halfway through the trials, he was amazed to find everyone had 'gone native' and grown beards. Although a good many were ultimately sacrificed in the interests of domestic harmony when the owners returned home, several beards were proudly and enduringly retained as evidence of having served in the Azores campaign! The smooth running of the operation was underlined by the fact that FRL's aircrew were now in possession of uniforms, these having arrived in a progressive piecemeal fashion from England! Of note is the fact that the cap badges embodied for the first time the Company logo that has since become familiar throughout the aviation world – the symbolic representation of two aircraft

in refuelling contact, and a design based on BOAC's own Speedbird insignia (see Footnote).

The South Atlantic Trials, as they were officially known, revealed the need for more reliable electrical and radar equipment and for FRL's radio operators to become better trained in trans-oceanic procedures. Two cases of engine failure also occurred, one on receiver G-AHJT, which required the pilot to make an unscheduled landing at Santa Maria, and the other on tanker G-AHJW just after it had completed refuelling the last east bound receiver.

Fortunately none of these events had a detrimental effect on Cobham's claim, keenly endorsed by Don Bennett, that in-flight refuelling was a practical concept that had once again been demonstrated for all to see. Sir Alan knew that it was most important to capitalize on the success of the trials as quickly as possible and he therefore lost no time in starting to plan the third and final phase of the proving programme – tackling the old enemy, the North Atlantic, this time in conjunction with BOAC.

Discussions with the airline reinforced the fact that the Company's aircrew fell well short of understanding the niceties of international flight procedures. Both Cobham and Latimer-Needham were, on their own admissions, well out of their depth when it came to discussing operation and communications requirements in detail, and usually it fell to Brian Cape to interpret the airline's statements as best he could. It was therefore a significant step forward when Sqn. Ldr. C.F.Rawnsley, who had served with great distinction as Gp. Capt. John Cunningham's navigator and radar operator on many night fighter 'sorties', joined the Company as 'Interception Chief'. His experience and expertise quickly provided a balance in an area that had become increasingly difficult.

Although it had been necessary to recruit from outside the Company in order to close this specialist gap, the work situation throughout the factory area had become increasingly desperate by the end of 1947. With barely enough work to keep the Machine and Fitting Shops and the general administration ticking over, Sir Alan took the painful decision to cut his staff by two thirds. Despite the staff reduction, and the fact that firm orders were proving so elusive,

Footnote: The original Company logo showed the aircraft flying to the left, but this was changed following a dispute over the infringement of BOAC's registered design. Since 1963, the FR logo has depicted the aircraft flying to the right!

C.F. 'Jimmy' Rawnsley, sketched whilst in the Service, joined FRL as 'Interception Chief' in 1947.

Cobham had to plan for eventual success. It was with an eye to the future therefore that he negotiated the purchase of four more Lancasters, chosen from the Ministry's surplus stockpile at RAF Kemble for £1000 each, along with spare Merlin engines at £100 per unit. Whilst considering the need for extra aircraft, Sir Alan was also facing the fact that Ford was now proving totally unsuitable for flying work, largely due to the lack of hangar facilities, and although he was willing to build his own, the Admiralty were again reluctant to provide a permanent site. Added to this, the airfield was desperately needing general repairs, and frequent closures necessitated the Company having to negotiate the temporary shared use of nearby RAF Tangmere. Cobham now found himself on the horns of a real dilemma! Although currently working in conjunction with the civil airlines and mindful of the probable long term associations, there was clearly no possibility of sharing a civil aerodrome such as Heathrow. Sir Alan's appeal for airfield facilities had to be made through the defence authorities and they were, at least for the time being, indifferent to his needs. This was, however, a problem that was not going to go away, and Sir Alan had to devote much time and effort into trying to find an airfield of the right size, and in a location that would suit his purposes. Flying with Tom Marks in the Company's Hornet Moth, Cobham visited many airfields, including Membury, Welford, Lasham, and Dunsfold, before deciding that Tarrant Rushton, near Blandford in Dorset, would meet his needs.

For once the Air Ministry had no serious objections, and at a meeting held there in May 1947, Cobham attempted to secure a tenancy on favourable terms. He pointed out that as the Company's presence would preclude the need to retain an experienced resident Service care and maintenance party, he was in effect doing the Ministry a favour, and this ought to be reflected in a nominal rent. Counter arguments were put forward, the Ministry claiming that the fair economic rental of an airfield that had cost £1 million to construct in 1943, would be £10,000 per year. Sir Alan soon realized that in order to keep outgoings down to a minimum, he would only be able to transfer a skeleton organisation down to Dorset, leaving the factory and training school at Ford and the administration at Littlehampton. With a compromise eventually reached whereby each hangar used would attract a rent of £1020 per annum, Cobham despatched an advance party under Ron Roberts to carry out the preparatory work.

Although still requisitioned by the Air Ministry, the RAF no longer flew from the airfield, but the Army base at Blandford frequently used the runways and perimeter tracks for motor cycle and truck driver training, and local farmers were also permitted to plough the land and graze cattle and sheep. With no authority to order anyone off the airfield, and with a great deal of renovating and maintenance work to be done at Cobham's expense, there were still formidable obstacles to be overcome. Working with local contractors, Roberts's team, now increased to twelve by the addition of local labour, made progress in restoring the site. Harry Hunt and the Adams brothers started off their employment in this manner before becoming the familiar respective custodians of Security and Transport in later years. By September 1947 the four Kemble based Lancasters had been made airworthy by Airwork Ltd. and flown in for storage at Tarrant Rushton.

Unfortunately the work being done to ensure the hangars were 'vandal proof' had not been completed before the aircraft arrived, and it was not long before enterprising Army personnel saw an immediate source of extra income in the aircrafts' loose equipment. Cobham complained strongly to the Air Ministry that despite his watchmen's best efforts, parts of the aircraft, especially compasses, were regularly disappearing, and although the Army were using the airfield for training in order to keep 'death off the roads' Sir Alan stated it would be a case of 'death on the airfield' if he caught the culprits. In February 1948 the four South Atlantic Trials aircraft were also stored alongside the Kemble aircraft, offering even more attraction for the raiding parties. On one occasion, four soldiers, when challenged, scrambled out through a hole cut in the side of a hangar. Although three got clean away, one was caught by the watchman, but even he managed to foil the investigators by giving a false name before being released. This kind of aggravation only came to an end when the Army was finally ordered to cease training on the airfield soon afterwards.

Throughout all the talks which preceded the North Atlantic Trials, BOAC's representatives had made it clear that only a winter trial would provide a thoroughly practical demonstration. The westbound flights would involve a receiver-tanker link up over Shannon before the transatlantic crossing, and another over either Newfoundland at Gander or Labrador at Goose Bay, before the receiver flew on to Montreal.

The assumption was made that if weather conditions closed in over Gander (the first choice) the alternate refuelling base at Goose Bay would be open. Only a single refuelling operation over one of the western bases was considered necessary for the return trip. The Lancasters used on the previous trials were deemed inadequate for the North Atlantic Trials, as it was essential to provide tankers that could offer the crews a reasonable degree of protection against the severe cold, as well as having powerplants and systems that could resist icing conditions. It was to prove a fortunate coincidence that at this time Trans-Canadian Airlines were planning to terminate the use of Lancastrian aircraft which had served to get their post-war operations underway, and had actually flown an aircraft to England in order to give demonstration flights to interested bidders. Convinced by Sir Alan that the aircraft would prove to be an ideal tanker, Jack Eaton directed him to travel to Canada and strike the best deal he could. Upon his return, pleased at having struck a bargain, he was soon surprised to find himself along with Eaton in the middle of a bureaucratic tussle, because it had been belatedly discovered that it was not

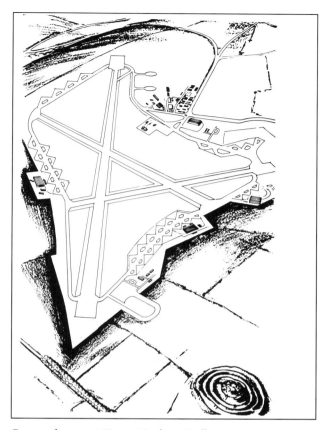

Runway lay-out at Tarrant Rushton. Badbury Rings, iron-age fort, is shown in the foreground with the main Wimborne to Blandford road cutting across the lower left-hand corner. (Wimborne is to the right). No.1 Hangar is at the top, and Nos. 2, 3 and 4 are positioned clockwise.

accepted policy for a person outside the Civil Service to buy equipment on behalf of the Ministry. However, presented with a *fait accompli* the Ministry withdrew its objections, the row eventually subsided, and it was decided that a team of Company pilots would fly over to Canada in the Lancastrian still in England, in order to ferry the new purchases back to Ford.

Along with Prowse, Taylor, Hanbury, Jeffrey, Large, Beaumont and Elliott went Michael Cobham who, after completing his service in the Royal Navy had resumed employment with the Company in May 1947. Now, because of Prowse's known shortcomings outside his flying skills, he was to act as purser for the trip, and faced the task of diplomatically handling all the administrative affairs en-route. The flight took place on 3rd September 1947, and no-one thought that warm clothing was

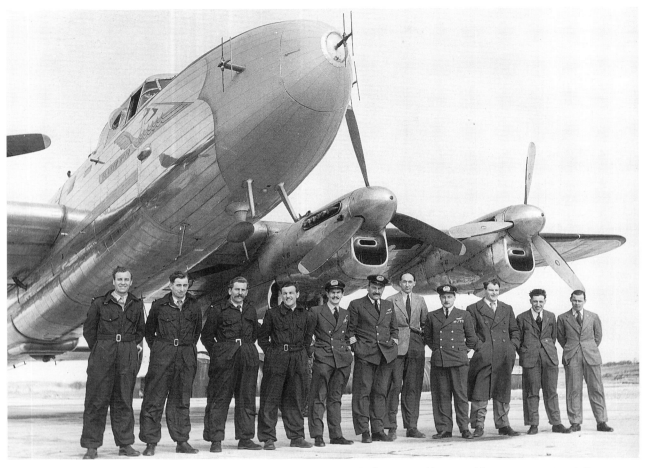

FRL's staff at Shannon during the North Atlantic trials. From the left; W. Ashall, J. McLachlan, F. Baldwin, A. Watts, W. Jeffery, D. Prowse, L. Thornhill, R. Beaumont, R. Bullock, V. Griffiths, R. Elliott. The aircraft is Lancastrian tanker G-AKDO.

necessary for the trip, which was scheduled to fly via the Azores to Newfoundland. David Prowse, who had crossed the Atlantic fifty six times during his wartime service, had predicted that 8000 ft. was the ideal flying height, as this was above the low cloud and below the light variety usually encountered. On this occasion however the weather clamped down, and the flight was re-routed over Iceland and Greenland, with Prowse finding it necessary at one stage to go up to 18,000 ft. in order to clear storms. Everyone in the main cabin suffered from the intense cold when the Janitrol heaters failed, and all available newspapers were in great demand for packing inside shirts and trousers in a desperate attempt to retain body heat.

Within a short time all the aircraft were safely delivered to Ford, and following conversion were allocated the new civil markings G-AKDO,

G-AKDP, G-AKDR and G-AKDS. Up at Prestwick, Scottish Aviation lent support to a Company team which, headed by Mike Goodliffe and including Roy Tier, carried out the receiver conversion work on a Liberator II, G-AHYD, allocated by BOAC. Hugh Johnson, now an accredited 'old hand' at setting up tanker bases, took overall charge of the arrangements at Shannon, Gander and Goose Bay, two crews along with support personnel being allocated to each station. In certain respects, living conditions had changed very little from when Johnson first visited Gander in 1939, but those at Goose Bay were undoubtedly the worst. With no communication with the outside world, except by air, the isolation often had serious effects on personal behaviour, and the RCAF having experienced several suicides, generally regarded it as a punishment centre. Both at Goose Bay and Gander, outside recreation was a physical impossibility during the winter months, and there was no question as to who had drawn the short straws when FRL's personnel postings were announced.

The trials commenced on 4th February and continued until 29th May 1948, with the Liberator flying one return service a week. Out of the forty five planned refuellings, forty two were successfully carried out, and three failures were recorded. The first of these was due to the BOAC pilot declining to carry out the operation, although the tanker aircraft was in radar contact at a distance of fifteen miles. Cobham's pilots later stated that BOAC's co-operation frequently failed to match that previously obtained with Don Bennett's crews, and relationships were not improved when inexperienced observers in the Liberator commented adversely on the tanker formating techniques. Cobham bluntly regarded the dissention as stemming from the attitude held by the airline's older 'million miler' pilots, which did not encourage other aircraft to be within one mile of their own for any reason! The second failure occurred during a refuelling at night, when fuel failed to flow with the tanker in an experimental refuelling position. The receiver however, although having sufficient fuel to reach its destination, was diverted due to bad weather. The third instance was due to a failure of the tanker's REBECCA radar and also the breakdown of the cabin heaters which rendered everyone on board immobile with the cold. The tanker captain requested the receiver to abandon the operation, whereupon both aircraft returned to Gander. After repairs, the operation was duly completed. Despite the differences of opinion concerning flying techniques, there was little serious criticism of the equipment which now pumped fuel to the receiver instead of relying on gravity flow, and Cobham had every reason to believe that the adoption of his brainchild by at least the more enlightened civil operators was now imminent.

As the move from Ford to Tarrant Rushton got underway, Cobham decided to close down the Staverton site that still housed the equipment and materials produced for the 'Tiger Force' contract. Works Manager Cook had long been of the opinion that all of it could be purchased from the Ministry for a relatively small sum, and that failing being used for its intended purpose, it would still fetch a good price as scrap.

A favourable deal was concluded in March 1948, but Sir Alan's ability to raise the few thousands of

BOAC Liberator G-AHYD refuelling at night during North Atlantic trials, 1948. The fast exposure time used in the photograph has resulted in the propellers appearing to be stationary.

Walter Hill OBE, who served as Shell's representative on FRL's Board.

pounds required was severely strained by another drain on his pocket — that of personally buying back the Company from Shell. A year previously, Walter Hill, Shell's Aviation Manager and representative on FRL's Board since 1937, had indicated that in light of its other interests, Shell would be prepared to sell its share in the Company for £40,500, the price it had originally paid. Now, unwilling to let the opportunity slip, but all too aware of his own and the Company's precarious financial position, Cobham elected to gamble on a successful purchase.

Walter Hill, who left the FRL Board at this time but rejoined it for the five years prior to his death in 1961, was widely respected in aviation circles. He literally controlled the allocation and supply of aviation fuel throughout a large part of the world during WW.II, and Sir Alan had good cause to be grateful for the influence he exercised in keeping the Company in being throughout the war years.

Always keen to promote FRL's interests, Hill was directly responsible for bringing about a big turnaround in the Company's fortunes when he brought Shell's General Doolittle down to Ford on a flying visit. This chance encounter, just prior to the start of the North Atlantic Trials, resulted in a USAF conference decision to launch in-flight refuelling as a Service operation.

The Americans had come to the conclusion that in order to be able to attack key targets in Russia by day or night, a bomber would be required that possessed twice the range of their existing B-29s. When asked how long it would take to design and develop such an aircraft, industrial representatives replied that production could be achieved in seven years. This unacceptable situation was resolved when Doolittle offered the solution — to refuel in flight! Despite some local objections, interest was quickly aroused, and in April 1948 a B-29 landed at Ford aerodrome, carrying Colonel Warden and other officers to find out all about the system that had so impressed the General. The Colonel however, had arrived with the idea that the British Government was about to make a present of the equipment, drawings and 'know how' at no cost. Sir Alan rapidly explained that far from this being the case, the successful trials currently being carried out on the North Atlantic, were the result of much private development that had 'cost millions' and therefore the system was subject to normal commercial safeguards. Colonel Warden and his team immediately withdrew to the US Embassy in London, for advice on the next step.

Meanwhile, Sir Alan, contemplating the slice of sheer good luck that had secured the ownership of the ex-'Tiger Force' equipment and material only two weeks previously, considered the implications of the prize about to fall into his lap. The Americans had expressed a need for the immediate delivery of three complete sets of equipment, with a rapid follow-up of an extra thirty seven sets. With a depressed skilled work force, meeting the required production deadlines was clearly going to be a problem. Cobham and Chris Tonge debated long and hard whether to sell the manufacturing rights and let the Americans produce everything, or to take the risk of defaulting on deliveries. Sir Alan contacted his old colleague, F.E.N.St.Barbe, de Havillands' Commercial Director, and long familiar with dealing in the USA. Cobham began to realise the size of his asset when St. Barbe advised him not to sell the 'know how' for anything less than a quarter of a million dollars — a significant sum in 1948 — and especially so when set against the Company's perpetually dire financial situation.

After a week of intense discussions which finally led to the contract being signed and sealed in the early hours of Good Friday morning, Colonel Warden's team set out that night on their homeward journey to Dayton, having left behind an order worth one and a quarter million dollars. This covered an option to manufacture all parts in the US (not taken up), and the supply and assistance with the installation of the initial sets of equipment. Latimer-Needham, Smith and Allison then spent several weeks during March and April assisting in the design of the KB-29 and B-50 systems, and at Ford the production line soon got into its stride. The USAF was amazed that deliveries were so consistently ahead of schedule, Sir Alan having failed to inform them of his trump card — the sizeable number of ex-'Tiger Force' parts and components simply awaiting final assembly. The order was later extended to one hundred sets, and due to the rosy future prospects thereby created, the order was referred to in-house as 'The 4711 Contract' — as it smelled as sweet as the famous '4711' brand of Eau de Cologne (see Footnote).

Footnote: Subsequently Boeing converted 92 aircraft to KB-29M tanker configuration; 74 B-29s, 57 B-50As and most of the B-36s were also modified as receivers for the looped-hose system.

SIX

Russian Roulette

Sir Alan decided to exploit the fact that equipment deliveries to the USAF were proceeding well ahead of schedule, and in mid-1948 paid a visit to the test centre at Wright Field, Dayton, Ohio. Following his arrival, he soon found himself the centre of attention at a luncheon arranged in order that he could meet senior officers associated with the project. The conversation centred mainly on the merits of the looped hose method of refuelling, and Sir Alan was caught off guard when General Crawford, the most senior officer present, announced that what was also needed was a new and automatic method of refuelling single seat fighters. He stressed the fact that although the looped hose system was a practical proposition for supplying multi-crew aircraft, it could not be used for a fighter where the pilot was already fully occupied in simply controlling his aircraft. Somehow a method would have to be devised which would transfer all the work to the tanker crew. Full of wine and confidence, Sir Alan replied that back in England his team was working on that very thing!

Fortunately the luncheon soon ended and Cobham deflected requests for more details, but General Crawford soon cornered him and introduced General Carroll who, it transpired, was due to visit England in the forthcoming spring. When pressed to provide a demonstration of the new system, Sir Alan — his bluff called — could only put on a brave face and indicate that he would be delighted to do so. Having no idea at that stage how the problem could be overcome, he appreciated that he had only a few short months in which to come up with something, and, that, with the stakes so high, the job would have to be given top priority.

Before leaving England, he had noted with concern the increasing Russian threat to seal off all the land and river trade routes into Berlin. Accordingly he had offered the aircraft and four crews, newly returned from the North Atlantic Trials, in support of the military aircraft already starting to transport supplies into the city. However, no formal acceptance of the offer was received from the Foreign Office before the time came for him to leave for the USA. Now, pre-occupied with the heady prospect of supplying the whole of the USAF with refuelling equipment, Sir Alan was only loosely aware of the rapid escalation of political events in Europe. It therefore came as a shock when Hugh Johnson telephoned him to say that the Russian threat had become a reality, and that the Foreign Office now urgently wished to take up his offer of support.

Apart from the immediate need to provide men and machines capable of carrying fuel, Johnson had little information on which to form a plan. What was evident however, was that the Company was being tasked with a vital role, as its cargo would be the life blood that enabled the ground distribution system to operate. At this stage no-one seemed to know the whereabouts of the fuel the Company had agreed to ferry, where it had to go, or how it was to be handled. The rate for the job had still to be decided, and it was anyone's guess how long the operation would continue. Despite the uncertainties, Johnson instructed Arthur Watts to start modifying the only two serviceable Lancastrian tankers to ensure that the motor spirit and diesel oil that had to be carried in the bomb bay tanks was isolated and could not contaminate the aircraft's normal fuel supply. Following this instant modification, G-AKDR, piloted by Captain Hanbury and with Maurice Jenkins as Flight Engineer, took off on 27th July 1948 bound for Berlin, which was now truly 'an island in a red sea of military might'. This flight meant that FRL became the first of the twenty-five British private contractors that made a civil contribution to the airlift, now codenamed 'Operation Plainfare'.

FRL eventually deployed a total of twelve converted Lancasters and Lancastrians on the Airlift, which became massive by any standards. With much already written describing the hardships, heroics and the logistics generally associated with the Berlin Airlift, it is unnecessary to repeat them — however, the statistics relating to the Company's aircraft which operated initially from Buckeburg,

The Link Trainer used for 16 hours a day at Tarrant Rushton to ensure flight crews maintained peak proficiency.

then Wunstorf and finally Fuhlsbuttel, are contained in Appendix IV.

At Tarrant Rushton the staff level rose from 207 to a peak of 652 in May 1949, and, in carrying out the continuous repair, overhaul and maintenance of the aircraft returning after 50 hours (later 75 hours) flying, No.4 hangar could lay equal claim to the London Windmill Theatre's proud boast – 'We never close!'. Maurice Jenkins, after some two hundred flights into Berlin, returned to indoctrinate new flight engineers as part of the special facility set up to train the crews now arriving.

Ted Alsop joined the Company on the 16th August 1948, when the Airlift was already in full swing, and one of his earliest recollections is of the noses of the participating aircraft being painted 'Cobham Blue' prior to a local artist adding the Company logo.

Tom Marks was asked by Johnson to take one of the first aircraft to Gatow, and once there to obtain 'local details' from Roy Elliott, another FRL pilot. It was only after a vain chase around several airfields, which culminated in being driven in a van on a mystery tour – as Marks put it 'halfway round Germany'- that the link up was finally made. One 'local detail' was made clear to him straightaway, and

that was that there was no question of his returning to Tarrant Rushton in another aircraft as planned, as both he and all available aircraft were urgently required. Equipped only with 'one of everything' he stayed for six weeks – a typical experience shared by several others. During this initial period, there was little visible overall organisation and the FRL crews, left to fend for themselves, flew virtually when they felt like it, usually two trips a day, the main difficulty being the obtaining and loading of fuel, which, in Marks's view, took a disproportionate amount of time. Once 'topped up' however, it was off to Gatow, stay for lunch, return to Buckeburg and then fly a second sortie before dusk. This degree of informality did not last long however, and with an enormous number of aircraft becoming involved, flying discipline, especially regarding the close timing of approaches and departures, tightened up considerably. In ex-Flight Engineer Frank Russell's words, 'the old wartime "press on regardless" spirit was very evident, and rather than lose a place in the never ending line up of aircraft waiting to leave Gatow, the usual practice, should an engine problem occur, was to take off with all four on full power, then cut the offending engine once airborne!'

Despite the meticulous timing that attended every

Forty-five years on! Berlin Airlift veterans Pat Hornidge (left) and Frank Russell pictured in 1993.

landing and take-off, it was a simple fact that such a dense concentration of aircraft in a confined airspace introduced a high risk of mid-air collision. Pat Hornidge, an ex-Bristol Aeroplane Company test pilot, who joined FRL in October 1948, has told of how during his 132 sorties to Berlin there were many occasions on which his aircraft was violently rocked after encountering another transport's slipstream, and also how fallible the overstrained ground controllers could be at times. He counted himself lucky to have avoided a serious accident when, returning from Gatow to Wunstorf, he relied on a ground controlled approach for landing through low, dense fog. Requested from the tower to fly straight ahead and land, he was astounded, on breaking through the mist, to discover the runway displaced some six hundred yards to the left!

As the Airlift got into its stride, and with FRL operating daily from Wunstorf (and, from mid-April 1949, Fuhlsbuttel airfield at Hamburg), it became necessary to appoint experienced administrators to run key areas of the operation. The man put in charge of the civil side was British European Airway's Edwin Whitfield, but unfortunately his appointment and level of authority was not made clear

immediately to Hugh Johnson and other charter company representatives. It was not long before Johnson at Tarrant Rushton realised that he was faced with a hopeless task in trying to keep aligned with changing conditions in Germany, and this fact, coupled with his somewhat contemptuous regard for Whitfield's attempts at control, led to many strong

Opposite top *FRL's Operational Site at Fuhlsbuttel.*   Above *'Fox-Fox' ready to roll.*
Opposite below *Briefing in the Company's Control Room.*

altercations. Matters finally came to a head when the RAF introduced an aircrew duty cycle which required less effort than that demanded by the Company, and this resulted in an initial refusal to fly at night by FRL's crews developing into a total strike.

Obviously it was now time for a strong personality to take charge and repair the Company's image – and in the end it fell to Johnson to do the job himself. He arrived at Wunstorf in February, and Whitfield commented later that a great improvement on the civil side was undoubtedly due to Johnson who re-vitalized FRL's effort. Johnson's problems were shared to some extent with the other charter companies and largely brought about by having to take on a number of ex-RAF aircrew who, probably disenchanted with menial civilian employment, suddenly found themselves back in a well paid flying environment. Knowing that it wouldn't last for ever, a hard core of recruits was determined to enjoy it to the full with little or no regard for the cost to the Company – and no concern as to how their brazen attitudes to authority would, in official eyes, dilute the efforts of the more responsible crews.

Whitfield even made adverse comment on the performance of Airflight, Don Bennett's organisation, which also suffered from a shortage of trained personnel. The company had lost its Chief Pilot, Captain Utting, in a bizarre accident in which he was killed by a refuelling truck on Gatow airfield. This had led to Bennett, the only other pilot qualified to fly Tudors at night, flying three sorties a night without a break for two months – another Herculean effort so typical of Bennett when an objective had to be achieved, but it was more than even he could do to meet the agreed flying quotas single handed.

Inevitably, fact and fiction have become entwined over the years and many stories, no doubt suitably embellished, have become part of the Airlift's folklore. It is true however, that one crew, returning to its billet after a night out in Hamburg came across a workmens' hut, and seizing the oxy-acetylene torches welded all the tram points they could find, causing Hamburg's trams to end up in a section of the city from which they couldn't get back!

Equally true, are events which involved the irrepressible David Prowse, whose off-duty behaviour was totally unpredictable! On one occasion, Hugh Johnson's deputy, Major Burton Gyles, having called for the bar to be closed – no doubt for good reason – suddenly found himself challenged by a very irate Prowse, who then nearly choked the life out of him by hanging him out of the window. But his wild

101

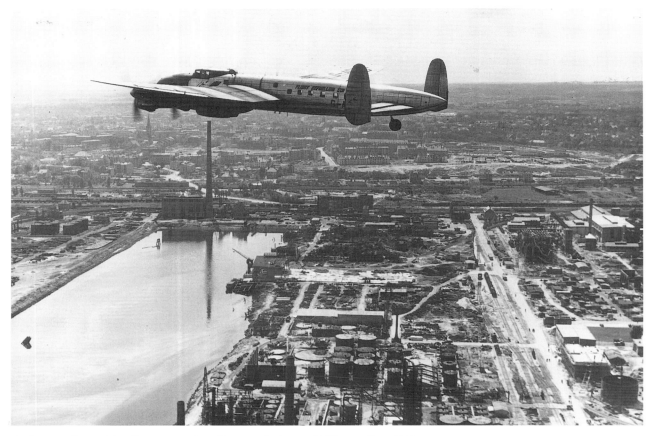

A Company Lancastrian flies over war-torn Germany during an Airlift operation, 1948.

escapades inevitably caught up with him following his decision to commandeer a German steam locomotive and take it as far as his limited engine driving experience would allow. This proved too much for the Group Captain in charge of RAF Wunstorf, and he ordered Hugh Johnson to remove him from the Airlift. Johnson wrote out his termination notice, and handed it to Prowse after he had piloted him back to England that same evening. Johnson later told of the appalling weather encountered on the flight and what a strange irony it proved that, having relied on Prowse's skill in getting the aircraft down safely at fog-bound Hurn Airport, he had to dismiss him! So ended a colourful career with the Company, but not, it seems, in other areas, for it was alleged that, prior to his death, Prowse continued his search for adventure in illicit gun running to the Middle East.

Perhaps the story most associated with FRL's personnel concerns the time their hotel caught fire. It was customary to house FRL's main contingent in the T-Force hotel at Bad Nenndorf, an establishment which contained two bars run by a former German Merchant Navy skipper and an ex-Wehrmacht captain, and, with very little else to do in off duty hours except drink, some excitement was provided when flames and smoke caused a sudden evacuation. Having bundled their gear outside, the British then assisted in trying to save the furniture, but as fast as they piled it on the pavement – other German civilians stole it! A further comic touch was added when a bus, with an FRL member standing on top training a hose on the flames, slowly moved off, causing him to move along the roof until his well-meaning effort terminated in an undignified contact with the ground. 'Uppy' Upward, clerical assistant to FRL's resident Chief Engineer, Frank Brobyn, also nearly came to grief when, running into the hotel with a bucket of water, he stood in a puddle that concealed a live cable – but somehow lived to tell the tale.

Although on occasions personnel 'hitch-hiked' home for leave in the Lancasters or Lancastrians

returning to Tarrant Rushton for servicing, it was the usual practice to fly in the Dakota chartered for this purpose from the Kearsley Charter company. Upward had an unusual experience on such a trip, when the pilot descended through cloud to find himself, as expected, over land. Some confusion resulted however, when it was noticed that the traffic below was proceeding on the right hand side of the road. Eventually, finding an airfield, the pilot landed and duly produced the journey log book to a policeman who had cycled over. Not wishing to indicate how totally lost they were, the pilot waited until the official stamp had been made in the log, and thus discovered he was in Belgium! With blame squarely placed on a faulty compass, and professional pride restored, everyone retired to the Belgian Air Force mess and drank beer with the fighter pilots until it was repaired. They were considerably overdue in reaching Tarrant Rushton!

The deliverance of the city was not achieved without significant sacrifice, and over the fourteen months of intensive flying, seventy eight American, British — and German — lives were lost, as well as several aircraft, including two belonging to the Company.

The first of those losses was later described as follows in the FRL Staff Magazine (Summer 1964):

'On the afternoon of November 22, 1948, Lancaster tanker G-AHJW "Jig Willie" took off from Wunstorf, in the British zone of Germany, and headed due west for Tarrant Rushton. Carrying two crews and three captains of FR's Berlin Airlift staff, the aircraft was returning to England for overhaul, and the crews were looking forward to a welcome spell of leave. It was dusk as "Jig Willie" flew across southern England: visibility was clear below 5,000 feet, but for patches of haze. Somewhere over Hampshire,

Above left   *The Ill-fated Lancaster G-AHJW which came down in Conholt Park, Andover, whilst returning to Tarrant Rushton.*

Above   *Captain 'Pop' Taylor who, along with six others, lost his life when Lancaster G-AHJW crashed in fog, 22nd November 1948.*

the aircraft went off course. Some believe that the pilot may have been homing on the beacon at Netheravon, instead of Tarrant Rushton, both beacons having similar codes. Near Andover, "Jig Willie" flew into a patch of haze and hit a hilltop. All but one member of the crew were killed. Had the aircraft been a few feet higher, it would have cleared the hill. The seven men who died that evening were among the seventy-eight who were killed during Airlift operations. Last month, on the fifteenth anniversary of the end of the Airlift, a remembrance ceremony was held at the memorial at Tempelhof Airport, Berlin, in honour of those who gave their lives for freedom of the city. In the crash at Andover — the only fatal accident in the company's history — the following aircrew were killed, and their names are amongst those inscribed on the memorial at Tempelhof:

Navigational Officer — A. J. Burton, Navigational Officer — M. E. Casey, Captain — W. Cusack, Captain — R. M. W. Heath, DFC, Radio Officer — D. W. Robertson, Flight Engineer — K. A. Seaborn, DFM, Captain — C. Taylor, DFC, AFM'.

Senior Captain Cyril Taylor (who was not flying the aircraft) had served in the RAF throughout the war, and was, at 34, ten years older than most of his

Headstone in St Mary's Churchyard, Andover, for the fliers who perished.

flying colleagues, thus earning himself the familiar appendage of 'Pop'. Prior to this he had been known within the Service as 'Tak' on account of his having flown on the Takoradi Trail, the hazardous 3,600 mile wartime supply route for allied aircraft which led down the length of Africa, through the Sudan and into Egypt. He now rests along with three of the others who perished on that fateful flight, Captain Heath, Radio Officer Robertson and Navigating Officer Burton, beneath a combined gravestone in St. Mary's churchyard at Andover.

The only survivor was Radio Officer Stanley who suffered severe burns and shock. Unfortunately he was unable to throw any light on why the aircraft had ended up some twenty five miles off course.

The other incident which involved the loss of a Company aircraft occurred on 10th May 1949, when Lancastrian, G-AHDP, force landed in the Russian Zone – but this time, fortunately, there were no casualties. The Russians naturally took the opportunity to examine everything in great detail, particularly the radar installation which had proved so invaluable on the earlier flight refuelling trials.

Finally, twenty four hours were allowed to remove the crashed aircraft, which meant that it was merely cut up, transported out, and was, of course, never used again.

In presenting a final impression of the Airlift, it is appropriate to invite the comments of the only person still associated with the Company who experienced conditions at first hand – Michael Cobham. Acting on Sir Alan's suggestion, he temporarily put aside his work assisting Bill Free in the Performance Office and joined Flight Refuelling Operator Bill Woodus, at Gatow in the early summer of 1949. His strongest recollections of the visit are of the strange atmosphere created by the close proximity of the ever vigilant Russian troops, and the combination of coal and flour dust which seemed to permeate

FRL was invited to carry the 100,000th ton of liquid fuel into Gatow. Flight Captain Hanbury with A.O.C.in C. British Air Force of Occupation and the Deputy Mayor of Berlin, 31st May 1949.

every nook and cranny on the aircraft, crews and ground handlers. FRL's personnel duly considered themselves relatively fortunate that they were only required to load and transport liquid cargo! In underlining the comments made by others that copious amounts of cheap alcohol certainly oiled the wheels of the labour force, Cobham added that it probably helped to make more palatable the fact that every meal prepared at Gatow was exactly the same! After some forty-five years, Michael Cobham still remembers the unremitting noise created by the many aircraft and trucks. Only at four o'clock each morning did a strange silence descend all too briefly on the airport, before the roar of engines bursting into life signalled again the start of another day's push to sustain the city's tenuous freedom.

After more than a year's miraculous effort by the Western allies, the Russians conceded a propaganda defeat and re-opened the normal routes into the city. This resulted in the civil airlift formally closing down on 16th August 1949, and FRL, the first in, and amongst the last six operators to withdraw, able to reflect proudly on its contribution and unsurpassed achievements.

SEVEN

New Horizons

In early 1949, the USAF was embroiled with the US Navy on problems of range and the future role of the large aircraft carrier. These discussions eventually led to a demonstration in which a Boeing B-50A – 'Lucky Lady II' – of the 43rd Air Refuelling Squadron, undertook a non-stop round-the-world flight. Taking off from Carswell Air Force Base, Texas, on 26th February 1949, the aircraft returned on 2nd March after having flown a distance of 23,108 miles in 94 hrs. and 1 min. Using the looped hose system, fuel was received from two tankers at each of four refuelling areas over the Azores, Dhahran, the Philippines and Hawaii. Percy Allison, by now FRL's Technical Service Manager, was specially commended for the invaluable assistance he provided for this top priority project. It was in the late Forties that the Boeing Airplane Co. which had installed FRL's equipment in the record-breaking

aircraft, was also called upon by the USAF to investigate other methods of transferring fuel in flight.

Boeing adopted a totally different design approach, and produced the 'Flying Boom' system, which essentially consists of a long telescopic tube which pivots on an attachment point under the tail of the tanker. An operator (invariably called 'Clancy') steers the tube and nozzle into a reception coupling located in a convergent channel on top of the receiver's fuselage. Sideways or vertical movement of the tube is achieved by the differential or collective deflection of a pair of aerofoils fixed to the tube. Many arguments have ensued over the years concerning the relative merits of different refuelling systems, but forty-five years after their entry into service, both the flexible hose and rigid boom methods are still employed today by the US armed services,

Boeing B-50A 'Lucky Lady II' is refuelled from a KB-29M using the 'looped hose' system. This was a training mission for the record round-the-world non-stop flight in March 1949.

Aerial refuelling – Boeing style! A boom-mounted nozzle is steered into a B-47 receiver's receptacle.

each vigorously defended by their respective practitioners! But with the record breaking flight again underlining the military benefits of refuelling in flight, Sir Alan's main concern, as the weeks ticked by, was the looming threat of General Carroll's visit, scheduled for late April.

Following Sir Alan's return from Dayton, many schemes had been investigated, including a Meteor equipped as a looped hose receiver, before design attention gradually centred on a method which involved a probe mounted nozzle on the receiver entering a coupling contained in a tapered funnel fixed to the end of the tanker's supply hose. The first attempts to define a suitable size and shape for the funnel involved towing a triangular fabric 'kite' at 'high speed' down the runway behind designer Peter Macgregor's car, but eventually the first airborne test took place with Lancaster G.33.1 streaming a cone-shaped 'drogue' at the end of a wire-reinforced canvas hose. The convergent entry provided by the drogue was found to be necessary, not only to guide the probe into proper alignment during the final stages of contact, but also to stabilize the hose when fully trailed, and only after a variety of cones had been deployed behind the Lancasters (including one aircraft actually engaged on the Airlift) did an acceptable shape emerge, the others having shown a propensity for performing alarming gyrations before having to be jettisoned into the sea!

Although the new principle appeared promising, one major difficulty remained, and that was how to prevent the hose from looping and whipping when the receiver pushed against the funnel. It appeared to

Goodliffe's team that the problem of taking up the slack in the hose was just too difficult to overcome, and despite having come so close to producing a viable system, another totally different approach would have to be made. This however, was easier said than done, for it seemed at this late stage that all the other possible options had been exhausted – nevertheless, a way forward had to be found! The answer came when Macgregor, reputedly lying in bed one Sunday morning, considered the principle of retraction used in spring blinds and measuring tapes.

Early calculations soon revealed that the installation of any kind of mechanical spring balance device would be far too heavy. Fortunately, further design work showed that a hydraulic solution was possible, and a Lancaster tanker was quickly modified to accept a suitable motor attached to the hose drum unit. This provided a continuous tendency for the extended hose to wind in against the drag load, thus allowing it to remain in a straight line when the receiver closed in from behind. The term 'probe and drogue' was a simple descriptive term that gained immediate acceptance, and one which has, over the years, become every bit as familiar as its American rival, the 'Flying Boom'.

When, at their first meeting, General Crawford had mentioned to Sir Alan the need to refuel fighters, clearly he had meant jet fighters, and Cobham now had to tread the familiar corridors at the Air Ministry in search of a suitable aircraft to serve as a receiver. However, his pleas that the use of a jet fighter would be of direct benefit to the RAF fell on deaf ears, for there was no official requirement to be met! Long since accustomed to meeting walls of resistance, Sir Alan persevered, and was eventually rewarded with the loan of a Gloster Meteor Mk.3, EE 397. Although not the latest variant, its arrival at Tarrant Rushton was greeted with great enthusiasm and allowed the Company to claim that it was matching the pace of jet airframe and engine development. But, with the ground and flight tests still to be carried out as March approached, it was going to be a race against time to have the new system developed in time for General Carroll's arrival. Mike Goodliffe well remembers how every spare moment was taken up with solving design problems, and recounts how he and Macgregor figured out the probe and drogue toggle locking system by 'doodling' in beer in the Littlehampton Labour Club!

Cobham was understandably alarmed therefore to be notified that the General, keener than ever to

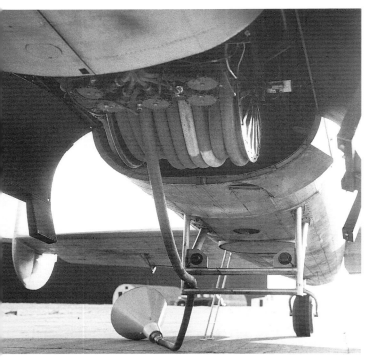

Mk.7 Hose Drum Unit and 'solid' drogue installed in Lancaster tanker G-33-2.

The business connection. Probe installation on Gloster Meteor Mk.3, EE 397.

Trusty team! (left to right) FRL's Bill Ashall, Tom Marks, Brian Cape, Peter Macgregor and Maurice Jenkins.

witness the demonstration, had brought forward the date of his visit to 6th April. It was only following a tremendous effort by all concerned that on Saturday, 4th April, with only two days to spare, Tom Marks piloting the Lancaster, and Pat Hornidge the Meteor, took off and conducted for the first time a series of dry contacts using the revolutionary 'probe and drogue' method. To everyone's relief, all went surprisingly well, although system refinements and adjustments required further flying throughout the weekend. When Monday dawned fine and clear, both tanker and receiver were polished and lined up on the hardstanding along with a Lancastrian that was to take the viewing party aloft. At precisely 10.00 a.m., General Carroll and his entourage of fifteen USAF Officers and one RAF Wing Commander arrived in a large bus, and the demonstration got underway. Cobham later recalled that although the system performed very well on the day, and impressed the American delegation, snags appeared immediately afterwards which rendered it impossible to repeat the success until over a month later. Notwithstanding this, a series of seven demonstrations was immediately put in hand with invitations extended to leading representatives of the RAF, the airlines, the major aircraft constructors, and many foreign officials.

The first of these special flights alongside which the VIPs were flown in a Viking aircraft chartered

Peter Procter demonstrates the probe and drogue principle to the USAF delegation at Tarrant Rushton, 1949.

from Airwork Ltd., was carried out before the system had been restored to full working condition, but Sir Alan, always keen to impress, had laid claim to the fact that it was perfectly capable of transferring fuel at 600 gallons per minute whilst flying at 400 knots and 35,000 ft. After landing, one officer pointed out that following contacts at only 130 knots and 2,000 ft., he couldn't understand why it was necessary to refuel the Meteor immediately it got back on the ground. Sir Alan, a veteran of many conversational tight corners, managed to convince the sceptic that a small and temporary snag had unfortunately curtailed that particular demonstration!

It was clear nevertheless, that demonstrations at high altitude were going to be restricted by the Lancaster's inability to operate much beyond 20,000 ft. This limitation was overcome, however, when Air Marshal Sir Alec Coryton, one of the VIP's intrigued by the possiblities offered by the new method, undertook to provide an Avro Lincoln, RA 657 and a Meteor Mk.4, VZ 389 for more advanced trials work. By this time, almost a year had passed since Sir Alan's initial visit to Dayton in connection with the looped hose system. On that occasion, and in conjunction with George Woods Humphrey, he launched a new offshoot company, Flight Refueling

Incorporated (FR Inc.), with offices and a workshop located at Danbury, Connecticut. It was here that spares would be produced to support the looped hose equipment operated by the USAF. Following a visit from the US Navy however, the fledgling company soon found itself busy also providing winch and coupling equipment for installation in dirigibles which allowed the transfer of fuel from the decks of ships.

As it had been with FRL before it, so the creation of FR Inc. in 1948 was based on the assumption that work carried out would revolve around the production of equipment specifically intended for refuelling aircraft in flight. In 1948 however, a new agreement was signed by the American, British and Canadian authorities, which affected the outputs of both FR Ltd. and FR Inc. Termed the 'ABC Agreement' it defined standards for the equipment and methods used for passing fuel into aircraft on the ground, and specified that the fuel pressure at the fuel hose-aircraft interface should not exceed 50 psi. No longer was it acceptable to rely solely on the traditional but hazardous and inefficient over-wing gravity filling of an aircraft's tanks through individual filler caps. All new designs, except very light models and trainers, now had to embody a single-point pressure refuelling system which incorporated proportional distribution and means for automatically shutting off the supply when the tanks became full.

The total effect this ruling would have on the fortunes and structure of the Company was not foreseeable at this stage, but the design and production of 'ancillary equipment' was now about to assume an importance which would provide a vital source of income over the years to come. Peter Procter recalled how, faced with this wonderful breakthrough, the attentions of all the leading British aircraft design teams soon focused on the expertise already existing within the Company, which having the additional advantage of possessing a range of equipment already developed for in-flight refuelling, was now acknowledged to be the leader in the field. Although flying boats had previously employed combined single-point and overwing-filling methods, the first British aircraft capable of being refuelled solely by the new 'closed gallery' system was the Armstrong Whitworth AW.52 Flying Wing which, with a wing surface entirely devoid of filler caps, pointed the way forward for contemporary designs. At first, aircraft such as the Apollo, Tudor and Hastings were fitted with refuelling control valves operated by mechanical float devices, but development work soon led to their replacement by

Ground refuelling the hard way. Overwing filling was slow and potentially hazardous. (DC-4 at Dallas).

An unusual aircraft, the Armstrong Whitworth AW.52 'Flying Wing', had no filler caps fitted for individual tanks, and was the first aircraft to be refuelled by a single point closed circuit system.

The Armstrong Whitworth AW.55 Apollo feeder liner was also one of the first aircraft to be pressure refuelled.

electrical solenoid-operated valves, and the Comet was the first aircraft to be so equipped.

The Vickers Viscount however, was the aircraft which gave a much needed initial boost to the Company's component production — a measure of which can be deduced from the number of rubber-sleeved pipe connectors able to withstand fuel pressure that were required, some two million eventually being produced! From this time onwards the Company relied heavily on the cash generated from component manufacture to underpin other activities, and every aircraft of significance that rolled out of the British factories carried FRL's system equipment. Inroads were also made into the European market, and components for aircraft such as the Caravelle, Vautour, Transall and Etendard were eventually made in France under a licence agreement reached with Carburateur Zenith in 1954.

Graham Marriette started work as a junior draughtsman at Tarrant Rushton in August 1949,

Above *The Drawing Office at Tarrant Rushton.*

Left *Graham and Mary Marriette – proud tenants of 42 Rushton Heights, Tarrant Rushton.*

Below *Internal 'General Arrangement' drawing of 42 Rushton Heights.*

and retired as Director and General Manager of the Aerospace Components Division in 1988. In recounting the working atmosphere during his early years, he keenly remembers the enormous team spirit and enthusiasm that pervaded all parts of the Company. He points out that this was due, in large measure, to the close-knit living arrangements provided on the airfield for employees' families. In addition to the 'communal' and caravan sites, there were two main housing areas, generally referred to as 'Rushton Heights' and the 'ex-WAAF site', and each consisted of a large number of wartime Nissen Huts converted into 'cottages', each having two bedrooms, a bathroom, toilet and kitchen, and a living room with a brick built fireplace.

The conversion of some ninety huts took place as a short-term measure, with the local authorities sharing the cost, until, over a five year period, sufficient new housing could be provided in the Blandford district. With Sir Alan sparing no effort to establish social and shopping facilities on site, and providing also a free daily bus service to Blandford, the area soon took on the character of a village in its own right, with a prize even being awarded for the best kept garden. With local accommodation in such short supply, 'Jimmy' Rawnsley and his wife, Micki, lived for several years in Tarrant Rushton's Control Tower!

The work force thus counted itself generally well cared for, but all was not well on every front, and sadly, events were clouded by a contractual misjudgement associated with the Berlin Airlift. In carrying out its flying duties, the Company had undoubtedly acquitted itself well and the impression had been given that its services would be required beyond the formal closedown in August, and, most probably until Christmas. On this assumption, extended contracts were given to the majority of the pilots, which resulted in a major financial problem for the Company when the Foreign Office announced that operations were to cease after only one week into the anticipated three month period. There was no way in which the team of pilots, radio and radar technicians in Germany, as well as the maintenance operation at Tarrant Rushton, involving some 900 men in all, could be wound down so quickly, and with the organisation costing over £25,000 per week to run, the monetary blow to the Company was a heavy one. After having so carefully built up the levels of technical expertise required, it was with deep regret that Sir Alan issued the following notice:

FLIGHT REFUELLING LTD
BERLIN AIRLIFT

The management regret to announce that we have received notice from the Foreign Office to reduce our efforts on the Berlin Airlift much sooner than anticipated. Contrary to all our estimates from available information the cessation of the major part of the Berlin Airlift has been a sudden surprise to the Management.

The majority of the civil Charter Companies will cease to operate after next week but Flight Refuelling Ltd. will continue on the Berlin Airlift. Unfortunately, we shall be operating on a much reduced tonnage that will not necessitate or employ our full fleet of aircraft.

We had always hoped that the Berlin Airlift would bridge the gap until we were able to start the organisation for our permanent tanker stations but unfortunately despite the strenuous efforts on the part of the Management to induce the Corporations and Ministry of Civil Aviation to go ahead in the immediate future with the operation of Flight Refuelling services on the Atlantic and other parts of the world, it has not been possible to get this scheme in operation quickly enough to act as an immediate follow on to the Berlin Airlift.

No one regrets this more than the Management because although this tanker service will start eventually, the gap between the cessation of the Berlin Airlift and the start of the tanker services is going to be so great that it will be impossible for us to bridge it with supplementary work. If we could have got some odd contracts or any indication of when our tankers might be required, the Management would have speculated to the extent of preparing the aircraft in advance, in any endeavour to keep their valuable team of crews and engineers together.

It is going to be a very difficult task for us to differentiate between those who we are going to ask to stay with us and those whom we are going to reluctantly inform that their services cannot any more be employed, but we shall endeavour to do it with as much fairness as possible, taking all circumstances into account. However, the Management realise the predicament that individuals might find themselves in, and instead of giving the customary one week's notice we are going to give two week's pay in lieu of notice. Thus, with the past week's pay and the holiday pay due and the fact that this pay will be free of income tax, in many cases it will mean that the individual worker on leaving this organisation will find himself with over a month's pay in his pocket, which we trust will help to reinstate him without undue hardship. We want to assure everybody that the Management deeply regret this unavoidable reduction in the establishment and they have been doing everything possible to avoid having to take such action, but it is the only course open. To those that are leaving us we extend a very sincere thanks for their loyalty, co-operation and good workmanship. We wish you all good fortune and success in the future.

Signed: Alan J. Cobham.

Following its involvement in the Airlift, it seemed a natural progression to move into the growing air charter business, and the Company purchased cheaply two Mosquito aircraft, G-ALGU and G-ALGV, for this purpose, which were flown primarily by Roy Elliott and Roly Beaumont. Sir Alan also acquired a couple of Tudor aircraft with a view to operating freight services to South Africa and Singapore. This scheme was not pursued however, as A.V.Roe would not approve FRL's proposal to cut the fuselage for the fitment of larger cargo

doors. Michael Cobham offers the view that simply possessing the crews and a maintenance base would never have guaranteed success in the charter field. He adds that the Company did not possess the right mix of aircraft, but more importantly it lacked the commercial skills needed to bring in the business.

1949 proved to be a year of fluctuating fortunes, but one very notable event was the establishment of an endurance record for jet aircraft on 7th August. This stemmed from a casual discussion between Marks and Hornidge, when, in considering how the probe and drogue system could be dramatically exploited, they decided to establish a world's 'first'. It was arranged that the flight would

Tom Marks refuels Pat Hornidge's Meteor over Poole, Dorset, during a 12 hour endurance record flight, 7th August 1949.

Pat Hornidge takes on fuel over Christchurch during his endurance flight. The Isle of Wight can be seen in the top left corner.

take place within easy range of Tarrant Rushton, and, in the event, Hornidge flew a continual orbit in the Meteor Mk.3 over Bristol, Devon and Dungeness in order to meet Marks's Lancaster, G-33-2, which continued to fly around the Isle of Wight. This routine resulted in ten refuellings taking place before a stiff pilot got out of the Meteor after 12 hrs. and 3 mins. in the air. Radio contact was maintained throughout the flight, and Rebecca/Eureka was used for the final link-up only after a rapid deterioration in the weather. Halfway through the day, Marks flew back to Tarrant Rushton and topped up his tanks before re-appearing over The Needles in time for Hornidge's next arrival. Pat Hornidge, being of large build, found the Meteor's cockpit most restricting and with little room to stretch cramped legs – but his discomfort was compounded when the locally added 'pee tube' was found to be vented to an area of positive

pressure – causing him to 'get his own back' in no uncertain manner all over the 'office' floor! Apart from getting his feet wet, and having run very low on engine oil, Hornidge reported that the aircraft had behaved well and that the normal oxygen supply had just been sufficient.

The flight took place whilst Sir Alan was back in America, discussing with General Putt how to implement a probe and drogue conversion programme on USAF aircraft at Tarrant Rushton. The first thing Cobham knew about the new record was when the General handed him a newspaper and expressed surprise that he had kept the intended flight such a secret. It was impossible to convince the assembled officers at Dayton that he had known nothing about it! Pat Hornidge received many telegrams and cables of congratulation from test pilots all over the world, and wondered how the Post Office accepted some of the sentiments they contained. Perhaps one that indicates the general theme — 'WELL DONE — WHAT A MAN — TEN CONNECTIONS IN TWELVE HOURS!!!' said it all.

It must be remembered that in parallel with all the excitement generated by the success of the new system, deliveries of looped hose equipment were still progressing smoothly from Site A, back at Ford, and by the middle of 1949, the USAF was regularly carrying out air refuelling exercises with B-29 tankers of the 43rd Air Refuelling Squadron operating with B-50s based at Marham, Sculcoates and Lakenheath in East Anglia. The Americans however did not use a gun to fire a grapnel across the receiver hauling line, preferring to use the 'cross over' method used by the Company in the middle 1930s. Poor results were being achieved and, with confidence in the equipment at a low ebb, the Company was requested to send a team of its experts to discuss and assess the problems. Tom Marks, accompanied by Messrs. Woodus, Rawnsley and Jeffery, after seeing the operations at first hand, soon pinpointed the reasons for the failures. The Americans' equivalent of FRL's Rebecca/Eureka interception radar was shown to be hopelessly inadequate, and led to crews relying on visual sightings – referred to as the 'See You over Cromer' approach, and with no manuals, or special tools, lack of proper maintenance had led to frequent malfunctions. The situation was seriously at odds with normal USAF practice and called for formal, if belated, training of all concerned. Accordingly, a familiarisation programme was set up at Tarrant Rushton which led to greatly improved performance by the Squadrons, and a glowing commendation for the Company's assistance from the Commanding General of the 3rd Air Division. Fortunately the profits generated from the sale of looped-hose equipment helped to counterbalance a corresponding loss from the Berlin Airlift — but it became evident that steps would have to be taken to avoid incurring a massive tax bill. At the end of 1949 Cobham achieved this by selling a majority holding in the Company to merchant bankers Robert Benson, Lonsdale and Co., who, whilst retaining his services as Managing Director, proceeded to carry out a dividend-stripping operation!

Also at this time, and as a result of Sir Alan's discussions with General Putt, four B-29 Super-fortress bombers and two F-84 Thunderjets were sent over to Tarrant Rushton for a probe and drogue conversion programme initially codenamed

With a world endurance record 'in the bag', Tom Marks and Pat Hornidge pose for posterity, 7th August 1949.

'Operation Layette', but later changed to 'Operation Outing'. The first B-29 to arrive had a Mk.8 Hose Drum Unit (HDU) installed in the rear fuselage, enabling it to become a 'single point tanker', and to be re-designated as a KB-29T. Two of the innovative features included in the conversion work were FRL's first electrical float switch, and an electrically-operated pump specifically designed for the fuel transfer system. Two of the B-29s were equipped as receivers by having probes fitted which extended forward through the upper cockpit glazing panels above the co-pilot's head. The original intention was to fit the newly designed 'ejector probe' which, upon pilot selection, allowed three pneumatically-operated rams to shoot out and engage the drogue unit. Although limited testing was carried out on a Lancaster, it was considered to be an unnecessary complication and the project was scrapped. The most ambitious work programme was that carried out on the second B-29, including the installation of an electrically-driven Mk.11 HDU at each wingtip in addition to the unit mounted in the fuselage. Now transformed into the sole YKB-29T, this aircraft thus gained the distinction of becoming the first 'three point' tanker to enter service. Following the fitment of a probe to the wing leading edge, both F-84s appeared more impressively in the USAF inventory as EF-84Es.

The conversion work proved to be far more difficult and protracted than originally foreseen, and problems for the design team began the moment service panels were removed and the bomb doors opened to reveal just how complex the aircraft

The sole YKB-29T, 'three-point' tanker, at Tarrant Rushton.

were. One designer, faced with installing a pipe run from the fighter's wing-mounted probe, commented that it would require a mouse with a string tied to its tail to find a way around the existing densely-packed equipment! FRL finally met its commitment, but at a cost far beyond that submitted in the fixed-price bid, and Sir Alan freely admitted later that it had been a mistake to estimate the work based on familiar but less sophisticated British aircraft, and that personnel should have gone to the US in order to carry out a first-hand survey. Now, faced with another heavy loss following hard on the heels of that incurred by the Berlin Airlift contract, Cobham saw financial question marks in every direction, and the Company was only just saved from liquidation by eventually selling the rights to manufacture the probe and drogue system in the US for approximately the amount of money which had been overspent on the contract. With fortune's pendulum swinging first one way, then the other, Cobham had to rely heavily on his inherent optimism – and famous luck – as the Company entered the new decade!

On the lighter side, the arrival of the American contingent certainly had an impact on both the Company, and the local neighbourhood. Enterprising coach companies ran tours to Tarrant Rushton in order that people could see the novel B-29s parked in front of the hangars. Officialdom soon prevailed over commercialism however, and large canvas screens were erected to thwart the enthusiasts. Many ex-employees remember the occasion when the local hunt galloped across the airfield. The Americans simply could not believe it, and with Senator McCarthy's Communist witchhunts then in full flow, the sight of the offenders dressed in red, threw real doubt on Britain's commitment to security!

The early stages of the conversion work on the USAF aircraft were confined mainly to the design office, and it became desperately difficult to keep the men remaining in the maintenance hangars usefully employed, until one day, a Coastal Command Lancaster, experiencing difficulties, landed at Tarrant Rushton. Willing hands soon had the aircraft in the hangar, where following inspection, more problems were discovered. Arthur Watts discussed the situation with the crew's Commanding Officer, who cheerily gave the go-ahead to put things right. The aircraft was then given a thorough going-over, including a respray and polish, and looked brand new when the time came for delivery. The Squadron's CO was delighted with FRL's effort, but the problem now was that it made all the other Squadron aircraft look shabby. Someone then hit on the idea of sending each in turn for similar treatment. All went well until Cobham, on one of his visits to the Air Ministry, was approached by an official who informed him that an arrangement already existed for the overhaul of Service aircraft by the parent design firms. This clearly presented a serious threat to the continuation of the refurbishment work, and Sir Alan immediately telephoned 'Tiny' Thomas, then the Aircraft Engineering Superintendent at Tarrant Rushton, who informed him that three Lancasters, as yet untouched, were in the hangar. Rather than run the risk of aircrews arriving to remove them without warning, it was decided to dismantle them immediately, and to inform Coastal Command that the only sensible action would be to complete the remedial work. Cobham readily admitted to having 'pulled a fast one', but claimed that it was a measure of his desperation in trying to secure every ounce of work he could during a troubled period!

EIGHT

Tales from Tarrant Rushton

As the Company completed its move from Littlehampton to Tarrant Rushton towards the end of 1949, Cobham was fortunate to engage the services of Tom Jones who, as the original aerodrome superintendent, was totally familiar with all its general services. His knowledge was invaluable in converting the wartime airfield into one which combined the activities of a peace time factory with civil flying operations. The old plotting room became a Materials Testing Centre, and other areas were adapted to provide a Drawing Office, along with Machine, Fitting and Instrument work shops. Because the airfield's facilities were so widespread it was not possible to congregate all the various activities under one roof, and virtually every section of the factory ended up having its own building. Although this arrangement had its disadvantages, Sir Alan always maintained that these were offset by the pride and friendly rivalry which developed among the various factions.

One of the new faces that appeared as the Fifties got underway was that of Arthur Hagg, recruited by Sir Alan as a Consultant Technical Director. Hagg was a designer of considerable experience, having been responsible for such beautiful aircraft as the de Havilland Albatross and the Airspeed Ambassador, and his arrival certainly added weight to that of Smith, Macgregor and Goodliffe but his appointment was not received well by Latimer-Needham, then Chief Engineer, who eventually decided (and was actually encouraged) not to take up a regular post at Tarrant Rushton. Hagg was soon called upon to get involved in discussions with de Havillands regarding the new Comet airliner. Great hopes rested on the success of this aircraft, regarded as the flagship which would ensure Britain's lead in commercial jet transport design and operation, and thereby counterbalance the growing dominance of American civil types. Its range, however, would not permit it to cross the Atlantic without refuelling and so Cobham, mindful of earlier unproductive dealings with BOAC, focused his energies on getting de

Havillands to use their influence in calling for the aircraft to be equipped as a receiver. Many meetings took place with de Havilland's chief designer, R.E.Bishop, and chief test pilot, John Cunningham, and test flights eventually took place in late 1950 and early 1951 involving the second Comet prototype, G-ALVG, and FRL's newly-arrived Lincoln tanker RA 657.

The early Comets displayed poor longitudinal control at lower speeds and Cunningham was understandably concerned about the handling difficulties likely to ensue during a refuelling contact. To overcome this, a reverse refuelling scheme was proposed that involved the Comet trailing a hose and drogue and flying on a steady course ahead of the tanker. It was intended that the tanker would carry out all the contact maneouvering and, with the probe engaged, pump fuel forwards. Limited flight tests were then carried out using a Tudor Mk.1, G-AGRI, loaded with four tons of concrete ballast in lieu of fuel, to determine its suitability for the role of tanker. However, the basic idea was discontinued when it became clear that heavy equipment required to be carried in the Comet's tail section would have exacerbated the existing control problem.

Arthur Hagg who joined FRL as Consultant Technical Director.

118

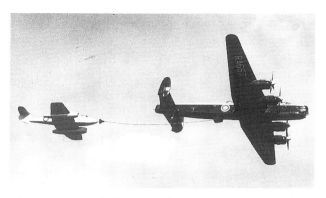

Above *Tom Marks flying Lincoln RA 657, and Pat Hornidge in the Meteor Mk.4, VZ 389, carried out the first public demonstration of probe and drogue refuelling at the SBAC Flying Display, 1950.*

Right *USAF Colonels Ritchie and Schilling flank FRL's Bill Woodus prior to the first non-stop jet crossing of the Atlantic in 1950.*

Pat Hornidge flew with Cunningham in the Comet and although entirely unfamiliar with the aircraft managed to achieve several consecutive successful dry contacts. Cunningham however, chasing a lively drogue attached to a very small diameter hose in turbulent conditions failed to make consistent engagements, and BOAC observers on board duly reported that passenger reactions to such an oscillating experience were hardly likely to be favourable. The trials were abandoned at this point, and with airliners becoming progressively larger and possessing greater performance, this proved to be the last attempt to introduce flight refuelling into civil operations.

The Lincoln gradually took over the tanker duties from the Lancasters, and it was this aircraft, along with the Meteor Mk.4, that, provided the first public demonstration of the probe and drogue system at the 1950 SBAC Display at Farnborough.

As a novel experiment the pilots' R/T dialogue was relayed over the public address system, a good idea only thrown into doubt when, upon separation of the aircraft, a wave of fuel washed over the Meteor's windscreen and Hornidge's forceful expletive came over the air loud and clear!

Immediately after the Farnborough demonstration, two USAF Colonels, Dave Schilling and Bill Ritchie, undertook the first in-flight refuelling crossing of the Atlantic by jet aircraft. This took place following the attendance of Schilling, a much decorated wartime Mustang pilot, at one of the many demonstrations at

Tarrant Rushton. Impressed by what he had seen and aware of the two F-84s undergoing conversion to receivers, he applied at once for permission from higher authority in the US to attempt the record flight. His arrival back in this country, accompanied now by Ritchie, led to an early meeting with Sir Alan who, equally enthusiastic, promised all his support for the venture. The plan was for Schilling and Ritchie to fly from the American base at Manston in Kent to Mitchell Field on Long Island, New York, refuelling en route over Prestwick, Keflavik in Iceland and Goose Bay, Labrador. Three weather-reporting aircraft, and six rescue aircraft were also to be positioned over the long water stretches to assist, should emergencies arise. The final preparations involved a sizeable working party from FRL, led by Ted Alsop, along with Tom Marks and Lancaster G-33-2 being located at Manston. Last minute snags were inevitable, and Bob Leonard has etched firmly on his memory the long uncomfortable periods spent down the intake of an F-84, after having been pushed in with a broom, in order to adjust highly inaccessible float switches. Electrical specialist Ken Wickenden also recalls the frustration he experienced when, after a total of eighteen hours spent in similarly cramped conditions with flashlight and tools tied to the wrist, it was decided to change an engine which allowed immediate, but belated, access to the offending equipment!

Eventually everything appeared to be ready, and on 19th September 1950, Marks took off and positioned the Lancaster tanker under a low cloud base over the Mull of Galway. The fighters followed, but Schilling, who made the first contact, expressed dissatisfaction with the tanker's equipment and elected to return to Manston. Marks landed at Tarrant Rushton and after the repair of some minor damage, flew again to Manston. During the time the Manston-based aircraft had taken to fly to the first refuelling point, Pat Hornidge had taken off from Keflavik in the Lincoln tanker. However, coincident with raising the undercarriage, a fire warning light illuminated to indicate a problem on the starboard inner engine. Aware of the effect his return to base would have on the mission, Hornidge instructed his crew to observe the engine closely from various vantage points for signs of the fire spreading over external surfaces, but none appeared. Encouraged by this, he elected to continue the flight, but upon being informed of the fighters' return to Manston, he in turn flew back to Keflavik. Examination revealed that an engine exhaust stub had shattered allowing flames to play down the inside of the cowling and causing considerable damage to electrical cabling and over-heating of the engine bearers. A new powerplant had to be flown out from England in a Dakota, and was installed the following day!

Although Schilling was suffering from a very bad cold and even had an inhaler clipped to the control column, the record flight attempt, code named 'Fox Able Four' got off to a better start on the 22nd September, and despite radar problems the first interception with Marks's aircraft took place successfully over Prestwick at the planned height of 18,000 ft. The radar equipment continued to cause difficulties with the second refuelling interception although good VHF radio contact was established, with Schilling at one point enquiring of Hornidge 'Say, we're at 42,000 ft. near a hole in the cloud with water underneath — you anywhere near that boy?' Hornidge and the fighters agreed to home in independently on the 'cone of silence' directly above the Keflavik radio station and, with visual contact made, the aircraft flew westwards in formation until Schilling came in for the first refuelling engagement with the Lincoln. Perhaps as a result of feeling generally unwell, his positioning after each of several contacts was poor, necessitating repeated requests from the tanker's operator for corrections to be made to avoid putting strain on the equipment. Ritchie, on the other hand, maintained a perfectly calm attitude, refusing to be hurried by Schilling's urgency.

It should be explained that following engagement of the probe, the receiver pilot had to select open a hydraulically-operated valve in the probe nozzle, and to close it before separation. On this occasion Ritchie's disengagement occurred before the valve closed, with the result that the valve stem was bent,

Bob Leonard.

Ken Wickenden.

120

allowing a steady stream of fuel to exit from the probe. The fact that strong headwinds were encountered at this stage, making the decision to continue hazardous, caused much critical debate after the flight, but Ritchie who tried, but was unable, to refuel from the third tanker, a B-29, elected to gain as much height as possible, thus allowing him to commence a long shallow glide towards land after his engine finally cut. At 20,000 ft. he found himself in an opaque mist, but he broke through at 12,000 ft. above water and birch-covered hills; whereupon Goose Bay informed him that he was above Melville Lake, 40 miles inland. He restarted his engine, but the last drop of fuel quickly dried up and the turbojet's roar died away when he was 30 miles from Goose Bay. After sending a message to his wife in New York via Schilling, Ritchie jettisoned his canopy and ejected at 3,000 ft., the aircraft falling into Melville Lake. The pilot slid down a tree that had hooked up his parachute, and awaited the rescue helicopter.

Schilling continued his journey and landed at Limestone, Maine, after a flight time of 10 hrs. 8 mins. A strong advocate of flight refuelling and a good friend of the Company, his support was sorely missed when, sadly, he was killed in a road accident within a year of his record flight. Following the loss of Ritchie's aircraft, the Company's designers recognised that the method of engaging the receiver's probe into the drogue coupling and separately selecting the fuel valve open and closed was inadequate. Accordingly a new Mk.6 nozzle was developed which allowed the fuel valve within it to operate automatically, but this was the last variant to be designed as an original component by the Company. Inevitably, international standards were imposed and after the Shultz Coupling appeared in America as the 'definitive design', FRL produced an Anglicized version known as the Mk.8 nozzle, which is still in wide use today on the RAF's receiver aircraft.

Despite the considerable sums spent on the 1945 'Tiger Force' contract and the immediate post-war trials, the British Air Ministry had appeared reluctant to take advantage of the improved method of flight refuelling. Now however, aware of the growing American interest in Cobham's equipment, and also influenced by the recent demonstration at Farnborough, the Ministry decided to enter the fray. Air defence policy at this time required the RAF's fighters to maintain standing patrols off Britain's east coast, but this proved to be thirsty work for the

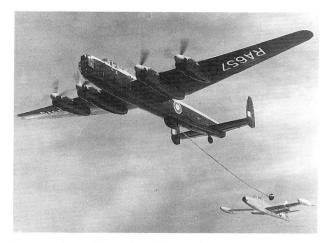

Pat Hornidge in the Lincoln tanker, refuels an F-84 during the transatlantic crossing.

engines of the day, and little time could be spent 'on station' before the aircraft had to return to base to refuel. As a result, the suggestion was made that No. 245 Squadron's sixteen Meteor Mk.8s be equipped with receiver probes, and trials carried out to assess refuelling interception techniques with and without radio contact and GCI assistance, formating sequences and pilot fatigue levels.

The trials, code named 'Pinnacle', officially commenced on 8th May 1951, with Lincoln RA 657 undertaking the tanking duties, and Lancaster G-33-2 covering the periods when the Lincoln was grounded for inspection. A second Lincoln SX 993, became available on loan from the Air Ministry in early October, but a third Lincoln tanker, RE 293, arrived too late to participate. The exercise was completed by the end of October and was regarded as having been very successful. Frank Russell described one incident however, in which the turn-round of the tankers on the ground at Horsham St. Faith had not been properly timed to accommodate the arrival over the airfield of a section of Meteors desperately low on fuel. A sudden call to 'scramble' saw Russell's Lincoln airborne in nine minutes, and the first Meteor in contact as the tanker commenced its climb away from the runway.

The B-29 tanker conversions had by now been completed and flight testing started at Tarrant Rushton, but following the departure of the two F-84s with Schilling and Ritchie, there was a marked shortage of receiver aircraft. It was of course essential that three fighters be made available for demonstrating a simultaneous 'hook up' behind the

The YKB-29T 'three-point' tanker refuels two Meteor F.8s from No.245 Squadron and FRL's Mk.4 (centre).

new 'three point' tanker, and the problem was neatly solved when two Meteor Mk.8s and pilots were temporarily seconded from No. 245 Squadron to join the Company's Meteor Mk.4. Sir Alan was determined to obtain maximum publicity from the flight, and, in addition to the cameras on board the tanker, no less than fourteen were also packed into an accompanying Lancaster. This 'photographic special' flight resulted in an excellent cine film being produced, and a well known Canadian actor, Robert Beatty, was engaged to provide the commentary in tones which would appeal to audiences on both sides of the Atlantic!

It had been Sir Alan's hope that such a large scale evaluation by the RAF under representative operating conditions would demonstrate once and for all the advantages of aerial refuelling. The Air Staff's decision however, largely influenced by Air Marshals Sir Basil Embry and Sir Ralph Cochrane, was against introducing such a facility mainly on economic grounds as the provision of tankers would simply result in fewer fighters. This proved to be a lengthy deferment, for another ten years were to

elapse before Javelins and Lightnings became the first RAF fighters in squadron service to have receiving capability. Although this was a disappointing outcome, Cobham was encouraged when informed by Air Vice Marshal Geoffrey Tuttle that air-to-air refuelling systems were to be incorporated into the new aircraft intended for Britain's bomber force (see Footnote).

And so, by the end of 1951, in addition to collaborating with the airframe designers on the installation of ancillary equipment, other, secret discussions, were taking place regarding the provision of

Footnote: Bill Free, then working in Latimer-Needham's Performance Department, was always convinced that this decision was highly influenced by a report he compiled, which, in addition to showing the extended ranges and bomb loads possible due to refuelling, also depicted the location of Soviet armament factories. The Chief of the Air Staff expressed great alarm that this information was available to a civilian contractor, and immediately restricted the report's circulation, even denying permission for Sir Charles Craven, Chairman of Vickers, one of the key companies involved, to have a copy!

in-flight refuelling systems in the Vickers Type 733, Avro Type 698 and Handley Page HP.80, soon to be better known as the Valiant, Vulcan and Victor. It is perhaps interesting to note that the talks with Vickers led to a price of £85,000 being submitted to cover all the design and manufacture of three complete sets of tanker and receiver equipment!

Until his resignation, Latimer-Needham, greatly assisted by a small team of analysts, which included his daughter, Barbara, provided theoretical cost and performance comparisons for virtually every civil and military aircraft either in, or projected to enter, service. In order to obtain basic data it had of course been necessary for him to liaise with the various company design organisations, whereupon with Bill Free's considerable assistance, brochures and books were circulated which showed the advantages to be gained from flight refuelling. This had generally worked very well, and the torrent of economic and technical information produced was an essential aid in Cobham's never-ceasing sales campaign.

During 1951 however, an incident occurred when Latimer-Needham's meticulous analysis backfired rather badly. Instead of using the official performance data prepared by Avro for the Shackleton maritime reconnaisance aircraft, he relied on pessimistic assumptions provided by the Ministry of Supply, to prepare a report entitled 'The Black Pit' (a reference to the infamous mid-Atlantic area). In the report, unfavourable conclusions were drawn which implied that the aircraft was incapable of performing a useful patrol mission of any kind – unless it could be refuelled in flight! Avro's Chairman, Sir Roy Dobson, responded strongly to the doubt cast on his aeroplane, and in a particularly aggressive letter to Sir Alan, he pointed out that 'as the Prince of Salesmen – you should have had enough sense to get in touch with us first'. Cobham realized that he could not afford to remain at odds with one as influential as Dobson, and made every effort to heal the breach – but although the prototype Shackleton was equipped as a looped hose receiver, and design schemes were later discussed, the production version was never equipped for flight refuelling.

FRL began to move through the Fifties on an increasingly broad front, but patchy periods persisted which required its executives to explore all avenues in the search for subcontract work. Sir Alan's badgering of officials coincided with the Ministry of Aircraft Production belatedly realizing that the introduction into service of the Hawker Hunter

and later variants of the Gloster Meteor was going to be much delayed. Consequently, the RAF, having allowed its existing Meteor overhaul programme to run down on the assumption that they would soon be taking delivery of these new aircraft, now found itself in a predicament, aggravated by the large numbers of aircraft operated at weekends by the reserve Air Force, whose maintenance also had to be taken into account. The result was that Glosters, now committed to producing the Javelin all weather fighter, could not cope with any overhaul work and subcontractors were invited to tender for the job.

It was decided to allocate nine Meteor Mk.3s to each of three companies – Westland, Scottish Aviation and FRL – with the final decision for the complete job resting on their respective performances. Fortunately, there were several employees in 'Tiny' Thomas's maintenance organisation who had worked with various Service Maintenance Units during the war, and they were quickly despatched around the country in a search for Meteor spares. They knew the system better than many of the new storemen, and on one famous occasion, having been told that certain items didn't exist, FRL's progress men walked down the long racks full of parts and immediately located items they had themselves stored away years previously!

Capitalising on this advantage, FRL was able to turn the aircraft round quickly, at a fair price, and it was a happy relief when the Managing Director of Glosters informed Sir Alan that Tarrant Rushton was to become the main subcontractor for Meteor overhaul work. Over a four-year period the Company undertook Category 4 Servicing (rehabilitation) and Category 4 Repair (of crashed and damaged aircraft) of more than four hundred Meteor aircraft, turning out an average of ten per month during the peak years and with a mean turn round time of three months for each airframe.

By its very nature, flight testing can produce some nasty surprises, and Pat Hornidge experienced two instances on which the cockpit canopy of the Meteor he was checking out suddenly disappeared! The first time this happened he was at 37,000 ft. and though it was disconcerting, he had ample time to assess the situation. The second occasion was far more threatening, for it occurred when Hornidge was carrying out a high speed run, low over No. 2 hangar. Following a loud bang, he received a blow on his head which was only protected by a leather helmet, and an egg-sized swelling came up on his temple

Above *A KB-29T tanker equipped with a 'quickie' conversion kit refuels a B-50 off the English coast.*

Below *Gloster Meteor F.8 undergoing a thorough strip and overhaul at Tarrant Rushton.*

within seconds. Quickly gaining altitude, he determined that no other damage had resulted, then landed — to find his goggles embedded three inches into the tailplane fairing!

On the other side of the world, in-flight refuelling rapidly became an operational necessity as the Korean conflict got underway in 1950. In 'Project Hightide' (later 'Texaco'), the USAF initially deployed KB-29M tankers fitted with looped hose equipment, and later eight KB-29T tankers converted at Tarrant Rushton to incorporate the so-called 'quickie' probe and drogue conversion kits. FRL's technical representatives Woodus, Russell, Roberts and Wickenden all flew regularly with the USAF crews that formed the Japanese Air Defence Force throughout the three year campaign — making sure the Company's equipment and reputation remained in good order. Whilst receiver aircraft usually carried a probe attached directly to the main airframe, a novel arrangement was employed when wing-tip tanks equipped with refuelling probes, were fitted to F-80 Shooting Stars, F-86 Sabres and F-84 Thunderstreaks. To 'top up', the pilot simply engaged the drogue, waited until fuel was seen to exit from a relief valve on top of the tank, then repeated the procedure with the opposite tank. This expedient method of refuelling allowed USAF Major Harry Dorris to carry out a remarkable exploit over North Korea on 28th September 1951. Leaving his Japanese airfield at 5.10 a.m., in an F-80A carrying a full warload of bombs, rockets, guns and cameras, Dorris attacked targets well outside the range of the normal single engined fighters. The ciné film he brought back showed a series of well co-ordinated strikes at low level — where fuel consumption is at its highest. He made eight refuelling interceptions with a KB-29T tanker, involving sixteen separate contacts (eight for each drop tank), before eventually returning to base at 7.25 p.m. In exceeding Hornidge's endurance time, Dorris established a new record for turbojet aircraft of 14 hrs. 25 mins., this time under combat conditions, and having observed radio silence throughout!

The air war over Korea also demonstrated to the US Navy and Marine jet fighter squadrons operating from the carriers, the need for increased range and endurance, and they readily adopted the probe and drogue method of refuelling as the most flexible way of meeting requirements. The first carrier-borne aircraft to be operated as a tanker was the North

The first carrier-borne aircraft to be operated as a tanker was the North American AJ-2 Savage, seen here refuelling a Grumman Panther.

American AJ-1 Savage which had an FR Inc. built A-12 HDU installed in the bomb bay. The success of this aircraft followed by the Cutlass in supplying the Panthers, Cougars and Banshees led later, in 1956, to the arrival of the mighty Convair R3Y-2 Tradewind flying boat tanker, which was capable of providing fuel to four fighters simultaneously from podded units located under the wings. Only a few of the Tradewind tankers were introduced into the US Navy's Fleet Logistics Wings, before problems with the Allison T-40 turbo-prop engines caused them to be withdrawn from service.

Unquestionably, the B-29 Superfortress played a key role in introducing flight refuelling to the USAF in the early Fifties, but it was becoming difficult for the ageing tankers to keep up with the new generation of aircraft beginning to enter service. As a result, the USAF began to investigate the use of faster and larger tankers and the highly experienced Allison, Woodus, Russell and Wilf Goddard were in constant demand in Seattle, Fort Worth and Eglin Air Force Base to commission installations of the higher performance Mk.14 HDU in aircraft such as the Convair KB-36, and Boeing KB-47. Frank Russell remembers one particular KB-47 flight when it was necessary to jettison the tanker's trailed hose. What made it memorable was the fact that he had to position himself over the open bomb-bay, without a parachute — and holding onto a convenient bit of the aeroplane with one hand, file slowly through the hose steel reinforcement wire!

Woods Humphrey had by now, established FR Inc as a truly going concern with the main manufacturing effort concentrated on producing equipment based on the British designs but incorporating American standards. By late 1951 however, it had become clear that if the increasing demands were

Above *In September 1956, the R3Y-2 Tradewind became the first tanker to refuel four aircraft simultaneously. The receivers are Grumman Cougars of the U.S. Navy.*

Below *FRL's hose drum equipment was fitted as a trial installation in the Convair KB.36 — not, however, in this particular aircraft, which undershot the runway at Boscombe Down in 1952.*

Boeing KB.47s carried out limited testing in the Fifties using probe and drogue equipment.

Harry Smith, FRL's Chief Designer in the late 1940s and early 1950s.

going to be met, high level technical reinforcement would have to be forthcoming.

Confronted with Woods Humphrey's plea for assistance, Cobham reluctantly parted with Chief Designer, Harry Smith, who left to become the Chief Engineer at Danbury, with Mike Goodliffe automatically filling the position he vacated at Tarrant Rushton. But other changes were also about to take place that would be far more reaching. The US government had for some time been expressing concern that FR Inc., a wholly-owned foreign subsidiary, was undertaking top secret work in America. Both Woods Humphrey and Cobham had sensed a growing resistance in official quarters, so it came as no real surprise to Sir Alan to be summoned to a meeting in General Putt's office, where it was explained to him that an American partner would have to be found and allowed to take effective control. Faced with this ultimatum, Sir Alan undertook a search that proved to be long and difficult, until, late in 1952 he came into contact with Lawrence Rockefeller. Under high level pressure to tie up a deal, Cobham agreed in January 1953 to an arrangement that still left 40 per cent of the shares with FRL, but split the remainder between

Rockefeller, Reaction Motors and other associated financial interests. With the transfer of control secured, the Rockefeller organisation soon insisted on appointing its own man to run the company, Woods Humphrey having to make way for Watson Newhall, who became the new President.

One of the first major decisions made by the new Board was to expand and relocate the factory to Baltimore in anticipation of large contracts being placed. Cobham frequently commented later how impressed he had been with the efficiency which had allowed such a swift resumption of production to take place following the transfer, and only nine months after the intention to move had first been discussed.

It was disturbing to note however that despite the US Navy's interest in probe and drogue equipment, the USAF, having invested close to ten million dollars in support of Boeing's 'Flying Boom' system on the KC-97 tanker, was now clearly regarding it as the preferred standard method. There was no question that the Boeing designed equipment could handle significantly higher flow rates than the FRL system, but it seemed to Cobham's colleagues, and to many others in the USAF, that the method of making contact was inelegant, clumsy and decidedly dangerous. The head of Strategic Air Command, General Curtis Le May was determined that any tanker force that was going to support the future bomber force of B-52s and B-58 Hustlers, would sit firmly within his Command structure. He achieved this by excluding probe and drogue equipment (which would also have supplied the Navy's aircraft) from the specification he placed for 200 jet tankers in 1953. Lockheed, Convair, Douglas, Fairchild and Martin were all invited to submit designs, but Boeing played its trump card in having a prototype, Type 367-80, ready to fly in mid-1954. Forerunner of the Boeing 707, it demonstrated its potential tanker capabilities to full advantage and led to an immediate order in September 1954 for twenty-nine 'Boom' equipped aircraft to be designated KC-135 (see Footnote). The USAF's policy was now clear, but it was a deeply disappointing decision for Cobham and his colleagues to digest, and difficult for them not to draw the conclusion that political rather than technical considerations had carried the day for Boeing.

It seemed as if the American authorities were determined to put obstacles in the way of progress, for during 1954 the Department of Defense adopted an isolationist stance by issuing new security regulations. These stated that a 'plant licence' could only be granted to a company whose Board consisted entirely of naturalized US citizens. This led to the resignation of Sir Alan and Christopher Tonge from the Board of FR Inc., but they retained their 40 per cent shareholding, and technical information continued to be exchanged.

Added to his problematical American affairs, Sir Alan found his hands full coping with events gathering pace at Tarrant Rushton. With the advent of the Gloster overhaul contract, the sight and sound of jet aircraft had already become commonplace, but with the formation of No.210 Advanced Flying School (AFS) at Tarrant Rushton, the skies above the airfield were almost permanently occupied by Meteors and Vampires.

This additional activity had come about in an attempt to ease the strain on the RAF's Training Command, already fully stretched in carrying out the extra pilot training caused by the Korean crisis. Word had also spread in official circles that the Company was thoroughly conversant with the Meteor and of course, was in possession of a first class airfield, particularly suited for training purposes. Sir Alan was gratified therefore, to be offered a contract which required the Company to service and maintain the Flying School's aircraft, and provide full living facilities for the instructors and pupils. Gp. Capt. Judge was the officer who conducted the first on-site discussions with Cobham, and much to Sir Alan's surprise he produced a hazel twig and used his skill as a water diviner to discover the whereabouts of numerous underground springs on the south side of the airfield. Despite his recommendation that living accommodation be built on the area, it was decided that a disused army site at nearby Grimsditch could be restored and renovated at far less cost!

The school opened in November 1952 with a mix of Meteor Mk.3s and Mk.7s, Vampire Mk.5s and an Airspeed Oxford. At its peak the establishment housed thirty-six aircraft, and, in flying an average of 150 sorties per day, a total of 16,500 hours was amassed before the school was finally closed in March 1954, the only serious incident during this

Footnote: A total of 820 KC-135 aircraft were eventually produced in tanker and other roles and in 1961 Le may's Strategic Air Command tankers extended their activities to support all other USAF Commands, using special probe to drogue adaptors attached to the boom when supplying probe equipped aircraft.

A Bristol Brigand undergoing conversion to T.4 trainer configuration at Tarrant Rushton.

period being the fatal crash of a Meteor north of Reading, and the 'write off' of a Vampire following a take-off mishap in June 1953. Sir Alan's organisation and the instructing team received an official commendation for having consistently achieved the highest serviceability (75 per cent) and the best safety record of any AFS operating in the United Kingdom at that time.

Before leaving 210 AFS, the reader may find it of interest to read two letters which were exchanged between the C.O. of another RAF unit, and the C.O. of the School at Tarrant Rushton, Wg. Cdr. Hyland-Smith. His reply to an official query as to whether the elevation of the airfield was 300 ft. or 301 ft., is an absolute gem, and is included in Appendix V.

The sound of piston engines frequently intermingled with the distinctive whine of the jets over Tarrant Rushton, for Sir Alan had also managed to secure a Ministry contract to convert ten Bristol Brigand Mk.B.2 bombers to Mk.4 trainers. When asked by one of the Air Ministry directors if he thought FRL could handle the job, Cobham, with unabashed confidence, had replied that not only could the Company do it, but could do it better than anyone else. Evidently the remark was well received and the work commenced in 1953.

Pat Hornidge told how the Brigand was nearly his undoing. It was the usual thing on Christmas Eve for everyone to retire to the Mess and enjoy a drink or two. On this particular occasion, Hornidge, feeling most relaxed after a pleasant lunch, was surprised and somewhat dismayed to be told that one of the Brigands was ready for flight. Rather than refuse to fly, he decided, against all his professional instincts, to carry out the tests. Once in the air, however, his festive mood prevailed and resulted in a spectacular 'beat up' of the airfield at eighty feet! He added that he had been most unwise when, having feathered the propeller on one engine, he had carried out a turn towards the dead engine — a manoeuvre not to be recommended at low level. Needless to say, everyone fully enjoyed the impromptu display!

Early in 1952, Cobham was approached by Ron Ashley, with whom he had formed Skyways Ltd. in 1946. It now appeared that Ashley had managed to obtain a sub-contract from Armstrong Whitworth Aircraft for the manufacture of rear fuselages for Hawker's new Sea Hawk naval fighter. He had however, underestimated the job and did not have the resources to go ahead. In a bizarre offer to Cobham, he proposed to sell the sub-contract to FRL,

Over four hundred rear fuselage assemblies were produced at FRL for the Hawker Sea Hawk naval fighter. Shown is a Sea Hawk FGA.6 of the Fleet Requirements Unit at Hurn in 1968.

but still wished to run the project as an outside agent! Alerted by his previous experience of Ashley's strange ways of conducting business, Sir Alan came to an uncomplicated arrangement with Armstrong Whitworth, who were only too relieved to find a safe pair of hands to take on the work.

An Airframe Construction Shop (ACS), which was really a continuation of what originally had been Site 'A' at Ford, was set up on the north west corner of the airfield, and it was here that production controller 'Gilly' Moule supervised the assembly of 415 fuselage units – followed later incidentally, by 90 sets of wing drop tanks for the ill-fated Vickers Supermarine Swift.

It can be appreciated that with the success of such widespread activities, Sir Alan's financial situation had undergone a dramatic improvement. At this point therefore, it is appropriate to consider how this initiated the transition of Cobham's Company from private to public ownership.

NINE

Coming of Age

FRL's new-found prosperity had allowed Cobham and his City partners to recover their original investments, but differences gradually developed over management policy. The merchant bankers were, in Cobham's energetic view, too concerned with matters of the moment and unwilling to invest in technical innovations that would secure the Company's future. These differences culminated, in 1952, in the Robert Benson, Lonsdale directors offering to sell their total shareholding for £30,000. At such a low price, Sir Alan keenly seized the opportunity to regain total ownership of the Company. In order to raise the capital, it was necessary to sell a substantial property he owned in the Bahamas, and all appeared to be going well until, with all the other formalities completed, the moment arrived for him to sign the cheque. Then, with almost theatrical timing, the telephone rang and Sir Alan's secretary informed him that the Bahamian property sale had fallen through at the last minute. Absolutely stunned by this turn of events, Cobham now had to take drastic action. After a few minutes' thought, he put on a brave face and, radiating a confidence he certainly didn't feel, returned to the table and signed the cheque.

After handshakes all round, he bid everyone a quick farewell, and without delay took himself off to see a man who had always taken a keen interest in his ventures – Sir Charles Lidbury, at the Westminster Bank. To his relief, Lidbury took a sympathetic view of the situation and gave his assurance that the cheque would be honoured, but as Cobham pointed out, it was a close run thing, for had he had to deal with anyone else, he could have ended up in a highly embarrassing situation!

Thus in July 1952, Sir Alan again became the sole shareholder in the Company, and immediately invited his son Michael, newly qualified as a barrister, to join the Board as a non-executive director. Michael Cobham recalls the difficulty he faced early on when, without wishing to appear self-seeking, he had to advise his father that such a monopolistic share arrangement introduced a potentially ruinous

death duty situation for the family. Sir Alan, mindful of the need to safeguard the family's position, discussed the situation with his long time trusted financial adviser, Gerard Kealey, who had joined FRL as Company Secretary in 1938. Armed with his encouragement, Sir Alan resolved the problem by transferring 30 per cent of his shareholding to Lady Cobham, a further 30 per cent to Michael Cobham, and 7 per cent to his old colleague, FRL's Financial Director, Christopher Tonge.

This proved to be the first step towards his intention to make FRL a public company, and shortly afterwards in 1954, despite some apprehension over

Gerard Kealey, Sir Alan's financial adviser, and FRL director over many years.

the differences which had caused their separation, he sought the advice of Robert Benson, Lonsdale on how best to implement such a move. Fortunately, his fears of a frosty reception were unfounded, and, having listened to his wishes, the firm's directors were soon engaged in financial machinations which, he freely admitted, left him bewildered and decidedly out of his depth.

Eventually, a plan was devised which firstly required that a moribund company already possessing a quotation on the Stock Exchange be acquired for straight cash. This requirement was met when Robert Benson, Lonsdale arranged with merchant bankers Singer and Friedlander, for the purchase of Manitoba and North West Land Corporation Ltd., a 'shell' company which, though having no physical assets, still retained the desired quotation on the British Stock Exchange. In order to acquire this public company, the Cobham family borrowed some £230,000 from the bank. Then, having become the new owners of Manitoba and North West Land in December 1954, they used the money as part payment to purchase FRL, then estimated to be worth £475,000, the balance of £245,000 being left as a loan secured by other stock held by Sir Alan's family. With ownership now established, it was at a meeting of the Manitoba and North West Land Board on 12th May 1955, that Sir Alan, as Chairman, along with the fellow Directors Michael Cobham, Bonner Dickson, Gerard Kealey, Christopher Tonge and Harry Harrison, formally decided to change the name of the company to Flight Refuelling (Holdings) Ltd. Michael Cobham recalls that this was one of the last occasions when 'going public' by means of such transactions was allowed, as much stricter financial regulations were put in place soon afterwards. Sir Alan's famous luck had clearly not deserted him, and as a result of these manoeuverings he now had a far more viable and flexible organisation at his fingertips!

Although Michael Cobham had joined the FRL board in 1952, he had remained in Chambers at the Temple, and fully expected to continue as a practising barrister. However, following Contract Manager Leonard Rossiter's premature retirement due to ill health in 1955, Sir Alan saw an opportunity for Michael to join the Company in an appropriate capacity. For his part Michael felt no immediate compunction to enter industry, albeit in a Company in which he had such a substantial interest. Nevertheless, a combination of Sir Alan's persuasiveness and a

realisation by Michael of the realities of the situation, resulted in his becoming Contracts Manager in the early summer.

Turning attention once more to Tarrant Rushton, the variety of projects in hand was showing no signs of diminishing. A number of former BSAA Tudor Mk.I's, two more belonging to the Ministry of Supply, and three Mk.4's owned by Avro, were being stored on the airfield. Several of these had already been purchased by Aviation Traders in the summer of 1953, but Sir Alan was still seriously attracted to taking on some of the remaining aircraft to equip an associated company, Flight Charter. One of the schemes he had in mind for Tudors was the transportation of carcass meat within Central Africa. Cattle bred and fattened on the heights of equatorial Africa had to be slaughtered and flown quickly some eight hundred miles to the refrigeration plant at Brazzaville, but on closer inspection, the contract, which only allowed for a one way carriage of freight, was not as attractive as Cobham had first thought, and his interest waned.

In 1952, FRL was requested by RAE Farnborough to convert two Lancasters out of a projected batch of nineteen, into drone aircraft for use as targets in missile firing trials. The first aircraft, PA 343, was converted and flown on five occasions by Tom Marks with Maurice Jenkins as flight engineer, before it had to be acknowledged that excessive mainplane deflections and difficulties with Ultra Radio's modified throttle box made the Lancaster an unsuitable candidate for this kind of work. The second aircraft, PA 474, was thus spared what would have been an unworthy end, and, after carrying out other work which included underwing mounted rocket-firing trials, it left Tarrant Rushton for Cranfield in 1956. This particular Lancaster went on to become a national symbol as 'The City of Lincoln', flagship of the RAF's Battle of Britain Memorial Flight. The Lancaster exercise however, was merely the forerunner of what was to become a large scale Company involvement with drone aircraft conversions in the years to come.

In 1953, Cobham was approached by a Poole based company called 'Tingtuf' that required more capital to fund special purpose machinery for making tufted fabrics. Sir Alan became interested and authorized the setting up of a small unit at Tarrant Rushton to develop and manufacture the machines, and also to produce finished products including lightweight carpets for aircraft use, and domestic

Lancaster PA 474 of the Battle of Britain Memorial Flight pictured at Hurn in 1986. This aircraft narrowly escaped being converted to a drone target aircraft at Tarrant Rushton in the early Fifties.

'candlewick' quilts, and rugs. Rather late in the day, a market research exercise revealed that production of the machines had far exceeded the demand, and manufacture came to a halt. The product line looked promising however, and Sir Alan formed the English Stitchweave Company to gain entry to the textile industry, but, after two years in which considerable effort and money were injected into the company, there was still no sign of a profit. The General Manager, Hugh Johnson, back in this country after an unsuccessful couple of years in Canada, had again been taken on by Sir Alan to run the business, and he was convinced that a further investment of £10,000 would see the company through; Cobham's Board however, disagreed and closed the operation down. It appears that again, a technically promising speculation was undermined by a failure to appreciate the commercial realities, and the views expressed earlier by Michael Cobham concerning FRL's unsuccessful bid for air charter work, were strongly reinforced by this latest unrewarding adventure.

By 1955, the Canadian aircraft industry was showing every indication of becoming a major force, with companies such as Canadair (a subsidiary of General Dynamics) and the Canadian extensions of Bristol, de Havilland, Fairey and Avro, all heavily engaged in substantial design or repair and overhaul projects. All the signs pointed to the country breaking away from dependence on American products, and it was this that encouraged the formation of FR (Canada) Ltd. with Sir Alan's cousin, Arthur Cobham, later becoming its Managing Director. An English

expatriate engineer, Dennis Cunliffe, was engaged to make the aircraft constructors and operators aware of FRL's products, and its willingness to set up a manufacturing plant in Canada. Cunliffe's enthusiasm was dashed however, when, despite the declared general move towards technical independence, Canadair combined with Convair in the USA, and the equipment orders he had thought forthcoming for the CL-28 Argus maritime reconnaissance aircraft (a modification of the Bristol Britannia to meet RCAF requirements), went elsewhere. FR (Canada) Ltd.'s future now rested on securing business with Avro Canada, who in turn made it clear that they wished to see tangible evidence of sizeable production facilities before they would commit themselves to ordering equipment. Despite Cunliffe's untiring efforts, it proved desperately difficult to undercut American competition and it was eventually agreed by the Flight Refuelling (Holdings) Board that any future Canadian operations would be handled more efficiently by FR Inc. in the USA. The situation was eventually resolved however, when the Avro CF-105 Arrow supersonic interceptor was cancelled, and the company was finally wound up in early 1959.

Throughout the later Fifties, Cobham was also faced with other problems concerning factory expansion, and indeed, by 1954, clouds had begun to form over the continued use of Tarrant Rushton. The first intimation of trouble came when the formation of the English Stitchweave Co. was seen by certain neighbouring landowners as the possible start of

133

a general industrial expansion that would have a serious environmental impact on the rural area. Formal objections were raised which culminated in an action being brought in the High Court against the Air Ministry and FRL. The seeds of the problem had been sown as far back as 1940, when, following the death of her father Lord Alington, Mary Anna Marten, not then of age, had inherited the 7,800 acre Crichel Estate. This roughly coincided with an Air Ministry decision to requisition land on the plateau above Tarrant Rushton village to provide an airfield. This land included Rushton Farm, at that time part of the Crichel Estate, Abbeycroft Down – the property of the Tory family, and a further sixty acres belonging to the Crichel Estate. The requisitioning process appears to have been troublesome and difficult, so much so that the Trustee of the Estate decided to sell Rushton Farm to the tenant John Harding in March 1943. The conveyance of this sale however, included a restrictive covenant which stated that the land, once de-requisitioned, should only be used for agricultural purposes – and it was an apparent disregard for this restrictive clause that formed the basis of the eventual lawsuit.

After the requisition period ended in 1958, the Air Ministry in turn bought the land, and FRL continued to operate under lease with its flying activities generally accepted as merely an extension of the RAF's wartime occupation. The construction of what the Martens referred to as 'a carpet factory', was however, seen as something altogether more sinister

and the thin end of an industrial wedge. Fierce local debate ensued over whether Cobham's retention of a work force of over one thousand, albeit mainly engaged on work of national importance, unfairly denied the farming community the chance to build up its depleted labour force, and matters were brought to a head at a special meeting held at Tarrant Rushton in 1954 to resolve the issue.

At this meeting the Under Secretary of State, Lord De L'Isle and Dudley, without any warning, asked Sir Alan how many people he needed to employ at the airfield, and an arbitrary figure of eleven hundred was quoted. Commander Marten, by now managing the Crichel Estate for his wife, was given the firm promise by the Under Secretary that this number would never be exceeded. This limitation, and the ever-pressing need to expand, led Sir Alan to purchase a factory in Bournemouth's West Howe; but although machine shop activities were actually started up, the site proved impractical for many reasons and was soon disposed of.

Matters were finally settled when, in May 1961, a ruling was handed down from the High Court. This stated that the Company would be permitted to continue its flying and related industrial activities such as fluid system development work, under a revised ten year lease from the Air Ministry, and providing the number of employees did not exceed eleven hundred. [Michael Cobham subsequently negotiated a further ten year extension to this lease which allowed FRL's activities on the airfield to

The cancellation of the Avro CF-105 Arrow resulted in the demise of FR Canada Ltd. in 1959.

Sir Alan and a group of key executives, circa 1960. Back row: John Pochin, Peter Procter, Peter Macgregor. Front row: Mike Goodliffe, 'Harry' Harrison, Sir Alan, Chris Tonge, Ernie Rossiter.

continue until 1981.] The Company was now therefore at liberty to proceed in much the same way as before, but as they foresaw a time when flying-related work would be overtaken by manufacturing, Sir Alan and his colleagues realized that they had only gained a breathing space. In an attempt to keep the number of employees on the airfield to a minimum, the Commercial and Contracts Departments were moved into Eagle House in Blandford, and, in 1959, the Accounts staff transferred to converted wartime buildings on the twenty-six acres of land at Merley near Wimborne, purchased three years previously for use as a sports ground. These were the first tentative moves in what became a full-scale transfer of FRL's manufacturing and commercial facilities to Wimborne during the early Sixties.

Returning to more familiar territory, the Company was now about to end its long association with propeller-driven aircraft. In May 1953, and following the decision to equip the RAF's 'V' bomber force for aerial refuelling, Canberra B.2, WH 734, arrived on the airfield and after installation of the prototype Mk.16 HDU, then being developed for the Valiant tankers, it became Britain's first jet tanker. The first of several Canberras to be supplied to the Company for various trials, this particular aircraft was to remain on FRL's charge for the next thirty years!

The first British all jet aerial refuelling was carried out in 1955 by this aircraft in conjunction with an ex-No.245 Squadron Meteor Mk.8, WE 934. A second Canberra B.2, WK 143, was also received in March 1955. Initially equipped as a receiver to replace the venerable Meteor, it too later performed in the tanker role with the new Mk.20 refuelling pod designed for use with the Royal Navy, mounted as a trial installation under the fuselage.

As the certainty of equipping RAF and Royal Navy aircraft grew, so the pace of refuelling flight tests increased, and also in 1955 the first trials using a post-war British fighter, Gloster Javelin XA 634

Canberra WH 734 became Britain's first jet tanker in 1953.

A classic shot of a Valiant tanker carrying out refuelling acceptance tests with a Gloster Javelin 'all weather' fighter.

Christchurch built de Havilland Vampires were production flight tested at Tarrant Rushton. Three Vampire T.11s are shown flying in 1953.

The Airspeed Ambassador, which carried out trials at Tarrant Rushton during the mid-1950s.

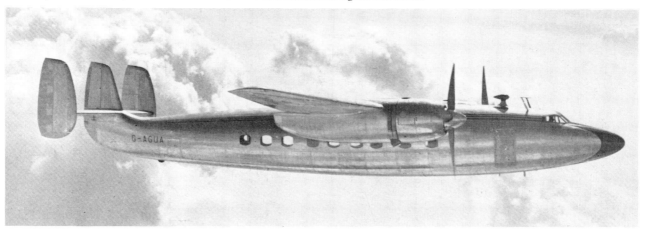

were undertaken. Over these years the Company's flying programme, already heavily committed to routine Meteor repair and overhaul work and aerial refuelling development, was further intensified when Vampire Mk.T.11s and Mk.T.22s were progressively delivered from the de Havilland-Airspeed factory at Christchurch, and also from Chester and Hatfield. A total of fifty-eight of these distinctive twin-boom trainers were put through their production paces at Tarrant Rushton before delivery to the RAF. Another welcome visitor from Christchurch was the elegant Ambassador, which carried out a series of radio, radar, and compass heading checks from the airfield. Flying control duties had, until this time,

been carried out by the Company's own flying personnel and by officers attached to the previously mentioned RAF jet training school. In late 1954 however, Eileen Towers, who was the first woman to join the Guild of Air Traffic Control Officers, applied for a permanent position, and was accepted. Having no radar equipment, Eileen Towers, as did her successor Shirley Boniwell, had to rely on visual contact and radio telephone for communication with the pilots, and informal though the arrangement was, it worked exceedingly well.

With the manufacturing side of the business by now relatively quiet, the Company depended strongly on the Meteor maintenance and overhaul

Not the best of friends! A refurbished Israeli Meteor F.8 looks decidedly ready for action – as does the one in the lower photograph awaiting delivery to the Egyptian Air Force.

programme which was expanding to include aircraft from the Middle East and Latin America, and with Israeli and Arab delegations now arriving at the airfield, much diplomatic manoeuvering of aircraft was called for! Over a five year period some six hundred and fifty Meteors were received for refurbishment and repainting, and FRL did indeed become the Design Authority for several variants following the eventual demise of the Gloster Aircraft Co.

One can easily appreciate the enormous contribution the Meteor overhaul programme made to the Company's finances, but another Meteor success story was about to unfold as the Fifties progressed. With the growing importance of the guided missile,

it became necessary to replace the ageing Fairey Firefly target aircraft with a drone possessing higher all round performance. Accordingly, a test programme was carried out in 1954 by the RAE at Farnborough, using a modified Meteor Mk.7, to assess its capabilities as a target. The tests proved promising, but Glosters, for reasons already described, were unable to take on further Meteor development work, and a conversion programme involving 119 Mk.4s and (later) 92 Mk.8s (from among the 1,085 Meteors to be built) was undertaken by FRL over an six year period.

The first automatic take-off by a Meteor Mk.4, RA 421, took place on 11th March 1955 at Tarrant

Top *Sir Alan Cobham with U.S. and Canadian members of the tripartite Target Panel Committee 1961. FRL's Ted Hall is third from the right, and John Reid is on the extreme right.*

Bottom *An evocative sight — Meteor U.Mk.16 pilotless target aircraft lined up at Tarrant Rushton.*

Rushton, and FRL and RAE continued working in close partnership to produce a serviceable drone variant, designated Meteor U.Mk.15 ('U' signifying 'unmanned'). Ted Hall, who left Saunders Roe Ltd. to join the Company when it moved to Tarrant Rushton, was appointed by Mike Goodliffe as Section Head of all work associated with RAE, and he consequently played a leading role in the Meteor conversion programme. So too did John Reid, who became leader of a development team modifying old Elliott Bros. control equipment for use in the Mk.8 conversion, now identified as the U.Mk.16. Reid himself had left the de Havilland-Airspeed factory at

Christchurch for a rather special reason. Facing a potentially disastrous financial future following the loss of the Comets, de Havilland decided to cease its subsidisation of flying club activities. Fortunately, FRL was not so imperilled and Reid's joining the Company allowed him to carry out a full restoration of his DH.60G Gipsy Moth in No.3 Hangar. With able assistance from Inspector Frank Hudson, the aircraft took to the air again in 1962, and more than thirty years later, G-AAWO still flies regularly over the southern counties.

Flight command of the drones was achieved by two operators, one of whom was located parallel to

139

The only surviving photograph of John Reid with the newly refurbished DH.60G G-AAWO at Tarrant Rushton. Deputy Chief Inspector Frank Hudson (left) gave valuable assistance, as did Mike Inskip, Surveyor-in-Charge of the Air Registration Board at Southampton, (centre).

Michael Cobham pictured with Ted Alsop, Dickie Dickenson and 'Tiny' Thomas.

the runway and the other at the end. Using binocular sights, they were able to transmit input signals via a radio command link to the aircraft's control surfaces and throttles, achieving, as their expertise grew, a high level of proficiency in take offs and landings. Each aircraft was refurbished, modified for acceptance of the drone equipment, and then painted in a highly distinctive red and yellow colour scheme. After the pre-assembled and tested 'drone kits' had been installed, Marks, Hornidge or 'Dickie' Dickinson, newly recruited onto the flying staff, would test the aircraft (see Footnote). With the pilot carrying out a preliminary series of flight checks, it was of course possible to determine whether any snags that arose were due to malfunction of the basic aircraft systems, or induced when receiving control inputs from Don Stubb's Special Equipment Section team on the ground.

The drones were duly despatched to the RAE's airfield at Llanbedr in Wales, the Royal Navy's test establishment at Halfar in Malta, and to Woomera in Australia. Another variant, the U.Mk.21 was produced by FRL to an Australian specification, and Fairey Aviation Pty. also modified many ex-RAAF

Footnote: It is interesting to note that although vacancies for extra pilots did arise occasionally in 1958, Sir Alan turned down such an application from the legendary Sqn. Ldr. Neville Duke!

Mk.8s to the same standard, with modification kits supplied from Tarrant Rushton.

Earlier, mention was made of the Company's initial entry into the drone conversion business using the Lancaster. Now, as the Meteor programme progressed, two Lincolns also arrived for modification to U.Mk.5 standard. The first of these, RF 395, undertook its first 'drone configuration flight' on 29th February 1956, by which time Avros had been requested to set twenty aircraft aside for similar treatment. Flight Engineer Jenkins remembers that unlike the Lancaster which required manually-controlled take offs and landings, the Lincoln was flown off in similar manner to the Meteor, i.e. by operators using the binocular sight. Pat Hornidge was the pilot who 'accompanied' the Lincoln on the test flights and he recalled that his hand rarely strayed far from the 'panic lever' which reverted the systems to manual control, during the critical take off and landing phases. As with the Lancaster however, the Lincoln proved less than ideal as a drone aircraft, and the Ministry eventually changed its mind, directing Avros which had originally made application to convert the remaining aircraft on their own premises, to release them for other purposes.

Whilst recording events which took place in 1956, a small digression must be made here to mention the party hosted by Sir Alan and Lady Cobham on 1st October that year to commemorate the thirtieth

Close up of a Meteor U.Mk.16 aircraft showing the miss-distance-indication equipment fitted to the wingtip.

Jock Kyle in command of a Meteor U.Mk.16 at Tarrant Rushton.

anniversary of his record-breaking flight to Australia. It was held in the Connaught Rooms in London, the place chosen thirty years earlier by his sponsor, Sir Charles Wakefield, to celebrate Sir Alan's triumphant return to England, and the list of over three hundred distinguished guests present that evening constituted a veritable 'Who's Who' in British aviation.

In 1957, the British aviation industry received a body blow from the Minister for Air, Duncan Sandys, when he delivered his (in)famous speech condemning manned aircraft. The new missile-replacement policy sent shock waves through the industry, and Ted Hall recalls the day when a despondent Cobham broke into his meeting with Mike Goodliffe to enquire what they could possibly do to meet the threat. Faced with a seemingly urgent need to diversify, a special group was set up to design electronic control systems for various industrial applications including Post Office letter sorting, and variable-speed factory conveyor belts. These and an individual paging receiver unit, the FR 'Clarion' were all developed and marketed at this time, but with limited success.

Without doubt however, the Company's most ambitious departure within the diversification plan, was its move into the field of nuclear engineering. Following a period at Southampton University for Mike Goodliffe and a number of selected students, a Nuclear Design and Development Department was set up in 1957. Roy Tier recalls how FRL's experience in refuelling technology and the design of special couplings and components proved highly relevant to the new work. In the early atomic power stations, such as Calder Hall, reactors had to be shut down during refuelling operations, but the use of a self-locking coupling design for standpipe closures supplied by FRL, later made this unnecessary, with a consequential saving in time, money and power. The experience gained in hose drum design proved particularly advantageous when a contract was received for transportable carbon dioxide purging trolleys. FRL's team worked closely with the Central Electricity Generating Board, whose long term plans included the construction of seventeen nuclear power stations. Other foreign organisations were also visited, and as confidence grew, the Company invested £50,000 in the machine tools necessary to carry out the work. The money was well spent, for the sale of its nuclear-related equipment contributed greatly to Company profits over the next thirty

years. As the Fifties came to a close, FRL had high hopes of marketing its nuclear equipment in the United States, and Mike Goodliffe, who became a Director in 1959, carried out negotiations with the Curtiss-Wright Corporation. Unfortunately the nuclear equipment discussions led nowhere, but it was agreed that FRL would become the European licensee for the Corporation's CWXL-1 engine sound suppressor unit, and in due course, tests on a jointly manufactured unit were carried out at the Ministry of Aviation's test establishments at Boscombe Down and Farnborough. Although it was never produced in quantity, the unit had the distinction of being the only one of several tested which did not blow up or disintegrate!

Before passing firmly into the Sixties it is important to review the progress made so far in the design and supply of fuel systems equipment. Mention has already been made of the effect the universal changeover from gravity to pressure refuelling had on the Company, but what may not be so widely known is the other exotic areas the design groups were called upon to explore.

In 1952-53, for example, there was much interest in the use of Hydrogen Test Peroxide (HTP) as a rocket motor liquid propellant. Used extensively by the Germans during the later war years, it was now intended for use alongside kerosene in the mixed rocket and jet engine power plant proposed for the Saunders Roe SR.53 Interceptor, and also in the propulsion system installed in 'Blue Steel', the H-Bomb delivery weapon carried by the Vulcan. As the designs progressed, it became necessary to build a special 'Clean Conditions' area and water rig, since it was potentially unsafe to carry out tests with such a volatile fuel, and FRL expended much effort in its endeavour to become the leading supplier of HTP equipment. However the SR.53 never went into production, for like 'Blue Steel' after it, the project fell victim to changes in defence requirements. Despite these disappointments, development work continued in conjunction with the RAE at Westcott and Laporte Chemicals, and equipment was supplied for the rocket motor systems installed in the S.Mk.50 Buccaneers delivered later, in the early Sixties, to South Africa.

With the advent of more sophisticated aircraft, and the growing importance of fuel management and control, FRL found its systems design expertise in even greater demand. This was especially true in the case of the Buccaneer, where the Company's increased design responsibilities included the construction of an articulated fuel system test rig. The rig allowed fuel flow behaviour to be observed under extreme flight attitudes, and this was followed by rig structures which simulated the Wessex helicopter and Germany's first post-war design, the HFB.320 HANSA corporate jet. Other rigs were also built and sent to operators such as BOAC, Kuwait Airlines and East Africa Airlines in order that they could conduct their own test work after overhaul and repair.

The advent of single-point pressure refuelling also dictated that the fuel suppliers' ground supply equipment would have to conform with standard requirements – and naturally Cobham was keen to secure a toe-hold in this potentially worldwide business. Accordingly, Ron Worlidge's team set out to design a nozzle that would attach to the end of the refuelling truck's hose, and engage with a coupling on the aircraft, regardless of type or country of origin. Fierce competition raged on both sides of the Atlantic to establish an acceptable basic design, and Sir Alan told of one Ministry meeting, at which a particularly heavy and cumbersome device produced by an American company, appeared to be receiving technical approval from an official deputising for the regular Project Officer, Mr. Bartell. Cobham's dismay was dispelled however, when Bartell, after being absent for a long period due to illness, miraculously reappeared at that precise moment, and, after a brief inspection, decided that the nozzle and coupling were totally unsuitable.

A formal requirement was then issued to six British companies, and with FRL and Avery Hardoll being adjudged the joint winners of the design competition, a split order for equipment was placed with the two firms. Graham Marriette recalls that in 1955, a vehicle equipped with a standardised coupling arrived at Tarrant Rushton for trials, and was connected up to a Swift drop tank that had its own pressure fuelling system installed. Unfortunately, the safety relief valve, which catered for tank overfilling, was located immediately adjacent to the pressure refuelling coupling that was the object of everyone's attention. As the reader will no doubt have guessed already, the tank overfilled, causing the valve to open – and the reviewing party were christened with a hundred gallons of kerosene, thus putting an unwelcome 'dampener' on the proceedings. It was noted that some modification would have to be incorporated in future designs!

The articulated Buccaneer fuel test rig at Tarrant Rushton.

Pressure refuelling had become a major activity in the Company, for in addition to designing and providing systems equipment for virtually every Western European aircraft, FRL found itself tackling many other applications outside the aircraft industry. The pressure refuelling of diesel railcars was undertaken for British Rail at Derby, and sea trials were carried out to assess the feasibility of refuelling Royal Navy coastal patrol vessels at speed: shown, unfortunately, to be impractical in rough weather. Ship-to-ship refuelling trials were successfully carried out however, when a special six inch diameter coupling, based on the in-flight refuelling probe nozzle was used which allowed a maximum flow rate of 680 tons per hour of fuel oil to be passed from the fleet oiler *Wave Borderer* to a frigate HMS *Grenville* – a far higher rate than had previously been achieved. FRL first began to investigate the refuelling of helicopters from ships in collaboration with Bristow Helicopters in 1956. Although this particular project did not go forward, the French Navy soon showed great interest and successful trials were completed at St. Raphael with a Westland Sikorsky S-58. Since that time Helicopter In Flight Refuelling (HIFR) equipment has been supplied for use with the Royal Navy's frigates, and for ships serving with a dozen other navies throughout the world.

One of the major problems that has always attended the refuelling process is that of absorbing the high surge pressure generated when large flow

A Royal Navy Westland Sea King takes on fuel from the frigate HMS Penelope *using Helicopter In Flight Refuelling (HFIR) equipment.*

rates are abruptly shut off. This problem began to receive urgent attention when, during the design of the Vickers Vanguard, it was realized that if all the tank refuelling valves closed simultaneously with 600 gallons per minute entering the aircraft piping, high instantaneous pressures were going to be experienced. Research at FRL had shown that high surges were largely due to the poor operating characteristics and the location of the pressure control valve fitted to the refuelling vehicle – and it was eventually agreed that if the pressure control point could be sited at the delivery system interface with the aircraft, the risk of damage to the aircraft would be eliminated. FRL therefore proposed to the oil companies that a pressure controller be fitted at the nozzle end of the hose, and with BP and Shell International in particular showing great interest, a flow demonstration model was produced in 1960 and full trials carried out on a vehicle in 1961. The Ministry however, followed its usual conservative approach and it was not until 1963 that they were

pursuaded to loan the Company a fueller, so that the many advantages of hose end pressure control could be properly displayed. Good design (and sense) prevailed eventually and FRL's Hose End Pressure Controller, still in manufacture today, has proven to be a key component in the Company's diverse range of products.

FRL's French licensee, Societe du Carburateur Zenith, also became interested in pressure control problems and after repackaging an FRL design, a regulator was developed for the hydrant fuel pit dispensers in use at certain major airports, which at that time included Orly and Moscow. Throughout the late Fifties, the Company found itself becoming increasingly involved with the supply of heavy-duty fluid handling equipment for use in non-aviation applications. This presented a problem, for the aviation related design work always seemed to demand first priority. To overcome this, and taking account of the different materials and testing requirements associated with industrial products, it was decided to set up a separate company within the FR (Holdings) Ltd. group. With Eddie Knowelden appointed as General Manager, Alan Cobham Engineering Ltd. (ACE) was formed in 1960, and established initially at Chestnut House in Blandford.

At this time FRL, having constructed a special test house and a simulated airport hydrant refuelling system on the airfield, was also engaged in the testing of filter manufacturers' products for British Petroleum. The Company itself later decided to embark upon filter manufacturing, and impressed by the superior quality of the items produced by London-based Broom Filters, it acquired the small firm in the late Sixties and transferred the production facilities to Tarrant Rushton. In 1970, it was agreed between the companies that all filtration work would become part of ACE's core business, although work continued on the airfield until, with its closure in 1981, all ACE activities and facilities were merged within a new purpose built factory in Blandford.

After the hesitancy shown post-war towards aerial refuelling, Service interest grew rapidly once the decision was made in 1952, to provide the new 'V' bombers with this capability. Although the Company's main design effort concentrated on the Mk.16 HDU for the Valiant tanker, schemes were also prepared for the Mk.19 HDU capable of delivering 1000 gallons per minute and intended for installation in the Vulcan, but the requirement was cancelled in 1957. In parallel with this, the Company began to

Entente cordiale! FRL and Carburateur Zenith's management teams meet to celebrate five years successful collaboration. FRL's Peter Procter and Mike Goodliffe are pictured on the left, Hugh Johnson is on the extreme right, Chris Tonge third from right and Sir Alan in the centre.

The Mk.16 Hose Drum Unit produced for the Vickers Valiant tanker.

address the Royal Navy's provisional requirement for a wing-mounted, jettisonable refuelling pod that could also carry fuel useable by the parent aircraft. At this time the Navy's prime concern was centred on being able to refuel aircraft that, having returned to the carrier, found the flight deck temporarily obstructed following an accident. Cobham however, had just returned from a visit to FR Inc. where he had been informed of the extensive use by the US Navy and Marines of what was termed the 'buddy-buddy' system of refuelling to achieve maximum range and increased warloads. This method involved single-seat fighter-bombers being refuelled, often by aircraft of the same type that had been converted into carrier-borne tankers, in a matter of minutes, by fitting self-contained refuelling pods onto wing or fuselage mounted pylons. Although various 'buddy' stores were developed, the Douglas D-704 refuelling pod was to become the unit most widely used by the US Navy, entering service in 1957, and being initially carried on the AD-6 Skyraider and subsequently on the A4D-2 Skyhawk. The Company therefore submitted its Mk.20 pod proposal to the Ministry which, whilst taking full account of the basic requirement, also drew on the Americans' hard

Above *Canberra WK 143 carrying out flight trials with the first Mk.20 pod.*   Below Sea Vixens in line astern!

won experience to emphasize the additional tactical benefits bestowed by the 'buddy-buddy' concept. No opportunity was lost to impress upon the Naval planners that means now existed to multiply significantly the range and striking capability of a relatively small force, and this resulted in orders being placed to equip initially one third of the Scimitars and Sea Vixens about to enter service, as tankers.

By 1958, both types of aircraft had also carried out 'receiver clearance' flights, firstly in conjunction with a Valiant tanker operating from Boscombe Down, and subsequently with Canberra WK 143, carrying the prototype Mk.20 pod. By the time the aircraft fully entered Squadron service in the very early Sixties the operational flexibility afforded by the 'buddy' technique, made the Mk.20 pod a

fundamental tool in the Navy's inventory. Intensive flying trials with the new equipment were undertaken by No.899 Squadron's Sea Vixens at Yeovilton, and the speed with which the crews became accustomed to air refuelling was underlined by the masterly demonstration given at the 1961 Farnborough Air Show – only seven days after receiving their first Mk.20A units!

By this time the Blackburn B.103 (Buccaneer) project was also well established at Brough, and it was intended from the outset that all production aircraft would be equipped with a receiver probe. The first design featured a 'swan-neck' unit that retracted to lay flush across the nose just in front of the windscreen, but this proved unsuccessful, and was replaced by the now familiar fixed device.

Design consideration was also given to installing a 'tanker' pack incorporating a Mk.21 HDU in the Buccaneer bomb bay. A mock up was constructed at FRL and plans were in hand for the HDU to be flight tested in a Canberra when the requirement was withdrawn. However, following the introduction of the Mk.20A pods on the Scimitars and Sea Vixens,

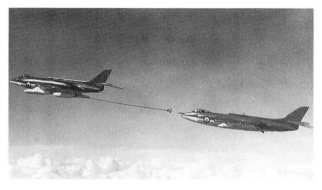

Royal Navy Scimitars in close harmony.

A Buccaneer S.Mk.2 featuring a full range of underwing stores including a Mk.20c refuelling pod.

the Mk.20C pod was developed for the Buccaneer, which then served admirably in the 'buddy-buddy' tanker role throughout its career with the RN, and subsequently with the RAF. Interestingly, a design study was also embarked on using the bomb bay unit intended for the Buccaneer to convert the Sud Caravelle airliner into a tanker, but the only practical aerial refuelling work carried out with the French involved Pat Hornidge flying the Canberra WK 143 tanker during trials at Istres and Bretigny with the French Air Force's Etendard and Vautour receivers in 1957-58.

The first Valiant tanker trials got underway in 1956, and after clearance for Service use was obtained from A and AEE, No. 214 Squadron was nominated as the RAF's tanker trials and development unit in 1958. During the subsequent two year evaluation period, the Squadron was commanded by Wg. Cdr. Michael Beetham, who, after a highly successful career which culminated in his becoming Chief of the Air Staff in 1977, eventually retired from the Service as Marshal of the Royal Force in 1982. After giving their first public demonstration of

air-to-air refuelling at the 1958 SBAC Flying Display, the Valiants were involved in many long distance proving flights, and Sir Michael recalls that he was particularly inspired to make a two-way, record-breaking flight from England to South Africa in 1959, by Sir Alan's journey to the Cape thirty-four years earlier. His Valiant was the first aircraft to fly to Capetown and back, non-stop in each direction, being refuelled by two Valiant tankers over Kano, Nigeria on both flights. Valiants, positioned over Cyprus, Karachi and Singapore, later enabled a No. 617 Squadron Vulcan, flown by Sqn. Ldr. Beavis, to complete a record-breaking non-stop flight from Britain (Scampton) to Australia (Sydney), a distance

Opposite page top Sir Alan Cobham, Pat Hornidge and Dickie Dickenson visit No. 214 Squadron, Marham, on 10th June 1959. Squadron Commander. Wg. Cdr. Michael Beetham (centre) is accompanied by Station Commander Gp. Capt. Wilf Burnett and Flight Commander Sqn. Ldr. John Garstin.

Opposite page bottom Wg. Cdr. Michael Beetham (left) and the crew of the Valiant which undertook the first non-stop flight to Cape Town, 1959.

Below Sir Alan presents a silver trophy to Wg. Cdr. Bastard, O.C. No. 617 Squadron, after a Vulcan achieved the first non-stop flight from England to Australia, 1961.

of 11,500 miles, in 20 hrs. 3 mins. at an average speed of 573 m.p.h. in 1961.

At separate functions held to commemorate their achievement, Sir Alan presented trophies consisting of a silver globe surmounted by the Company's emblem to the Officers Commanding Nos. 617 and 214 Squadrons. In his congratulatory speech, the old pioneer was quick to point out when comparing the new record with the thirty-six days he had taken on his outward journey — that it was his aerial refuelling system that had made it possible. Mischieveously, he purposely glossed over certain other improvements in airframe, powerplant and navigational systems that might have contributed just a little to the Vulcan's feat! However, there was no denying the pride felt by everyone in the Company that its famous double 'Speedbird' logo was now incorporated in the Squadron's emblem emblazoned on the fins of the tankers. In August 1960, No. 90 Squadron became the second Valiant tanker unit, and was also based at Marham.

In 1958 and just prior to relinquishing his position as Contracts Manager, Michael Cobham, accompanied by 'Tiny' Thomas, attended a meeting in Brussels. The visit was in response to an invitation by the Belgian Ministry of National Defense to discuss the undertaking of aircraft overhaul work, and in light of the Company's experience on Meteor aircraft, it was assumed that any forthcoming work would be on the same type.

It therefore came as an enormous surprise to both men when General Detige, impressed by the Company's previous efforts involving BAF aircraft invited FRL to bid for an 'Inspection and Repair As Necessary' (IRAN) programme for one hundred and fifty American F-84F Thunderstreak and RF-84F Thunderflash aircraft. In the event it was only after overcoming strong Belgian political resistance that a contract covering one hundred and nineteen aircraft was awarded, the first of several including one for sixty-six T-33 Shooting Stars which in total, resulted in a ten year Company association with the BAF. All the aircraft were delivered directly to and from Tarrant Rushton by BAF pilots, except for six RF-84Fs which arrived via a more circuitous route. These aircraft had languished for some time under a scorching desert sun at the USAF storage base at Tucson, Arizona, until purchased by the Belgian authorities in 1962. 'Tiny' Thomas then supervised their dismantling and despatch in twenty-seven large crates, firstly by rail to New Orleans and then in the

Routine inspection of a 214 Squadron Valiant. Note the insignia on the fin which combines the Squadron and FR emblems. The inset photograph is of Wg. Cdr. P. G. Hill who later commanded the Squadron.

FRL's Chief Test Pilot Dickie Dickenson DFC, receives the Queens Commendation for Valuable Service in the Air, from the then Minister for Aviation, Roy Jenkins, in 1965.

cargo steamer *Madam Butterfly* to Southampton. A police escort accompanied the 'packages' on the final leg of the journey to Tarrant Rushton. Apart from one aircraft being totally destroyed on the ground following an engine fire, the work programme proceeded smoothly – although Dickie Dickinson recalled an incident which, in his words, 'caused a little excitement'. This occurred during a supersonic dive from 45,000 ft. in a BAF Thunderstreak when the aircraft's landing-brake parachute suddenly

deployed. This produced some nasty moments before the attachment cable broke and the cause of the trouble went billowing into the blue!

In 1959, the FRL Board recommended that Michael Cobham, who, by this time had become Commercial Director, responsible for contracts, sales and after sales service, be trained for higher duties. This suggestion stemmed largely from three non-executive Directors, Gerard Kealey, Walter Hill and Bonner Dickson who had recently joined

Belgian Air Force Republic RF-84F at Tarrant Rushton.

A T-33 Shooting Star jet trainer of the Belgian Air Force.

the Board following his retirement as Director and General Manager of the Vickers Weybridge factory.

Accordingly, Cobham, greatly encouraged by such prized opinions, left the Company to take a general management course at Urwick Orr and Partners in London, afterwards spending a year at Solartron, a successful electronics firm founded by Eddie Ponsford (later to become a Director of Flight Refuelling (Holdings) Ltd.). This was followed by an equally rewarding year gaining City experience with old associates, Robert Benson, Lonsdale. Cobham admitted that he was sorely tempted to remain with the merchant bankers, but, well aware that his training represented a serious long-term investment by the Company, he returned to Tarrant Rushton as Deputy Managing Director and Chief Executive in the spring of 1961.

A Corporate Creation

1961 proved to be a year of mixed fortunes for the Cobham family. Within a few months of Michael rejoining the Company, Lady Cobham died following a protracted illness. In a forty-year marriage that could never be regarded as uneventful, she had always provided the stability necessary to off-set Sir Alan's sometimes impulsive actions and his phenomenally energetic drive. Whilst totally supportive of her husband's ventures, she had of course, undertaken many of her own, and her cheerful involvement with the Company's social events was to be sorely missed over the coming years. It seemed most appropriate that she should be laid to rest in the ancient church at Tarrant Rushton, since she had devoted much time and energy to its restoration. Friends attending her funeral on 26th October were legion, and there were many from Ford who chartered a special four-coach Pullman train to travel from Sussex to Dorset. Later, a memorial service was held in Bournemouth's St. Stephen's Church, at which Michael Cobham read the lesson, and the music was provided voluntarily by members of the Bournemouth Symphony Orchestra.

Immensely saddened by his loss, Sir Alan knew that not only was his personal life about to undergo a major change, but also that again his Company was facing a different future. With a reducing requirement for military aircraft maintenance work, and the end of the target aircraft programme in sight, a gradual run-down in the airfield-based activities appeared inevitable. It had now become imperative to concentrate the Company's resources on the production of systems equipment, and in order to achieve this, Tarrant Rushton's widely-dispersed manufacturing shops were going to have to be relocated in more suitable, modern premises. It was these factors which focused Sir Alan's attention on the creation of a new factory, and the day-to-day running of the Company fell increasingly onto Michael's younger shoulders.

As the site for the new venture, an eight-and-a-half acre plot at Wimborne's Leigh Park, alongside the River Stour, was finally chosen. This formed part of

Sir Alan and Lady Cobham attending a Company function in the late-1950s.

152

A Pullman Special bringing a large party from Brighton for Lady Cobham's funeral at Tarrant Rushton, October 1961.

Chief Chemist, Mick Tanner.

a larger area originally purchased in the Twenties by the Wimborne Urban District Council for some £2,000 for development as a council housing estate. Prior to the introduction of mains drainage to the town in the Fifties, the proposed factory location had served as a site for general refuse and sewage disposal, and the main approach road was, not surprisingly, called 'Dump Road'. Although it was intended that the factory would overlook the river and attractive open farmland, the planners nevertheless faced a challenging task in overcoming the somewhat unsavoury image long associated with the area.

Wimborne Councillor Sid Dennett, a long-serving member on many local committees, recalls that having agreed a purchase price of £17,000, the formal negotiations proceeded smoothly and were completed without complication. A Bournemouth company, Claude A. Barnes Ltd., whose Managing Director, Bob Manton, had worked alongside Sir Alan on previous projects at West Howe and Tarrant Rushton, was appointed the main contractor, and work began on levelling and marking out the factory foundations in October 1961. FRL's Tom Jones and Dave Remington were responsible for organising the layout of the internal facilities, and Chief Chemist Mick Tanner was intimately involved with the integration of the water and sanitation systems. Tanner recalls that Sir Alan, reluctant to pay a high price

for the installation and use of 'mains' water, decided to sink a 140 ft. deep bore-hole and pump his own supply. To many this seemed an unusual decision, but it resulted in a saving of many thousands of pounds over the years.

The move to the new factory began in 1963 with the transfer of the heavy equipment from the Nuclear Machine Shop at Tarrant Rushton, and under the able supervision of Dennis Bastable, General Services personnel over a six week period, dismantled, transported and re-assembled a total of one hundred and forty-two machines plus various compressors and other miscellaneous equipment. As accommodation became available, the Accounts and Commercial Departments, which had operated for several years at Merley and Blandford, also moved to Wimborne. The transfer of staff was eventually completed in 1965, when, following the reversal of an earlier decision to retain the engineering function at Tarrant Rushton, Mike Goodliffe's team took possession of a new drawing office and test facilities at the west end of the factory.

Whilst widening interests and new requirements on this side of the Atlantic necessitated this expansion, it was also recognised that the Company's association with its erstwhile protege, FR Inc., had now run its useful course. Reductions in US defence spending had made serious inroads into profits, and following a move initiated in 1961 by the Rockefeller organisation to sell FR Inc. to the Aeronca Corporation, the FRL Board (despite Sir Alan's preference for holding shares in Aeronca), accepted a cash offer for its shares in FR Inc. Michael Cobham recalls the relief he felt when, having had to overcome the strong reservations expressed by his father, his recommendation to take the cash offer was fully vindicated by a substantial fall in the value of Aeronca shares.

Whilst market forces inevitably exerted a major influence on the workings of the Company, natural forces also played their part during the exceptionally bad winter of 1962-63. Blizzards just after the Christmas break caused massive snow drifts and it was only the dogged determination of teams from the General Maintenance, Canteen, Transport and Works Police Departments that kept the essential services going, and prevented the airfield being totally cut off. Possibly inspired by Captain Scott's

Blizzard conditions in the winter of 1962-63 made it impossible for bus-drivers to get through to Tarrant Rushton.

Mike Goodliffe OBE, who was instrumental in the design and development of all the Company's engineering products over a forty year span.

heroic endeavours, many staff members resolved to 'get through at any price', and two men even tramped some twenty miles between them through the snow to reach Tarrant Rushton from Shillingstone. Mike Goodliffe recalls that the welding of extra reinforcing members onto the Company snow-ploughs eventually enabled them to clear a way to Wimborne, and incidentally to strike a profitable deal for moving the snow from the Town Square. Not only was it then important to keep Tarrant Rushton

Valiant bombers at Quick Reaction Alert readiness. Tarrant Rushton in the early-1960s.

FRL's Michael Cobham and Ted Hall (left) with Hamlin Inc. President, Ron Ferguson.

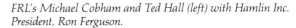

open for Company purposes, but the airfield was also one of several designated as emergency dispersal bases for the RAF's 'V' bombers. This was a time when East-West tensions were running high, and after the runways were lengthened and strengthened in 1959, Valiants and Victors taking part in Service exercises became familiar visitors.

The 'saga of the reed switches' is probably well known to anyone who worked at the Company during the Sixties. Until 1962, microswitches, which were notoriously unreliable, had been used to provide the electrical switching operation and indication for FRL's fuel system equipment; so when Harry Smith brought over from America a highly improved device called the dry contact reed switch, which was already in quantity production for telephone exchange circuitry in the US, it was welcomed with open arms. Although originally conceived in the Bell Corporation laboratories, American anti-trust laws required royalty-free licences to be granted to several smaller manufacturers, and it was to one of these, Hamlin Inc., based in Wisconsin, that Smith secured an introduction. The reed switch consisted simply of a pair of contacts in a sealed glass tube which opened or closed whenever a magnet, was moved across them. This basic principle offered immense possibilities to Graham Marriette's design group, and again the Cobham-Goodliffe team moved quickly to secure an exclusive agreement that allowed FRL to manufacture and market the Hamlin reed switch in Europe and the (then) British Empire (excluding Canada). Ted Hall, Experimental Shop

Foreman Bob Leonard, and Design Engineer Derek Henderson then visited Hamlin Inc. to familiarise themselves with the new technology, and, such was the perceived scope of commercial application, that an independent Industrial Electronics Division was set up on the new Wimborne site in January 1963. This arrangement fitted in well with the Company's general move towards a more diversified range of products, and the new Division also took on the responsibility for other electronic projects. The agreement originally secured with Hamlin Inc. proved successful until its President, Ron Ferguson, decided to cancel FRL's exclusive rights in Germany, introduced a manufacturing base to the British Territory of Hong Kong — and finally set up a rival production company in the UK. Such blatant disregard for the arrangements previously concluded in good faith resulted in the formal termination of the agreement in 1968.

As time went by it became evident that if the Division was to compete successfully in the commercial electronics market, it would need to adopt more efficient methods of component assembly. The purchase of expensive machinery was considered, but rejected in favour of transferring the assembly of less sophisticated components to a company called Dolam in Poland, where labour costs were particularly low. This company was already producing similar components, and an agreement was signed which allowed FRL to purchase these and also pursue at the same time its own market penetration into Eastern Europe. However, a succession of technical and quality control problems, coupled with the bureaucratic difficulties of dealing through the Polish government, eventually outweighed the other advantages, and the Company withdrew its interest. A more successful agreement, which lasted for many years, was reached with Southern Electronics — now renamed Reed Relay and Electronics (India), based in Madras. By 1969, this Division had become known as FR Electronics (FRE) and it remained at Wimborne under Managing Director Jock Dunlop until March 1984, when it was relocated to a nearby site at Ferndown (see Footnote).

Concurrent with the general upheaval and transfer of facilities to Wimborne in the Sixties, was a change of direction in the Flight Test Department at Tarrant Rushton, when Pat Hornidge retired as Chief Test Pilot. Dickie Dickinson was appointed to succeed him on 1st January 1962, and Pat Bolger, an ex-Shorts' test pilot with considerable target-towing experience, now joined the Company. As already mentioned, drone aircraft played an important part in the experimental and evaluation phases of Britain's

Footnote: As part of a product rationalisation programme, FRL has now relinquished its interest in this field, and the Electronics Division was finally sold to the Silicon Power Corporation in July 1994.

early guided missile projects. But as missile accuracy increased, it was feared that full-scale drone targets might prove far too costly and Ted Hall was informed by Ministry officials that future requirements would most likely centre on devices similar in concept to the sleeves or banners trailed behind target-tugs during W.W.II for anti-aircraft or fighter gunnery practice. For obvious safety reasons it would however, now be necessary to employ a far greater tow length, so Hall was sent on a 'fact finding' tour of America, where he visited the Hayes International Corporation in Birmingham, Alabama, a Division of which supplied targets to the US forces. The visit was rewarding and resulted in a handshake agreement for FRL to produce the Hayes T.17 and T.6 series of targets under licence. After Michael Cobham and Mike Goodliffe formalised the arrangements in 1961, two Meteor Mk.T.T.20s, WM 167 and WM 234, were allocated for target towing development work, and evaluation trials of the Hayes targets took place with these aircraft and, later, a Sea Vixen at Hatfield, using the American Del Mar winch. As a result, it was decided that the Hayes targets required significant modification and the Ministry placed a contract on FRL to undertake a virtual redesign, while still retaining the

Hayes target and launcher installed in Meteor TT.20 WM 234.

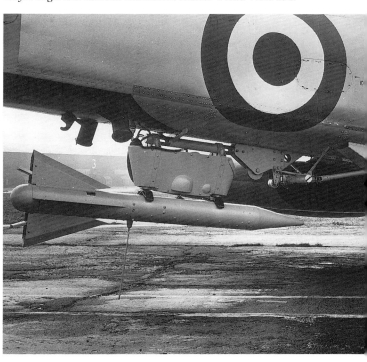

157

all-important centre of gravity towing attachment method patented by Hayes. With design office work at a low ebb, the new requirement proved most opportune, but Michael Cobham was acutely embarrassed when he had to explain to the Hayes executives that further to FRL not implementing the licence to manufacture the Hayes target as agreed – Peter Macgregor had now produced a competitive design, the aptly named 'Rushton' target!

Work also began at this time on a larger more powerful winch which could deploy and recover targets over a towed separation distance of up to eight miles, thus providing an adequate margin of safety when the attacking aircraft launched its heat-seeking missiles. The 'Rushton' winch which evolved from this development work made clever use of a series of winding capstans, along with stepped diameter towing cable to match the progressive change in drag-induced tension throughout the cable length. A setback occurred however, when Brian Bennett, then in charge of target and winch development, was killed in a road accident. Dennis Lewis was transferred from nuclear work to take over his duties, and thus began an association with airborne equipment and airfield services which led to his eventual appointment as Commercial Director of FR Aviation (FRA) – a company whose evolution is described more fully in a later chapter. From this development work came, first the Rushton target, and then, the Rushton winch which made clever use of a series of capstans, along with stepped diameter towing cable to match the progressive change in drag-induced tension throughout the cable length. Lewis accompanied British Aerospace's test pilot, Johnny Squier, in carrying out the first tests of the new winch installed in Canberra WJ 632 during September 1966. Paddy O'Brien, an ex-Boscombe Down pilot, had now joined the flying team, and the number of Goodliffe's designers and engineers was also increased to develop a range of devices, which, for example, improved the target's performance. Dave Langdon, then one of the target system development team, still claims to hold the British record for a towed-target separation distance – 48,000 ft. – the result of a mechanical failure during target deployment which allowed the towing cable to run out to its fullest extent.

Working closely with the Ministry's Trials and Ranges Department, the Rushton system was finally cleared for Service use in early 1970. After this, Bruce Sheppard, who later joined the Company's

flying staff, delivered several of the eleven Canberra Mk.T.T.18 aircraft flown from No.27 Maintenance Unit at Shawbury to Tarrant Rushton, where Rushton winch systems were installed. Following a period of aircrew conversion to the Canberra and several weeks of intensive systems training by FRL's instructors, Dave Langdon, Bob Campbell, Arthur Chant and Jock Kyle, Sqn. Ldr. Crumpton led a newly reformed No.7 Squadron in a fly-past over Tarrant Rushton before its departure for St. Mawgan in Cornwall, where it remained for the next ten years.

FRL's Canberra towing aircraft and Rushton equipment were also utilised in certain non-military activities, and in 1976 a special target fitted with radar-reflecting units was towed down the airways approaching Britain's west coast, thus enabling the CAA's Evaluation Unit to calibrate several major airport radar installations. Flights were also carried out to determine wave spectra for the Department of Energy's investigations into the use of wave energy as a source of power. On another occasion, a Company aircraft was held in readiness at Coningsby to record freak wave conditions similar to those thought to have caused the loss of two trawlers off Dogger Bank. It has to be said that the cancellation of this particular mission was greeted with mixed feelings given the certain prospect of flying very low in severe and turbulent weather.

The key combination of Canberra aircraft and Rushton equipment was also effectively demonstrated to the Indian Air Force (IAF) when Lewis, Chant and Sqn. Ldr. Nelson of No. 7 Squadron visited the sub-continent in 1974. The IAF, which already had several Canberra squadrons in service, subsequently bought six more T.4 aircraft direct from RAF stocks. Delivered in 1975, these were modified at Bangalore for target towing, and redesignated as T.T.418s. As Airwork's resident engineer-in-charge at St. Mawgan, John Stephens had a thorough working knowledge of No. 7 Squadron's Canberras and their target towing equipment, and his experience proved invaluable when he left Airwork to join FRL in 1978. Almost immediately he found himself on his way to India to support the setting-up of IAF's No. 6 Squadron as a target-towing unit. The task took eighteen months

Opposite page top *Meteor TT.20 WM 234 with a Rushton Target, note the Del Mar winch on top of wing.*

Opposite page bottom *First flight of the wing-mounted Rushton winch on Canberra WJ 632, September 1966.*

The Lightning's sharply swept wing necessitated the exceptionally long flight refuelling probe, produced by FRL.

to complete, but the unit remains in service to this day. With both No. 7 Squadron and the IAF successfully operating target-towing Canberras, the Company then provided similar aircraft conversion and crew training for RAE Llanbedr and the Fleet Requirements Unit (FRU) based at Yeovilton. FRU later became the Fleet Requirements and Aircraft Direction Unit (FRADU) and their Canberra T.T.18s continued in service until 1987 when they were superseded by the fleet of Dassault Falcon 20s operated by FRA.

During the early Sixties, provision of a two-point Valiant tanker using the naval standard pods was under consideration, but advanced fatigue damage was discovered in the main wing spars and by the end of 1964 the Valiants' flying days were over. To fill the gap caused by their withdrawal, urgent tanker conversion work already being undertaken on a number of Victor B1 bombers was speeded up, and as a consequence the first five Victor B(K)1A two-point tankers delivered to No. 55 Squadron at Marham in May 1965, whilst fitted with Mk.20B pods, still retained their bombing capability.

Although the Mk.20A pods had been in service for several years, naval tanker aircraft were rarely called upon to exceed an altitude of 16,000 ft. or a flight time of one and a half hours. As a result it was not until Victor flight trials involving 'cold soaking' at high altitude for long periods were undertaken that shortcomings in system performance and pipe connector sealing were revealed. Improvements were made and the new variant, the Mk.20B (or the 'Golden Pod' as it became known 'in-house') now capable of meeting the RAF's more demanding requirements for the Victor, was introduced.

By mid-1966, Nos. 55, 57 and 214 Squadrons were operating from Marham, still with Victor B(K)1A two-point tankers, and by January 1967, the first Victor K.1 three-point tankers (now also fitted with the Mk.17B HDU) had entered service with No. 55 Squadron; followed a year later by the formation of Strike Command, this enabled the Victor tanker force to demonstrate on a regular basis its ability to extend the range and flexibility of both RAF and Royal Navy aircraft. In one exercise, two Lightnings became the first RAF fighters to fly the Atlantic non-stop between Scotland and Toronto, a distance of 3,440 miles in 7 hrs. 22 mins. Shortly afterwards an entire squadron of these aircraft was, for the first time, deployed to the Far East and back in the biggest air-to-air refuelling exercise (Exercise Hydraulic) ever mounted by the RAF at that time.

This success showed clearly that Strike Command could rapidly reinforce the air defence capability in the Far East, and the Victor tanker force now firmly established itself as an indispensable operational component. A consultancy report produced in the mid-Eighties by Decision-Science Applications showed that a tanker fleet could, for example, increase the operational effectiveness of a fleet of eighteen Airborne Warning and Control System (AWACS) aircraft to that of twenty-six — a 44 per cent improvement — by simply extending the time on station and permitting increased coverage of the areas of operation. Such an increase in AWACS capability (and equally that of fighters) showed in-flight refuelling to be a 'Force Multiplier'.

The term 'Force Extender' entered the Service vocabulary when in-flight refuelling was used to permit the non-stop intercontinental flights of aircraft during strategic deployment; similarly 'Force Extender' referred to its use on aircraft with a vital role, e.g. Maritime Patrol, Command Post Duties or Search and Rescue helicopters, when facilitating their operation outside their unrefuelled radius of action. These emotive terms, forged out of front line experience, still serve to underline perfectly the old axiom that 'flexibility is the key to air power'.

Throughout the Sixties, with the advantages of air-to-air refuelling now fully appreciated by the Air Staff, Mike Goodliffe and his team were conducting other design studies; one such, being a 'tanker pack' for installation in the bomb-bay of the TSR-2. A mock-up was built featuring a Mk.26 HDU and a rigid guide tube, some twenty feet in length which, whilst normally stowed under the fuselage, could swing down to an angle of forty-five degrees. It was calculated that this arrangement would ensure adequate clearance between the hose and the tanker, but this interesting, though difficult, project had to be abandoned when, in 1965, the Labour Government cancelled this very advanced aircraft. It was for TSR-2 incidentally, that FRL also carried out its first development work on float-operated fuel tank equipment incorporating the new reed switches.

Another refuelling pod variant was the Mk.20D developed for the RAF's Armstrong Whitworth Argosy twin-boom freighter. This featured an unusual installation — the pod being mounted on a horizontal pylon fixed to the side of the fuselage — and although trials were conducted with an Argosy receiver during 1966, this aircraft never entered Squadron service as a tanker, and the pod requirement was withdrawn.

It is fitting to record here the death in 1964 of Sqn. Ldr. Bill Helmore, exactly thirty years after he accompanied Sir Alan on the Airspeed Courier's famous but abortive attempt to fly non-stop to India. Countless words have been written, and many photographs published relating to aerial refuelling,

Consideration was given to installing a 'tanker' pack in the bomb-bay of the TSR-2, seen here at the start of its maiden flight in 1964.

The Mk.20D pod was designed for use with the
Armstrong-Whitworth Argosy tanker, which did not see
Squadron service.

The unusual Mk.20D pod installation on the Argosy tanker.

but no picture is more instantly recognized than that
on the cover of this book showing Bill Helmore
braving the slipstream to guide the tanker's refuelling nozzle into the Courier's fuel tank. He was a man
of many parts, who, in addition to achieving the rank
of Air Commodore, had a degree in Chemical Engineering, was an MP, and also an accomplished
musician.

In the same year, Michael Cobham moved from

Tarrant Rushton to Wimborne and succeeded his
father as Managing Director, although Sir Alan
remained as Chairman for the time being. He recalls
that following his new appointment, Bonner Dickson
made the pithy observation that he could not regard
himself as a 'true' Managing Director, until he had
sacked someone at Director level for the first time.
He did not have to wait for long, for shortly
afterwards, Works Director John Burnett was 'occa-
sioned to leave the Company' which, incidentally,
created a vacancy that was filled by Michael Cobham
until Ken Saltrick arrived from Hawker Siddeley in
1966.

This came at a time when several new major
aircraft projects were taking shape, all requiring the
Company to invest heavily in research and development in order to win a major share of the fuel system
components business. In Europe, it was closely involved in the initial stages with the Concorde and
Multi-role Combat Aircraft (Tornado) and, also a
little later, with the Airbus design teams. With the
Mk.17 HDU and the Mk.20 pod projects the Ministry, having awarded development contracts, could
use the patents and the design, or allocate manufacture as it wished; for all the new ancillary projects
however, the components were to be developed
and produced under private venture funding. Today,
Michael Cobham stresses the fact that it was the
continued pursuit of this policy which proved to be a
key business decision, and that the Company's insistence on the retention of proprietary design rights

subsequently ensured many years of commercial success.

The extent to which FRL's equipment featured on the new Concorde was perhaps best illustrated by Shell's Managing Director, who pointed out that during a typical transatlantic flight, sixty-five tons of Shell products would be consumed, and in the process, fuel would be received on board the aircraft, transferred, controlled, balanced, cooled and heated, pressurized and de-pressurized, and measured – all by FRL's equipment, which included some two hundred separate assemblies and eighteen hundred fuel pipe couplings on each aircraft. Graham Marriette, then Chief Designer of the Fuel System Equipment Group, estimated that had the supersonic transport (SST) entered full-scale production, FRL's Machine Shop would have had to double in size!

The pipe couplings supplied by the Company for Concorde had to meet stringent design requirements, and were manufactured under a licence agreement negotiated with the Gamah Corporation in 1965. (This was a company formed in the Fifties which took its name from the initials of the co-founders, George A. Mahoff and Al Hass. However, Stanley Aviation had secured a controlling interest in Gamah in 1964, and transferred its operations to Denver, Colorado.) The new agreement followed a meeting between British Aircraft Corporation's (BAC) Tom Boucher, then Head of Fuel System Design at Filton, and George Mahoff, at which it was pointed out that although only Mahoff's superior product would meet the requirements, the terms governing the choice of Concorde equipment dictated that items had to be manufactured either in Britain or France. It was at Boucher's suggestion that Mahoff then discussed licence manufacturing with FRL – and a relationship was formed that had far-reaching effects, for eventually it led to FRL's acquisition of Stanley Aviation in 1981.

In 1966 the eyes of the aeronautical world turned westwards again, and in particular to Boeings in Seattle, where their supersonic transport and giant subsonic 747 airliner projects were starting to gather momentum. FRL's Board realised that it would not be possible for the Company to 'go-it-alone' in America, and decided to set up a reciprocal marketing arrangement with Simmonds Precision Inc. of New York which was anxious to sell its fuel-gauging equipment in Europe. The respective company heads, Michael Cobham and Geoffrey Simmonds, had known each other since their schooldays, and

the omens seemed good for a solid partnership. Goodliffe and Marriette, accompanied by Simmonds's engineers, had given several presentations to Boeing, and with the bulk of the commercial bargaining being left in Simmonds's care, the prospective team appeared to be favourably placed. Michael Cobham, however, recalls a meeting at the Renton Plant at which he and Geoffrey Simmonds realised the extreme difficulties they faced in attempting to overcome Boeing's total reluctance to procure equipment from outside the USA. Ironically, during a subsequent visit by Cobham and Goodliffe, the President of JC Carter, an American company situated on the west coast, offered to show how his equipment worked, but Mike Goodliffe instantly recognised the valves in question as being virtual copies of FRL products, which could only have been made using data supplied previously by the Company in support of project presentations. Belatedly it was concluded that all the effort had been based on false encouragement, and that FRL had displayed its technical hand to no avail.

In 1968, Michael Cobham's workload greatly increased when, in addition to his duties at FRL and those he undertook as Vice-Chairman of the SBAC's Equipment Group Committee, he also found himself appointed to the SBAC's Price Fixing Working Party – which later became the Joint Review Board Advisory Committee (JRBAC). This was a select panel of Financial and Commercial Directors from Rolls-Royce, Westlands, British Aircraft Corporation, Hawker Siddeley and Bristol Siddeley Engines whose brief was to negotiate with the government on behalf of the SBAC, the amended terms and conditions of contracts set up in the wake of the excess profits made (and subsequently repaid) by Ferranti on the Bloodhound missile contract. Cobham owed his presence on the committee to the insistence of the Equipment Group that the Price Fixing Working Party should include a member from the equipment sector of the industry.

It was later that same year that Sir Alan, upon attending the SBAC Dinner, discovered that Michael, having now taken over as Chairman of the Equipment Group, was required by custom and practice to dine at the President's top table. Sir Alan, seated at the Vice-President's table, wryly acknowledged this as clear evidence of Michael's increasing influence on industrial affairs, and that times, and his own long established role as senior partner were indeed changing!

During the Sixties, the character of the Company also changed significantly and FRL became almost entirely devoted to manufacturing, with only a small flight test team operating at Tarrant Rushton. Some 60 per cent of the fuel system components produced were exported to prime aircraft manufacturers in Europe, Brazil, India and Japan and from small beginnings, this side of the business had now become the primary money earner! It was this success that prompted Michael Cobham to consider making the Company's first business acquisition. Enquiries had revealed that the Saunders Valve Company, based in Hereford, would be willing to dispose of its Aviation Division, primarily because the specialised manufacture and testing requirements of some sixty motorised components being produced for each Concorde, rendered them time consuming and labour intensive compared to the company's other industrial products. Saunders had also found that the virtual monopoly they had previously enjoyed regarding the supply of lightweight valves to the aircraft industry had been upset by High Temperature Engineering Ltd. — a highly competitive company, of whom, more later!

It was against this background that Michael Cobham saw the chance for FRL to combine its existing range of servo-operated components with Saunders' motorised units. With Concorde at that time offering great potential for high volume production, such an opportunity was not to be missed, and the Division was eventually purchased for £480,000. Aware of the concern expressed by BAC that continuity of supply must not suffer as Concorde moved into its production phase, Goodliffe arranged for the transfer to Wimborne of some thirty key design and production personnel, including Chief Designer John Medgett, Chief Engineer Arthur Gower and Senior Designer Steve Roebuck. The team, aligned alongside Graham Marriette's component designers, resumed operations in November 1968, greatly assisting the Company's efforts to counter the growing competition from American suppliers in Europe.

The 50th anniversary of the first non-stop crossing of the Atlantic by Alcock and Brown was commemorated in May 1969 by the Daily Mail Transatlantic Air Race, and teams from the RN and the RAF, using whatever resources they could muster, from bicycles to jump-jets, covered the distance between London's GPO Tower and the Empire State Building in New York. Three Phantoms from the Navy's No. 892 Squadron achieved the fastest overall New York

– London time (5 hrs. 11 mins. 22 secs.) and in addition to the Daily Mail's cash prize, a magnificent Silver Cloud car was awarded to the Squadron by Rolls-Royce, manufacturers of the Phantom's Spey engine. Sqn. Ldr. Lecky-Thomson flying an RAF Harrier won the London – New York sector (6 hrs. 11 mins. 57 secs.) and this was the first operational occasion that a Harrier received fuel in flight. Both teams subsequently acknowledged the contribution made by the RAF's Victor tankers and a fly-past was arranged to take place over the Wimborne factory in recognition of the part played by the Company. On the appointed day, employees duly lined up on the old railway bridge close by to await the flight, but there was some degree of disappointment when the Victor, accompanied by two Lightning fighters, did indeed fly past — but over Hamworthy Engineering some four miles away, and unfortunately was barely visible to the naked eye. Although Sir Alan's comments following this navigational miscalculation are not recorded, Michael Cobham recalls an amusing sequel to the story; the Royal Navy, seeing an opportunity to press home an advantage, telephoned him to enquire at precisely what time it would be convenient for the Senior Service to conduct a fly-past. At the appointed time, three Phantoms and two Sea Vixens flew over Wimborne. After three pin-point passes with one of the Phantoms 'hooked up' to a Sea Vixen, the two Sea Vixens flashed past the factory so low, it is said, that waves appeared on the River Stour!

Mention of the Harrier immediately brings to mind a name forever identified with jump-jet pioneering — that of Tom Brooke-Smith, who joined the FR organisation in 1969 and succeeded Leslie Castlemain as Public Relations Executive. Having learned to fly in the Thirties, 'Brookie' served throughout the war years with Short Brothers flight testing hundreds of aircraft as they left the production lines. He had a long and distinguished career as a test pilot and was the first man to take off vertically in a fixed-wing aircraft, translate to forward flight, and return to the hover configuration for a vertical landing. He achieved this on 6th April 1960 in the Short S.C.1. VTOL research aircraft. Known throughout the industry and media alike as a colourful, flamboyant and charming character, 'Brookie' and his maroon 3.5 litre Rover, which carried his personal number plate — 1 VTO — remained an institution at the Wimborne plant until his retirement in 1985, by which time he had been elected Master of the Worshipful Company

Tom Brooke-Smith who undertook the first vertical take-off in a fixed-wing aircraft.

of Air Pilots and Air Navigators, as had Sir Alan twenty years previously.

The Company was again associated with a jump-jet the year after the Transatlantic Air Race, when a Hawker P.1127 Kestrel (forerunner of the Harrier) was delivered to Tarrant Rushton. This aircraft, XP 980, was fitted with wings from a crashed Harrier, XV 751, and a modified Meteor U.Mk.16 drone control unit prior to undertaking various trials during the Seventies. In 1971, using deck arrester wires specially set up on the runway, the aircraft carried out 'wire trampling tests' for A and AEE, Boscombe Down. These tests enabled the optimum flight deck taxying speeds for the Harrier (with its unusual wing-tip-mounted stabilising wheels) to be determined. The aircraft was then fitted with a dummy refuelling probe and a structure which represented the front fuselage profile of a two-seat Harrier, prior to leaving for barrier-net trials at RAE Bedford. XP 980 later returned to Tarrant Rushton

for further trials to evaluate carbon fibre brake and anti-skid control systems for rival companies Goodyear and Dunlop.

In 1969, Sir Alan finally announced his retirement at the Annual General Meeting following his 75th birthday, and Michael Cobham then became both Chairman and Managing Director of the Company. For many years Sir Alan had owned property in the British Virgin Islands, and now he was able to spend as much time as his still busy life would allow, enjoying the balmy sub-tropical climate.

Although he remained a Director and was elected Life President, his close involvement with FRL's affairs naturally eased, but he maintained a passionate interest in aesthetic matters appertaining to the Company. The progress and well-being of the trees and rose-beds that he had so carefully chosen ten years previously, and the selection of bushes and plants for the factory grounds remained an abiding interest until his death on 21st October 1973 —

The Hawker P.1127, XP 980, carrying out braking trials on a flooded runway at Tarrant Rushton, 1971.

Hawker P.1127, XP 980, fitted with dummy refuelling probe and structure representing a two seat Harrier profile for barrier-net trials.

Tarrant Rushton's churchyard — final resting place for Sir Alan and Lady Cobham.

twelve years, almost to the day, after that of Lady Cobham.

Throughout his life, Sir Alan had always shown an uncompromising desire to beat the odds and thereby achieve his goals. An instinctive businessman with little in the way of formal training, he attributed much of his success to a generous helping of good fortune. Stubborn and quirky to some, generous and benevolent to others, he was a pioneering legend who generated feelings of intense loyalty in staff and colleagues at all levels. In return, he created a Company that has grown and matured to become the cornerstone of an international corporate organisation.

ELEVEN

Flying Colours

The new heat-seeking missiles undergoing development in the early Seventies required an aerial target that possessed a good infra-red signature. The Ministry considered that the Sea Vixen FAW2 aircraft then being withdrawn from naval service would meet the requirement, and decided to convert twenty-five to the pilotless target role. A first batch of eight duly arrived at Tarrant Rushton in 1972, and were stored and maintained by Ted Alsop's team in No.2 Hangar. However, it was not until 1974 that Michael Cobham, in his Chairman's Annual Report, finally announced that work had started on the conversion programme.

The contract called for the development of an airborne control unit which, by responding to commands transmitted from the ground, operated servo-motors attached to the main cockpit controls. Whereas the equipment used in the U.Mk.15 and

U.Mk.16 Meteors had been spread throughout the aircraft, Phil Bunn was now charged with the ambitious task of designing what became the 'Universal Drone Pack' (UDP), and although it was intended to develop the unit in the Sea Vixen, the contract also called for ease of installation in a variety of other aircraft. Three Sea Vixens, XN 657, XP 924 and XS 577, were modified to D.Mk.3 standard ('D' signifying Drone) and used in a joint flight test programme with RAE Farnborough which started in 1978. By this time, the Company's test flying was in the hands of Dave Ashover – an ex-Empire Test Pilot School instructor who had succeeded Dickie Dickinson upon his retirement – and Bruce Sheppard, recently arrived from Short Bros. The trials programme began at Tarrant Rushton and continued after the Airfield Division transferred to Hurn in 1980, but the Ministry cancelled

Sea Vixen D Mk.3 prototype at Hurn, 1983.

Canberra WV787 was used extensively for development trials. FRL installed the water-spray bar under the rear fuselage which enabled the aircraft to serve as an icing tanker.

further development work in the autumn of 1983 when it concluded that the Sea Vixen did not, after all, possess the afterburning characteristics necessary for missile trials work. The three Sea Vixen test aircraft were eventually delivered to Llanbedr, where XP 924 (still in flying condition) and XS 577 played valuable roles in developing the data link and autopilot equipment used today in the Jindivik Mk.4A pilotless target aircraft. (Jindivik is an Aboriginal word meaning 'hunted one'.)

Following the cancellation of the Sea Vixen development programme, the Ministry turned its attention to drone proposals vis-a-vis the Lightning, submitted by BAe, and the QF-100 Super Sabre recommended by FRL in conjunction with an American company, Flight Systems Incorporated. In the event, neither type was chosen and the Full Scale Drone Target Aircraft requirement simply faded away.

An aircraft that undertook a series of unusual roles was A and AEE's Canberra WV 787, a hybrid B.2/B(1)8, which first put in an appearance at Tarrant Rushton in the mid-Sixties, and was fitted with a retractable water spray boom under the fuselage for use in icing trials in conjunction with other aircraft at Boscombe Down. Later, special role equipment was mounted for highly classified work at the Chemical Research Establishment at Porton Down. The aircraft returned to Tarrant Rushton in December 1973 for major modifications to the spray boom, namely an increase in size and delivery performance, which were instrumental in evaluating Concorde's airframe and engine anti-icing systems. After a varied test development career, WV 787 was finally purchased by the Newark Air Museum in 1985. Phil Syms, recalls that

the icing tanker exercise was the first of many which he subsequently fronted as engineering project leader.

At a later date Syms became involved with the FR 500, a small turbojet-driven, remotely-piloted vehicle (RPV) proposed by the Company as a replacement for the Royal Navy's ageing 'Chukar' target aircraft. The Ministry decided however, that the small number of targets procured annually did not warrant the cost of developing such a replacement, and the project was dropped.

Disappointing as this was, the experience gained by FRL's designers and performance engineers provided a sound basis for a later submission which met the Army's Rapier missile training requirement. British Aerospace and Short Brothers had already bid unsuccessfully for this contract, and it reflected much credit on all concerned when FRL, with GEC Avionics as its main sub-contractor, competed for and won an initial development order worth £1.5m in 1979. Originally referred to as the Advanced Subsonic Aerial Target (ASAT), the winning proposal featured simply-designed wings which were interchangeable, and surfaces which avoided expensive compound curvature. Powered today by a Microturbo TJA-24 jet engine, the target has a maximum speed in excess of 400 knots. Using a 'carousel' style circular launching track, and mounted on a tethered dolly, the aircraft can take off under its own power regardless of wind direction. It was the first British jet aircraft to employ this highly cost-effective and versatile method of launch – a fact directly attributable to Dennis Lewis's keen powers of observation when he saw this kind of system in operation as he overflew the Dutch gunnery range at Den Helder. Using simple rocket boosters which give an extra two tons of thrust over a short burn period, the aircraft can also be 'zero-length' launched from confined spaces such as ships.

The Ministry eventually decided to replace the aircraft's functional title – ASAT – with 'Falcon', but this incurred the displeasure of another target aircraft builder, Mr. Noel Falconer, who had understandably already claimed the name for his own range of products. Syms then wryly proposed 'Falconet' – the name of a cannon used in medieval times – and as the Army considered it a most appropriate choice, official approval was given. 'Falconet' was the first aircraft to be designed, built and flown entirely by the Company, and Mel Porter led the trials team which carried out the early development work on the specially constructed 'carousel' launching track at

Phil Syms (left) discusses the 'Falconet' demonstration model with David Brown of Aviation Week, *1981.*

'Falconet' ready for launch from circular track.

Larkhill on Salisbury Plain. Porter recalls the initial consternation felt when it was realised that a hill, adjacent to the track, would obstruct a clear take-off. However, the somewhat unscheduled removal of vast quantities of earth eventually overcame the problem and the first 'Falconet' finally took off on 14th February 1982. Although the Larkhill range was conveniently close to Wimborne, its size proved restrictive as it only allowed launch and recovery procedures and the low speed end of the flight envelope to be explored during the eighteen-month test period. The Royal Artlery's operational training range in the Hebrides was also less than ideally situated for the continuance of the trials, for many test vehicles were inevitably lost in the sea, rendering fault analysis impossible, and frequently poor weather conditions and the problem of supporting trials teams away from home for long periods introduced many difficulties. However, Service operations eventually began in August 1986 under FRL's Target Service Manager Dougie Braid, and with a thousand successful launches to its credit in the ten years since its 'Hebridian Overture', 'Falconet' now appears on course to remain in service until the end of the century.

In 1975, Michael Cobham was informed by Sir Harry Broadhurst that he had been nominated as Vice-President of the SBAC. This took Cobham entirely by surprise, for this appointment, which traditionally led to the Presidency a year later, was normally offered only to the most senior people within the large corporations, such as British Aircraft Corporation, Hawker Siddeley Aviation etc. Now, however, it was not considered appropriate for the position to be filled by a representative from any company about to be nationalised, and, as Cobham further pointed out, with Shorts and Smiths having recently supplied Presidents, the number of SBAC Council members left to choose from had become somewhat limited! Becoming President of the SBAC in 1976 clearly carried with it a high level of personal prestige and the honour was undoubtedly one of the most important events in Michael Cobham's career; but it also attracted a workload which, added to his duties as Managing Director of FRL and Chairman of Flight Refuelling (Holdings) Limited, began to cause concern amongst his colleagues on the Board. It was suggested therefore that a deputy be appointed, and Ken Coates became Managing Director of FRL in October 1977. Coates made an immediate impact on the Company as an outspoken, forthright

Ken Coates, who became Managing Director of FRL in 1977.

Ray Harris who took charge at Tarrant Rushton following the death of 'Tiny' Thomas.

individual whose declared aim was to expand what he regarded as a 'local Dorset-based concern' into a truly international group. He started by restructuring the organisation into four separate major product Divisions — Aerospace Components, Military Systems, Nuclear and Industrial, and the Airfield — each having dedicated sales and engineering personnel concentrating on their own unique customer environment.

The airfield activities at Tarrant Rushton came in for a particularly searching examination when, during his first week in office, Coates discovered the high cost of providing support services for as few as two or three flights per week, and as the Company's tenancy would shortly be coming to an end, he made it clear that in order to justify a search for another permanent base, a great deal more work would have to be generated. It was during this period of re-evaluation, and following the death of 'Tiny' Thomas, that Ray Harris, newly appointed as Airfield Director, and Dennis Lewis intensified a campaign to promote the sale of target-towing and airfield management services.

A major target presentation role then being undertaken by No.7 Squadron's Canberras was for the Royal Navy's Weapons Training School at HMS *Cambridge* near Plymouth. The Navy, however, had expressed growing concern not only with the high costs involved, but also with the difficulties encountered in making an accurate, instant assessment of the gunners' performance — a problem largely attributable to the old-style RAF sleeve targets,

FRL's Beech Baron towing sleeve target for an Egyptian Ramadan Class patrol boat off Portsmouth.

which were highly unstable and lacked any kind of miss-distance-indication (MDI). Naval dissatisfaction became even more acute when No.7 Squadron's target-towing duties were taken over by No.100 Squadron at Wyton in 1982, resulting in even more expense when aircraft were detached to St. Mawgan to operate over HMS *Cambridge*. Consultation with staff at HMS *Cambridge*, resulted in Lewis suggesting to the Ministry that target presentation costs would be significantly reduced if FRL were to undertake the work using its own twin-engined aircraft equipped with a simple Swedish winch and sleeve target fitted with MDI. This introduced a pioneering principle, for it was the first time the concept of 'Contractor-owned, Contractor-operated'

aviation services had been proposed by any company, and following acceptance by the Ministry, it subsequently formed the basis of many successful working arrangements. The aircraft chosen for this purpose was a Beech Baron, G-AZXA, and it was also used for target-towing work already contracted by shipbuilders, Vosper Thorneycroft. The importance of this breakthrough cannot be overstated for the establishment of the 'Co-Co' principle led to the eventual purchase of the Falcon aircraft used today by FR Aviation Ltd. not only for target-towing but also for Electronic Warfare and Threat-Simulation training.

In addition to developing the Rushton target and low-level height-keeping targets fitted with

Bruce Sheppard (FRL's last Chief Test Pilot), Dennis Lewis and Dave Ashover in convivial mood.

radio altimeters, during the Seventies the Company equipped several Canberras for carrying the supersonic Short Stilleto (a British version of the American Beech AQM-37A air-launched target). Under the terms of a contract placed by the Italian Meteor Co. in 1978, trials were then carried out in Sardinia to evaluate the improved NATO Hawk missile.

It was largely due to this increase in work that the search continued for a new permanent base, and Michael Cobham recalls that at that time, Exeter

Airport, despite being over seventy miles from Wimborne, appeared to be the only option. However, good fortune prevailed and in 1980, and just in the nick of time, Plessey decided to withdraw its operations from Bournemouth's Hurn Airport, leaving the way clear for Harris's thirty-six strong team to take over Hangar 46 and a number of adjacent buildings.

Dave Ashover made the Company's final flight out of Tarrant Rushton in a Sea Vixen on 3rd September 1980, and it then fell to Ted Alsop to supervise the demolition of over three hundred unwanted buildings, thus bringing to an end a most eventful chapter in the Company's history.

Following the move to Hurn, organisational changes led to the Airfield Division becoming the Aircraft Operating Division, which made an immediate impact with a successful bid to undertake the Ministry of Agriculture and Fisheries protection flights within the inshore Fisheries Exclusion Zone. These patrols had previously formed part of standard missions carried out by RAF Nimrod aircraft, and, once more, the proposal to provide a much less expensive specialist service by the use of contractor-owned aircraft and crews carried the day. A Britten-Norman Turbo-Islander, was chosen as the most suitable aircraft for this kind of work, and sporting the highly appropriate civil registration G-MAFF (denoting the Ministry of Agriculture, Fisheries and Food), it began patrol flying in September 1982.

Farewell to Tarrant Rushton's Control Tower, 1981.

The new Division, in collaboration with Radio Corporation of America (RCA) Services Division, was also successful in winning contracts to operate two important Ministry-owned facilities. Subsequently, Ted Whitley headed the FRL team at the RAE's weapons testing range at West Freugh in southern Scotland, when contractor operations commenced on 11th July 1982, and Jock Mancais was appointed FRL's Manager when FRADU, based at Royal Naval Air Station Yeovilton, came under the Company's control on 1st December 1983. FR (Services) Ltd. was then set up as a special company for handling the out-station administration, and immediately formed a close relationship with RCA (later to become SERCO Ltd.) which exists to this day.

Over the years, the Company has extended its target activities to include land and sea-borne projects. In 1970 for example, it was invited to consider the manufacture of target boats for the Royal Navy, although at that time FRL did not envisage marine products forming part of its future business, and it was as a consequence of this that John Reid, keen to set up his own boat-building company, left FRL's employment in order to take up the contract. However, by 1977, he had become a victim of his own success and his resources were severely strained. He managed to persuade FRL to take over his company as a going concern, and to re-engage him as a Marine Project Consultant on Seaflash, which he had developed as a high-performance radio-controlled launch used for naval gunnery practice. The Company subsequently built forty boats – mainly for India and the Middle East.

By the onset of the Eighties, the Aerospace Components Division, under its General Manager, Graham Marriette, had also become closely associated with shipboard activities of a rather different nature, for not only was its ship-to-helicopter refuelling equipment already in use with the Royal Navy and also the navies of Norway, Argentina, Indonesia and Italy, but work was in hand to supply several other countries. However, the Division was facing the significant challenge of securing a share of the component supply for the McDonnell Douglas (McAir) AV-8B (Harrier II) jump-jet, then in the project design stage at St. Louis. This was intended to be a generally more powerful, and longer-range version of the Harrier GR3 which, as the AV-8A, had been produced for both the US Marines and the Spanish Navy. The move to build the aircraft in the US carried no guarantee that equipment supplied

Graham Marriette (right) with Tony Ashley at the Paris Aero Show, 1983.

previously by UK companies would be incorporated in the American version. However, McAir was working in close collaboration with the Harrier design team at BAe Kingston, and the fact that FRL's components were well established on the British aircraft, clearly helped it to find technical and commercial voices willing to endorse the Company's products and credentials. It was at this time that Michael Cobham, in his capacity as SBAC President, flew to St Louis, ostensibly to pay a courtesy call on his American counterpart and head of McAir, Sandford McDonnell, but the visit had equal importance in backing up the efforts of Sales Manager Tony Ashley, whose perseverance and pursuasiveness during the proposal negotiations, led to McAir writing the fuel system components specification based on FRL's equipment. This placed the Company in a strong competitive position which led to orders for many key components. Based on its experience of having produced the refuelling probe for the Lightning fighter, FRL had initially indicated its willingness to compete for the retractable probe unit proposed for the AV-8B. However, McAir's specification called for an electrically-driven, rack-and-pinion method of extending the probe, and as FRL's engineers were not convinced that this was a sound design approach, the Company declined to bid, but suggested an alternative method. This was an hydraulically-driven system using telescopic tubes similar in principle to the swing-wing fuel and air joints already being produced for Tornado, and it was this proposal that McAir finally accepted as being the more practical option. Design engineers

JP233 Airfield Attack Weapon Systems, mounted under the Tornado, were used in the Gulf War.

Derek Sheldrake and Ted Smith then spent two months in St. Louis developing the concept and producing a set of drawings for McAir's approval.

Activity in America grew even more when, in the same year, FRL was appointed UK agent for Shaw Aero Devices Inc., a component manufacturer based on Long Island. Having established this situation, the Company, as mentioned in the previous chapter, then showed its determination to penetrate further into the US aerospace market, by purchasing Stanley Aviation Corporation – a company well known to FRL and one which was regarded as an ideal springboard for launching its products into America. However, Michael Cobham well remembers the strong opposition encountered from a powerful group of Stanley shareholders before the President, Jerry Ryan, finally agreed to Cobham's offer of £5.2m in July 1981.

In 1979, ML Aviation Ltd. (MLA) received a contract from Hunting Engineering Ltd. to develop a multi-weapon dispenser for the JP233 Airfield Attack Weapon System. Intended primarily for use on the Tornado, JP233 was designed to eject simultaneously, at high speed and low level, two complementary types of sub-munitions – the SG357 cratering weapon, which renders an airfield's operating surfaces unusable, and the HB876 area-denial weapon which poses a continuing threat to vehicles and personnel attempting to carry out runway repairs.

Faced with such a large task, MLA's Chairman, Michael Mobbs, decided to seek out a partner who could offer first class manufacturing facilities but who would not wish to become a competitor in the weapons dispensing business. Aware that FRL could meet the requirement, he approached Michael Cobham, and their discussions soon revealed a potential business opportunity for FRL of major proportions. Various work-sharing arrangements were considered before it was finally decided that FRL should concentrate solely on the production of structural items. Production Director Ken Saltrick then placed the responsibility for getting manufacture underway with John Eyres, who in the early stages relied heavily on Geoff Millman and Bert Metcalfe for production planning advice and support. Newly-recruited Keith Younge later took over from Eyres as Project Manager, and by the end of 1983 the first of over two thousand sets of structural parts was delivered. This turned out to be the start of a highly successful ten-year programme, worth £45m, in which FRL supplied all the structural items ranging from small detail parts to large complex machined side beams for final assembly at MLA. This was also the first of three major fixed-price manufacturing sub-contracts undertaken by the Company which have to some degree overlapped to provide production continuity over an eleven year period. (FRL's later involvement in the Tornado drop tank and VC-10

John Eyres, who undertook the setting up of manufacturing facilities for JP233 at FRL.

tanker conversion programmes are more fully described in the next chapter).

Throughout the Seventies, it became evident that the RAF's fast jet aircraft were demanding fuel at delivery rates well beyond the capability of the Mk.20B pods fitted to the Victor, and FRL was not surprised therefore, when, in 1977, a contract was placed for the design and development of a refuelling unit that would embody the latest technology and deliver fuel at 350 g.p.m. – twice the rate of the existing pod. To meet this, Peter Macgregor, who was awarded a well deserved MBE for his services to aviation in 1963, adopted an entirely new design approach, discarding the Mk.20B's mixture of hydraulic and pneumatic systems, and utilising the fuel within the pod to control delivery to the receiver and also regulate hose movement. The introduction of this 'fueldraulic' control, digital electronics, and a new automatic steel spring stored-energy system (produced by Tensator Ltd.) for taking up hose-slack during contact with the receiver, provided a major breakthrough in the design of air-to-air refuelling equipment. Sadly, Macgregor died in November 1978, and failed to see his final concept come to fruition.

The new Mk.32-2800 pod, so numbered because of its ability to deliver 2800 lb. of fuel per minute (350 g.p.m.), was lighter, simpler and easier to maintain than the Mk.20 pod series and was intended for installation on the nine ex-civil VC-10 aircraft (five Standard and four Super versions) undergoing tanker conversion by BAe at Filton. The first flight trials took place at Boscombe Down in June 1980 when the prototype pod, installed in Sea Vixen XJ 580

transferred fuel to Phantom and Buccaneer receivers (see Footnote 1). Full clearance however, was not achieved until 1982, when, with FRL's Ron Henson, Graham Orchard and Steve Thomas in close attendance, pre-production pods were flown on VC-10, ZA 141. On 25th July 1983, the C-in-C, Strike Command, Air Chief Marshal Sir David Craig, accepted the first VC-10K Mk.2 at Filton, and following the ceremony, the aircraft, ZA 140, complete with Mk.32-2800 pods, departed for Brize Norton (see Footnote 2).

It had been originally intended to replace the Mk.20Bs installed on the Victors with the new pod, but a general moratorium on defence-spending introduced by the Ministry in 1982 prevented this and the older equipment remained with the Victor until the end of its flying days in October 1993.

Concurrent with the tanker conversion work at Filton, an event took place on 2nd April 1982, which suddenly brought the Company's equipment into sharp focus – Argentina invaded the Falkland Islands! Britain's military response was obviously highly dependent on maintaining its extended lines of communication and all air operations from the nearest forward base, Ascension Island, had to rely totally on air-to-air refuelling.

With the main Task Force sailing towards the South Atlantic, intense activity got under-way at RAF Waddington, to prepare Vulcan B.2s for long-range action, including the reactivating of fuel receiving systems that had not been used for fifteen years. The immediate task facing the station's engineering branch was the replacement of components that had deteriorated with age, and how to overcome chronic leaks attributable to dried-out coupling seals. More problems followed when, during the initial system-proving flights, contacts with the tanker resulted in fuel-drenched windscreens, but the aircraft were soon made serviceable once FRL's Dick Tanner and Dave Ashenden discovered that the probe nozzles had been reassembled incorrectly! At the same time, BAe at Woodford and Marshall of Cambridge embarked

Footnote 1: Sir David Craig later became Chief of the Air Staff and subsequently Chief of the Defence Staff during the Gulf War.

Footnote 2: XJ 580, which had helped to blow up the crippled tanker *Torrey Canyon* on the rocks off the Scilly Isles, is now on permanent display outside the old Airspeed-de Havilland factory at Christchurch, Dorset.

Above *The Mk.32-2800 pod shown fitted to the wing of a VC.10.*

Left *The Mk.17B HDU installation on the VC.10.*

A No.50 Squadron Vulcan 'stop-gap' tanker tops up a Buccaneer, 1982.

on a programme of installing Mk.17B HDUs into six Vulcans and six C-130 Hercules, achieving results within six weeks that would normally have taken many months of peace time effort. These conversions were carried out to ensure that once the Victor tanker force had left Marham for Ascension Island, the RAF, working alongside the USAF's KC-135s, could still meet its home-based NATO commitments.

In addition, the work programmes included fitting refuelling probes for the first time to the Hercules and (also at Woodford) Nimrod MR Mk.2 maritime reconnaissance aircraft. In this limited time-scale it was possible to install basic systems only, and in the case of the Nimrod, bowser hose was used to connect the refuelling probe to collector tanks in the rear fuselage which fed the main fuel system. The Nimrod's new refuelling probe also aggravated a directional control problem, which necessitated the attachment of 'finlets' to the tailplane to increase the vertical fin area. The problems encountered were many and varied, and the task was only completed when refuelling probes were 'donated' by the Vulcans not earmarked for the Falklands operation. These included aircraft already removed from service and, in one instance, located as far away as the USAF Museum at Dayton, Ohio!

During this eventful period, both Denis Preston and Pat Collier headed works teams heavily engaged on the assembly and test of the Company's in-flight refuelling equipment and system components

at Wimborne. (At ACE too, there was feverish activity to ensure an adequate supply of fuel filters for the Royal Navy's Task Force vessels.) Noteworthy also was the considerable technical support given by designers Dick Tanner (who later received the MBE) and Roy Young, both at Woodford and Cambridge and at Boscombe Down where Roger Kilford of A & AEE supervised the 'Operation Corporate' flight clearance trials. Although No. 50 Squadron's Vulcan tankers were not deployed for overseas duty, the Hercules tankers did provide a vital spares supply service, and remained in the Falklands when the Victors eventually returned to the UK. The RAF still operates a total of five Hercules tankers at Mount Pleasant in the Falklands, and with the Tanker Training Flight at Lyneham.

The Falklands War brought the Tanker Force very sharply into focus for the first time since its formation nearly a quarter of a century earlier, and the public at large became aware of its strategic importance due to the extensive media coverage of its role. A brief glance at the operational statistics reveals its enormous contribution to the war effort. During the ten-week period of hostilities, Nos. 55 and 57 Squadron's Victors flew some 3,000 hours in carrying out 600 refuelling sorties, and transferring more than 12 million pounds of fuel. However, not all the Victor efforts were devoted to tanker duties, for immediately after their arrival at Ascension Island on 18th April, several fourteen-hour maritime radar reconnaissance flights were carried out which

A Tanker Training Flight sortie from RAF Lyneham. Hercules refuels Hercules, with the suitably impressed author of this book on board the receiver.

High and Mighty! Victors of No.55 Squadron.

provided the RN Task Force Commander with vital intelligence about surface contacts, icebergs and pack ice. Each sortie required the support of four tankers outbound and the same number for the return journey. The radar reconnaissance capability of the Victor was retained throughout the campaign, but the arrival of the probe-equipped Nimrod, with its superior radar, later allowed the Victor to return to its primary tanker role. During this time, tanker operations were retained under the overall direction of Gp. Capt. Jeremy Price who had relinquished his duties as Station Commander at RAF Marham, Headquarters of Tanker Force, to become the Senior RAF Officer on Ascension Island.

Although all the tanking activities took place over vast stretches of ocean, particular reference must be made here to the support provided by Victors which enabled No.1 Squadron's single-seat Harrier GR3s, led by Wg. Cdr. Peter Squire, to cover the 4,000 miles between St. Mawgan, Cornwall, and Ascension Island in nine-hour, non-stop flights.

During the ferrying operation, the Victors not only provided the essential fuel, but, having been specially fitted with advanced equipment (Omega), they also served as navigational platforms for the Harriers. The Harrier pilots, flying parallel to the coast of Africa had the comforting knowledge that they could divert to dry land should trouble occur. This was not the case however, for the pilots of four replacement aircraft who were later called upon to fly direct from Ascension to the Task Force carriers. Two Harriers arrived after a remarkable nine-hour flight, supported by Victor tankers. Nimrods also provided airborne Search and Rescue (SAR) and ships along the route kept listening watch, with the Royal Fleet Auxiliary *Engadine* acting as an emergency landing platform half-way along the 4,000 mile track. However, there was no suitable mid-point landing facility when the other two Harriers undertook the same long journey shortly afterwards!

An event which generated large headlines during the Falklands air campaign was the bombing of the airfield at Port Stanley, on 1st May 1982. The raid, code-named 'Black Buck 1', was not only the first occasion on which a Vulcan dropped its load in anger (in this case twenty-one 1,000 lb. conventional HE bombs) but also the longest and furthest bombing mission ever carried out — a round trip of 7,800 miles. Whilst it was the Vulcan's feat which captured the world's attention, not so well known was the

Tuxford's team. Tuxford (left), Wallis, Rees, Beer and Keable. Ascension Island, May 1982.

Michael Cobham, with Wg. Cdr. Andy Vallance (third from right) and crew of No.55 Squadron Victor K.2 XM 715, at Marham 19th May 1983.

drama played out by two of the Victor tanker crews which made the attack possible.

Pre-flight planning showed that a formidable sequence of refuelling operations would be necessary with tankers refuelling tankers, as well as the Vulcan aircraft. Eleven Victors were involved in the outbound leg and five on the return, and they undertook a total of eighteen successful contacts, all at night, transferring some 500,000lb. of fuel. At a point 2,750 miles south of Ascension Island, Sqn. Ldr. Bob Tuxford and Flt. Lt. Steve Biglands, were piloting XL 189 and XH 669, the only two Victors remaining with Flt. Lt. Martin Withers's Vulcan XM 607. The plan then called for Tuxford to pass fuel to Biglands's aircraft thus enabling him to accompany Withers to within 300 miles of the target. Problems occurred however, when, in appallingly turbulent weather punctuated by searing flashes of lightning, the refuelling nozzle on Biglands's Victor snapped

off – fortunately falling clear of Tuxford's aircraft – whereupon the pilots agreed to exchange roles. Tuxford then successfully took on the extra fuel needed to fly with the Vulcan, and Biglands turned for home. After the final transfer of fuel to the Vulcan, it became obvious to Tuxford that he would not be able to make it back to Ascension Island unless a tanker could be scrambled to meet him. He also realised that he could not break radio silence to request assistance until after Withers had made his surprise attack. Tuxford's navigator, Sqn. Ldr. Ernie Wallis, told how, even when it became possible to send a transmission, their troubles were not over. In transferring roles, the aircraft call-signs had not been properly exchanged, with the result that both aircraft, now finally on the homeward run albeit many hundreds of miles apart, were calling base using the same identification – Biglands indicating no serious problems, and Tuxford an emergency fuel situation! Fortunately all ended well, Tuxford made a successful rendezvous with the tanker, and he and his crew were appropriately fêted on their safe return.

Hindsight suggests that the enormous efforts involved in the attack on Port Stanley had hardly been worthwhile, but the raid did indicate that targets in the Falklands and on the Argentinian mainland were within the RAF's striking range, and aircraft were retained to defend Buenos Aires which would otherwise have been deployed to attack the British Forces. A total of five 'Black Buck' bombing and anti-radar strikes were carried out. All required extensive refuelling support, and the last took place on 11th June 1982, just four days before the Argentinian surrender.

In addition to the awards and decorations received by individuals within Tanker Force, further recognition of the Victor's role in the South Atlantic came when three tankers led the victory fly past over the City of London on 12th October 1982, an occasion celebrated in proper style in the 'Sir Alan Cobham' bar, appropriately located in the Officer's Mess at Marham (see Footnote).

During more than thirty years in service, Victor tankers, in addition to supporting front-line operations, carried out many hundreds of training sorties. Virtually all involved familiar, well-rehearsed procedures and were undertaken without serious mishap. However, hidden dangers attend even routine flying activities, a fact well illustrated by the tragedy that befell a No. 57 Squadron aircraft on 24th March 1975, when two Honington-based Buccaneers, flying at 20,000 ft. above the North Sea and some 100 miles off the East Coast, were receiving fuel from a Victor K.1A, XH 618, piloted by Flt. Lt. Keith Handscombe. All went according to plan until the pilot of the second aircraft, having misjudged his approach, found himself in the downwash of the Victor's crescent-shaped wing. His aircraft rolled, one wing striking the tanker's tailplane. This soon broke away from the fin and the aircraft, now without longitudinal control, went into a 'bunt' and disappeared into thick grey cloud. Within moments, a vivid flash, followed by a pulsating orange glow within the cloud, indicated to the horrified Buccaneer pilots that the Victor had exploded. The high 'negative g' forces prevented the co-pilot and the three crew members in the rear cabin leaving the aircraft. Miraculously

Footnote: This highly popular amenity was officially opened by Michael Cobham on 10th May 1974.

Sqn. Ldr. Keith Handscombe, the only survivor of Victor K.1A XH 618.

Handscombe survived, and was rescued from mountainous seas whipped up by storm-force winds by the combined efforts of brave crewmen from a No. 202 Squadron Whirlwind helicopter and the German freighter *Hoheburg*. To this day Handscombe remains uncertain whether he genuinely ejected from his aircraft – or was blown out when it disintegrated!

Events such as those experienced by the Handscombe and Tuxford crews are fortunately rare, but their tales illustrate only too well the hazards which occasionally beset the men of Tanker Force.

Whilst paying this tribute to the Service, it is also appropriate to mention the official recognition given to the Company after the Falklands air campaign. Following a visit in May 1982 by Air Marshal Sir John Curtiss, Air Commander – South Atlantic Operations, the Prime Minister, the Rt. Hon. Margaret Thatcher, then extended a pre-planned series of engagements in Dorset to include a visit to FRL and travelled to Wimborne on 16th July, accompanied by her husband. Denis, and a strong security

The Prime Minister, the Rt. Hon. Margaret Thatcher, with Michael Cobham and Frank Behennah, 1982.

and media entourage. Michael Cobham, who had already been honoured with the CBE for his personal services to industry, escorted her on an hour long tour of the factory where she was met with spontaneous outbursts of applause from the shop-floor.

Highly appreciative of this welcome, Mrs. Thatcher, in turn, expressed her sincere appreciation of the Company's efforts and products – without which military success would not have been possible. Clearly in her view, and those of its employees, Flight Refuelling Ltd. had met its commitments with 'flying colours'.

TWELVE

A Challenging Profession

The early Eighties ushered in a period of great change. Many familiar long-serving employees now faced retirement, one of whom was Tom Marks who had joined FRL as a test pilot in 1945 eventually becoming Commercial Director in 1973. He left the Company in May 1981 after thirty-six years' service, but regrettably his life was cut short only a few months later. He was succeeded by Robin Clark, who, at thirty-five years old, became the youngest member of the Board.

Clark arrived at the beginning of a period of organisational restructuring, in which Divisional Managers Graham Marriette and Frank Behennah, along with Chief Accountant Brian Moore, also became directors. More changes were in store however, for in October 1983, Managing Director Ken Coates, and Financial Director Nigel McCorkell, jointly tendered their resignations. At the time the shock announcement caught everyone off guard but with hindsight it was the inevitable result of strong disagreements concerning the running of the

Company. Coates maintained that his policy of 'divisionalisation' had revitalised the workforce citing the ten-fold increase in turnover achieved during six years in office as proof of his success, but not everyone agreed with his future plans to amalgamate newly-acquired companies such as Stanley Aviation Corporation and the Midlands-based Hymatic Engineering Company into FRL's organisational structure. Michael Cobham and other Directors strongly believed that firms such as these, providing they remained well run, should retain their independence within the FR Group, (Flight Refuelling (Holdings) Ltd. was re-named as FR Group plc in 1985). Following Coates's departure, Michael Cobham, still continuing as Chairman, took on the added role of 'caretaker' Managing Director, a situation that continued for the next eighteen months.

Attempts to recruit from outside the Company proved unsatisfactory and in due course Production Director Ken Saltrick was invited to take up the

Right *Technical Director, Frank Behennah, with the (then) Vice Chief of the Air Staff, Air Marshal Sir Peter Harding.*

Below *Robin Clark takes over from Tom Marks as Commercial Director, May 1981.*

Brian Moore, who joined the FRL Board as Financial Director in 1983.

Ken Saltrick, OBE, became FRL's Managing Director in 1986.

Gordon Page, who initially succeeded Ken Saltrick as FRL's Managing Director.

challenge, which he did on 1st January 1986 – the day it was announced that he had been awarded the OBE in the New Year's Honours List. His appointment was well received throughout the Company, and heralded a new sense of direction after what had been a disquieting time in the Company's affairs. When he retired in 1989, Saltrick was able to claim, with strong justification, that amongst other achievements, he had established one of the finest manufacturing centres in the country and, with Frank Behennah and John Medgett, had been fundamentally responsible for the introduction of Computer Aided Design and Manufacture (CAD-CAM) into the Company.

Gordon Page, former Commercial Director of Rolls-Royce's Military Engine Group at Bristol, was then appointed Managing Director, later becoming Chief Executive of the FR Group when Michael Cobham relinquished the post in 1992. His successor as Managing Director of FRL was Robin Clark who, having been at the forefront during a highly transitional period within both the Company and the aerospace industry, saw the ability to change in line with market trends as crucial to the Company's future. But FRL has long been familiar with change and challenge, as is shown in the following review of work undertaken within the Eighties.

The Falklands conflict had highlighted the RAF's need for a greater strategic airlift capability, and this led the MoD to purchase six ex-British Airways L1011-500 Tristar airliners, and a further three from Pan-American, for conversion into tanker-transport aircraft by Marshall of Cambridge.

FRL's designers, confident that the well proven Mk.17B HDU would be specified for the converted aircraft, were therefore shaken to discover that Marshall were already giving serious consideration to the installation of American refuelling equipment. Urgent discussions revealed that based on erroneous assumptions, Marshall had prematurely concluded that little could be done to install FRL's unit inside the confined space allocated on the Tristar. With Company pride and profits clearly at stake, it was quickly proved that by re-locating certain components, a satisfactory installation was possible and initial flight testing of what was now referred to as the Mk.17T HDU, was carried out in a Hercules. Two Mk.17Ts were then installed side-by-side thus providing improved system reliability in what became the standard Tristar installation. This was the first time an HDU had been installed in a wide-

A Lockheed Tristar equipped with Mk.17T HDU fuels a Tornado F3.

bodied aircraft, and the unique turbulence patterns created behind the aircraft introduced drogue instability problems not experienced before on the Hercules, Victor or VC.10 tankers. However, after exhaustive investigations, modifications were introduced which then enabled the aircraft to enter service with No.216 Squadron at Brize Norton in March 1986.

Although in the early Eighties, the Company re-entered the US market through its involvement in the AV-8B programme, an unsolicited attempt to displace the Sargent Fletcher Company, the incumbent American supplier of refuelling pods to the US Navy, was not so successful. This bid was submitted in association with Grumman, a renowned naval aircraft manufacturer based on Long Island, and offered the Mk.35-2 pod, which was essentially a re-packaged variant of the Mk.32-2800 fitted on the VC-10. Naval interest resulted in an official request for more formal proposals in 1982, but despite close technical co-operation with Grumman, the Company was unable to make a breakthrough.

In 1986 however, and with valuable assistance from the Defence Export Sales Organisation (DESO), another intensive sales campaign got underway when a strong Company team, including Ken Saltrick and Robin Clark, accompanied a No. 101 Squadron VC-10 tanker on a tour of selected

locations in North America and Canada, where this elegant aircraft already serving as a fully proven tanker with the RAF, was successfully demonstrated to McDonnell Douglas in St. Louis and Los Angeles, the USAF at Andrews AFB in Washington, and to representatives of the Canadian Armed Forces in Ottawa. In all cases it made a considerable impression on the decision makers.

The following year on 9th April, another VC-10, flown by No.101 Squadron's Commanding Officer, Wg. Cdr. J. Uprichard, this time with Michael Cobham on board, departed from Brize Norton and arrived in Perth 15 hours and 53 minutes later. This non-stop flight, which included refuelling from Tristar tankers based in Cyprus and Sri-Lanka, easily eclipsed the previous record set on 8th July 1963, when three No.101 Squadron Vulcans flew from Waddington to Perth in just over 18 hours. Cobham recalls that whilst their arrival in Australia had not invited the ecstatic welcome experienced by Sir Alan sixty years previously, it had aroused a great deal of local interest through the Australian media. The VC-10 then went on to give highly successful demonstrations, firstly in conjunction with the RAAF's F-18s, and then in New Zealand, where, coincidentally, the RNZAF was commemorating the fiftieth anniversary of its founding.

Following on the heels of the successful airborne

Phil Syms, who led FRL's engineering team on the Mk.32B pod programme.

exercises, the sales and engineering teams at FRL had to work very hard with the aircraft manufacturers, and the influential representatives of the various air forces who had the final say in the choice of specialist equipment. However, the efforts of all concerned finally paid off when the Company won a contract from McDonnell Douglas to supply sixty 'ship-sets' of wing pods and mounting pylons for the USAF's KC-10 tanker fleet. Throughout the contract negotiations, the Company laid great stress on the

fact that 'risk to programme' would be minimised wherever possible by the incorporation of existing Mk.32-2800 pod technology – an aim underlined by the retention of 'Mk.32' in the new variant designation, Mk.32B. However, it soon became evident that in order to meet the the demanding specification requirements, significant system and structural changes would have to be introduced. Both Phil Syms, who undertook the conceptual design, and Keith Younge, who was appointed the Programme Manager, later praised in particular the efforts of the electronics team which, within the remarkably short time available, developed a microprocessor-driven, digital control system which allowed the critical requirements to be met.

The first deliveries of what then became a 'new generation' mainstay product took place only fifteen months after receipt of 'go-ahead' instructions, and initial flight tests were conducted between October 1988 and May 1989. These showed that, as in the case of the Tristar, unexpectedly high turbulence levels were present, and aerodynamic modifications to the pods were needed to overcome excessive hose movement. Whilst this was the kind of problem typically encountered and cured during a flight test programme, a more fundamental criticism raised by the US Navy receiver pilots came as a most unwelcome surprise. They regarded the separation distance between the tanker and receiver aircraft as unacceptable, and refused to continue the trials, whereupon McDonnell Douglas eventually instructed the Company to extend the hose length from 50 ft. to 75 ft. It was August 1991 before flight tests were

A USAF KC-10 Extender fitted with original short-hose Mk.32B pods. Note the limited clearance between the tanker's tailplane and S-3 Viking receiver's wing.

A Royal Australian Air Force Boeing 707 'two-point' tanker refuels an F/A-18 Hornet off the southern coast of Victoria, 1990.

A Boeing C-135FR tanker displays its new Mk.32B pods for the camera.

A Canadian Forces CC-130T supplies a thirsty Hornet.

successfully resumed and as a result of this and other, largely political, 'stop-go' situations, the production pod delivery programme for the KC-10 now extends well beyond that originally envisaged. Across the Pacific, the Royal Australian Air Force, clearly influenced by McDonnell Douglas' choice of FRL as its new supplier, opted to instal the 'short hose' variant of the Mk.32B pod on four Boeing 707s, then about to undergo conversion to the tanker role by Israeli Aircraft Industries (IAI). Although the Company's equipment is also fitted on Boeing 707s flying in Peru and Columbia, it was the decision to fit the Mk.32B pod to the French Air Force's eleven C-135FR tankers that led to a significant re-association with Boeing. Robin Clark, mindful of the USAF's long stated intention to convert its own fleet of boom-equipped KC-135s to three-point tankers, pointed out at the first C-135FR hand-over ceremony in Wichita in December 1993 that, although there had been an unfortunate gap of some forty years since the B29s visited Tarrant Rushton, FRL was now back with Boeing, and intended to stay!

In addition to supplying equipment to McDonnell Douglas and Boeing, FRL now has a working arrangement with the Lockheed Aeronautical Systems Company, based in Georgia. Fitment of Mk.32B pods on the C-130H, the aircraft used more extensively than any other throughout the world, now gives it even more versatility by enabling it to function as a quick change multi-role tanker transport; five aircraft in this configuration, designated CC-130T, were supplied to and are currently operating with the Canadian Armed Forces.

As the Eighties progressed, Marshall and FRL jointly submitted feasibility studies to the Ministry for fitting wing-mounted pods (either Mk.32-2800 or Mk.32B) to the Tristar, but the proposals were rejected in favour of expanding the existing VC.10 tanker fleet, and in order to retain commonality of equipment, it was also decided to continue using the Mk.32-2800 standard pod. Accordingly, two separate Air Staff Requirements (ASRs) were then issued. ASR415 called for the complete refurbishment and conversion to three-point tankers of five ex-commercial passenger aircraft that had lain dormant at RAF Abingdon for many years. After conversion they were to be re-designated, VC-10 KMK4s. AR416 called for eight VC-10 C.Mk.1 aircraft – already flying as troop carriers with No.10 Squadron – to be fitted out as dual-role transport and two-point tankers, and to undergo a complete avionics upgrading. This variant became the VC-10 C.Mk.1(K).

The project clearly called for a blend of resources unlikely to be found within a single company, prompting Robin Clark and Dr. Maurice Dixson, then BAe's Managing Director of Commercial Aircraft at Hatfield, to agree to the submission of a combined BAe-FRL proposal. This logical pairing of companies which were the Design Authorities for the aircraft and the refuelling equipment, undoubtedly influenced the award of a contract in January 1990.

FRL, as principal subcontractor then formed a dedicated management team under Phil Syms, with Adrian Jackson appointed Programme and Design Manager, and Geoff Millman becoming responsible for all aspects of manufacturing. The Ministry later extended the number of aircraft scheduled for conversion to C.Mk.1(K) standard to thirteen, and the Wimborne factory was eventually required to undertake a manufacturing programme of major proportions which, including HDU's, pods and structural parts, amounted to some 77,000 separate items. At Hurn, FR Aviation was also tasked to carry out all the 'on aircraft' work, along with some avionic installation design for the two-point tankers, and at Filton, BAe undertook to transform the five aircraft flown in from Abingdon into three-point tankers. The conversion programme, due to be completed when the thirteenth C.Mk.1(K) aircraft is delivered from Hurn in February 1996, has been the most recent of three highly successful collaborative manufacturing ventures undertaken by FRL within the past decade.

The first of these as already described was the JP.233 project, which fortunately gained momentum at a time when the Company's nuclear work began to decline. The second, which also commenced in the early Eighties, resulted from an enquiry made by the MoD at the 1982 SBAC Exhibition. Entering a new field of manufacture, FRL successfully competed for the production of a large number of 2250 litre fuel

The 2250 litre drop tanks fitted on the Tornado's inner-wing pylons are shown to advantage in this imposing study.

The Falcon 20 took over the duties previously performed by FRADU's Canberra T.22s.

drop tanks for carriage on the Tornado. A teaming arrangement was then made with Lear Siegler Inc., an experienced tank manufacturer based in California, in which they agreed to supply technical information and special purpose machinery to Wimborne. Although the design and airworthiness qualification testing of the tank were carried out at Lear Siegler, the contract for almost 3000 tanks resulted in a dedicated production facility being set up at Wimborne, and, with monthly output averaging between 40 and 60 (peaking to over 100), supply continued for some 10 years. The nature of this project led to a gradual integration of the Nuclear and Industrial Divisions' engineering staff with that of the Military Systems Division during the mid-Eighties.

Of all the changes which affected the Company none was more far reaching than that which took place at Hurn following the transfer from Tarrant Rushton. As already noted, the Aircraft Operating Division was going from strength to strength and by 1982, was seeking an aircraft suitable for carrying out Threat Simulation Exercises with the Royal Navy. Dennis Lewis and Dave Ashover investigated several contenders such as the BAe125, Gates Learjet and the Cessna Citation, but in the end the French Dassault Falcon 20 was chosen, as, in addition to its excellent performance it offered the crucial advantage of having a military aircraft wing structure with pylon hard points, and it was the only contender with sufficient cabin volume to accommodate FRL's special role equipment.

The original intention was for the Ministry to purchase and the Company to operate the aircraft, but it rapidly became clear that problems would arise with the servicing and provisioning of spares for an aircraft type not then on the Ministry's inventory and a 'Co-Co' arrangement again proved to be the answer. Having located a fleet of aircraft which possessed a common modification standard, a 'purchasing panel' which included Robin Clark, Brian Moore, Dennis Lewis and newly-arrived FR Group Financial Director, Giles Irwin, completed the acquisition of seven aircraft from US based Federal Express.

At that time it was not possible for aircraft on the British civil register to be used for para-military purposes, so the Falcons were retained on the American register, but operated in the UK under a special long-standing agreement set up between the FAA and CAA. Frank Behennah, then FRL's Technical Director, recalls that these aircraft had been extensively modified to provide large access hatches in the side of the fuselage. The work had been carried out in the US under the supervision of an FAA-designated engineering representative, but the relevant design documentation in its original form was not acceptable to the British airworthiness authorities and it was only after further modifications were undertaken and confirmatory analysis provided by Dassault that Flight Clearance certificates were issued. Eventually, however, the Falcons took over the general ground support duties and Threat Simulation exercises previously performed by the FRADU's Canberra T.22s at Yeovilton, and a further three ex-Federal Express Falcons were purchased when the Threat Simulation work was extended to include Electronic Warfare.

Michael Cobham then took the view that the pace and nature of the changes at Hurn called for an independent company, and following the MoD's acceptance of the new organisation, it was a relatively short step to the formal creation, in January 1985, of FR Aviation Ltd. – a brand new company the prime function of which was to be the operation of aircraft and the provision of specialist aviation services. Michael Cobham placed the responsiblity for running the company into the capable hands of Colin Jones, following his return from the Far East where he had risen to become Chief Executive of the Hong Kong Aircraft Engineering Company, and incidentally, a Director of Cathay Pacific Airlines. The unfolding story of Jones's success and achievements, coupled with the extensive activities subsequently undertaken by his company, constitute a story that must be left to later pages.

A visit to China as part of an SBAC sponsored trade mission in 1979 made Michael Cobham very much aware of the enormous sales potential for western products which existed in the Far East, and the following year, the FRL's sales team attending the British Aviation Equipment Exhibition in Shanghai were similarly impressed by the intense interest shown in the Company's equipment. A follow-up visit to Wimborne by a delegation from the Chinese Flight Research Institute eventually led to the purchase of the Low-Level Height-Keeper target system, which by then, and following the loss of HMS *Sheffield* and HMS *Glamorgan* after Exocet attacks in the Falklands, was well established as the Royal Navy's sea-skimming missile threat simulator. At this time, the Chinese were also keen to develop an aerial refuelling capability, and requested the Company to prepare schemes which would convert the H.6 (Tupolev TU.16) into a tanker, and the F5 (MiG 17) into a receiver. So, by 1986, with the prospect of securing the sale of aerial refuelling systems looking particularly bright, Robin Clark, Peter Turner, Tony Ashley and Derek Sheldrake duly departed for China to discuss the Company's proposals and a deal was successfully concluded in Wimborne a short time afterwards. A major problem arose however, when

export licence approval was refused by the Co-ordinating Committee for East-West Trading Policy (COCOM) – a body consisting of members representing NATO countries and Japan. The Japanese raised an objection, backed, it was thought, by a US concerned about the increased projection of air power that aerial refuelling would afford China. Sir Geoffrey Howe, then Foreign Secretary, represented British interests in exchanges which subsequently took place at the highest level, but all to no avail, and the opportunity to enter this vast trading arena foundered on the rock of political pressure.

In the preceding chapter, a brief outline was traced of the Company's entry into the remotely-piloted-vehicle market with the introduction of 'Falconet' and the resultant partnership with GEC Avionics. This relationship was continued when, in 1980, the two companies agreed to enter a joint proposal for an unmanned target acquisition system ('Phoenix'), for the British Army. The requirement, which now called for a fixed-wing vehicle, had arisen in the wake of a programme in which Westlands had produced a succession of rotary-winged RPVs that had proved unsuitable for their intended role. Michael Cobham suggested that on this occasion, with FRL offering to produce the air vehicle and the launch and recovery modules, and GEC retaining responsibility for the surveillance package, ground links and flight controls, that GEC should become the prime contractor. This was the first time the two companies' roles had been reversed, and the agreement reached between Michael Cobham and GEC's Jack Pateman, was then endorsed at senior level by Sir Robert Telford.

FRL's Peter Turner, then Head of Performance, became the Company's Project Manager, and an 'A' model demonstrator was produced which, although not intended to meet full specification requirements, proved that it was possible for an unusual airframe configuration to fly in a conventional manner. A 'fly-off' demonstration between the two remaining competitors, GEC-FRL and Ferranti-Slingsby, in August 1984, eventually led to the award of a production contract to GEC-FRL the following year. Phil Syms, appointed Chief Designer Military Systems, and Roy Trim, Head of Performance, set to work immediately to turn the demonstration design into a 'B' model production variant, capable of meeting the speed, payload and endurance targets. Numerous technical delays were encountered however, which were further exacerbated by the

The Phoenix unmanned air vehicle is shown complete with launcher, ground control, and recovery equipment.

The Phoenix air vehicle and launcher are produced by FRL.

severe restrictions imposed by the limited size and availability of the Larkhill test range; it also proved far from easy to retain a clear sight of the original design objectives when constrained to working within the strict financial limits set by the fixed-price contract, but, in spite of all, design targets were eventually met, successful system acceptance trials completed and, in 1993 the 'go-ahead' was finally given for production to begin. 'Phoenix has a proven endurance of 4 hrs. and a radius of action of over 50 km. at altitudes up to 9,000 ft., and is expected to start a twenty-year service life with the British Army in 1995.

Although 'Phoenix' is also generating interest with other prospective customers from overseas, the Company cannot yet claim the same success for 'Raven' — a less sophisticated RPV which offers a low cost ground surveillance system. Hopes ran high for its adoption by the US Forces when a system was purchased for evaluation in 1990, but these were dashed when 'Raven' was unable to meet a late requirement imposed by the Joint Project Office, (JPO) that all close and short range surveillance systems had to use a common ground station. 1994 however, has seen new enquiries raised by the Defense Evaluation Support Agency, and following the recent dissolution of the JPO, it is hoped these indicate a renewal of American interest.

When Iraq invaded Kuwait in August 1990 signalling the start of the Gulf War, the Cabinet immediately announced its intention of deploying British Forces to the war zone (Operation Granby) and within twelve hours the first VC-10 tankers from No.101 Squadron had left the UK, and No.55 Squadron's Victors were instantly recalled from a Reconnaissance Air Meet in Texas to assist the movement of fast jets to the Gulf. Two Victors later led the first Tornado GR1s, equipped with JP.233, into Iraq, flying along the Olive Trail which ran south of the Iraq border before turning onto a short northerly leg, at which point the receivers were cast off into enemy territory. The Victor detachment flew 300 missions in support of attack aircraft and air defence patrols over the forty-two day war period, and did not fail to complete a single task or sortie. For many years the tanker squadron exercises had included inter-operational training with the allied air forces, and the refuelling sorties undertaken during the Gulf War, were greatly assisted by the US Navy's aircraft which employed the probe and drogue system. An impressive list of thirsty aircraft that 'hooked up' at some stage during 'Granby', in addition to the RAF's Tornados, Buccaneers, Jaguars, Hercules and Nimrods, included U.S. Navy and Marine Corps A-7 Corsairs, AV-8Bs, EA-6B Prowlers, F-14 Tomcats, F-18 Hornets and S-3A Vikings, as well as French Mirage 2000s, Saudi and Italian Tornados and Canadian CF-18 Hornets. The subsequent proud claim of the VC.10 Victor and Tristar tanker crews that "anything fitted with a probe was refuelled by the RAF", appears to have been well founded – and was a fine reflection on the personnel and equipment involved!

This level of aerial refuelling capability, obviated the need for an immediate tanker conversion as had occurred at the start of the Falklands war. However, the MoD did raise an urgent request on the Company for structural and system modifications to be made to the RAF's No.7 Squadron Chinook heavy-lift helicopters, prior to the installation of long-range fuel tanks for use in the Gulf. Each aircraft was later provided with three, 800-US gallon tanks, which not only greatly extended its own range, but also enabled it to provide a Forward Area Refuelling System (FARS), capable of ground refuelling two other helicopters simultaneously. Service Engineer Phil Francis, assisted by Inspector 'Daisy' Adams and

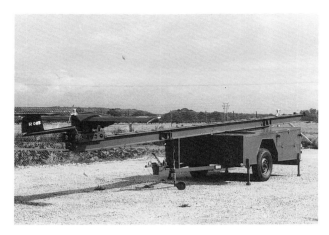

FRL's Raven provides a low cost ground surveillance capability.

Opposite page   No.7 Squadron's Chinook helicopters, shown here in normal guise, were equippped with special long-range tanks for Gulf War operations.

Fitter Supervisor Ken Foster, ultimately converted a total of 33 aircraft – initially at RAF Odiham, and subsequently at King Fiesal International Airport in Saudi-Arabia. (At a later stage they also carried out similar modifications to Chinooks in the Falklands.) It was with some surprise that each member of the team found that he had been awarded the Gulf Medal – and, for good measure, the Liberation Medals from both Saudi-Arabia and Kuwait! Francis is adamant that he deserved his for the severe airsickness he experienced in a Hercules when flying low to avoid possible missile attack!

Critical rush orders were also placed on FRL by the Ammunition Division of Royal Ordnance for Challenger Armament ammunition containers. Acutely aware that the supply of special tank ammunition depended upon containers being delivered on time, the Company formed a project team under Roy Poulter, Production Manager of the Containers Division. All containers were delivered either on or ahead of schedule, and Poulter's determination and dedication were recognised with the award of the B.E.M. Other Group companies also made significant contributions to the war effort, and in the special case of FR Aviation, the Threat Simulation and Electronic warfare training services which it provides for the Royal Navy were required both for the work-up of naval vessels whilst en route to the Gulf, and for training purposes in the war zone itself. These efforts once again demonstrated that in times of national emergency a capable, flexible and fully

responsive defence industry is vitally important, and that the industrial base is in fact an integral part of the UK's overall defence capability.

Within this scenario, FRL continues to strengthen its position as a leading contractor, and with the recent acquisition of High Temperature Engineers Ltd., now merged with the Aerospace Components team to form FR-HiTemp Division, under Director Richard Annett, it has now become the industry's main supplier of fuel and hot air pneumatic systems and components and also composite fibre components. Within its current military work programme the Division is providing equipment for the European Fighter Aircraft and the Challenger 2 Medium Battle Tank. On the civil side a total fuel system hardware and technical integration package is being supplied for the Indonesian NPTN N.250 airliner.

As the foregoing narrative has shown, FRL's success has been based on many diverse skills and products, and it is perhaps ironic that in parallel with producing 'state-of-the-art' equipment, 1994 has also seen a new lease of life for the Mk.20 series of pods originally produced in the Sixties. Not only are enquiries in hand regarding the supply of restored Mk.20B pods for installation on Canberras operating in South America, but a contract has now been awarded for the conversion of a number of ex-Victor pods for use on the RAF's Tornado GR.1. Designated the Mk.20H, the new variant, due to be delivered in 1996, will incorporate an enlarged 275 gallon fuel tank which, attached under the fuselage, will enable the Tornado to serve in the 'buddy-buddy' role recently vacated by the Buccaneer.

Pausing for a moment in this sixtieth year, all within the Company can reflect with satisfaction that Sir Alan's original wish for FRL to become the world leader in the design and supply of aerial refuelling systems has been well fulfilled — especially in view of the Company's recent take-over of its American counterpart and erstwhile rival, Sargent Fletcher. Serious negotiations aimed at purchasing this competitor began in February 1994 and soon led to intense discussions with the Committee for Foreign Investment in the US (CFIUS), a body strongly concerned with safeguarding American business interests subjected to overseas control. Although it was felt that the Company could confidently claim to be injecting technology into the US rather than extracting it, Robin Clark was mindful of the official resistance to foreign-owned

Richard Annett, Director of FR-HiTemp Division.

subsidiary companies engaged in defence contracts that had led to Sir Alan's disassociation with FR Inc. so many years previously. Fortunately Clark's concern was later shown to be unfounded, for assisted by supporting documentation from major aerospace manufacturers McDonnel Douglas and Lockheed, the merger eventually received full governmental approval.

As described in an earlier chapter, it was only by selling the rights to manufacture probe and drogue equipment to the US government that the Company managed to survive in the early Fifties. It was evident at the time that this was a high price to pay, and so it proved, when, with the rights subsequently assigned to Douglas and Sargent Fletcher, they became the suppliers of aerial refuelling equipment to the US Navy. Now however, with the new alliance with Sargent Fletcher successfully achieved, Robin Clark was able to report to his Chairman that 'the family silver had, at long last, been returned to its rightful home'!

Within a changing industry it has been suggested, that the name Flight Refuelling Ltd. implies an over-concentration on a single product area and its

Sir Alan and Michael Cobham pictured together at the SBAC Exhibition, 1972.

continued use has been the subject of some debate in recent times, but, as many colleagues world-wide have pointed out, 'everyone knows Flight Refuelling', and the adoption of a different image would be self-defeating. It is, above all, Cobhams' Company, and, standing proudly within the newly announced Cobham plc, it serves as a unique tribute to a father and son who have brought widely differing talents and made highly individual marks in a 'most challenging profession'.

THIRTEEN

Afterthoughts

This journey through the Company's history has in the main, encompassed its people, politics and products, but in bringing Part One to a close, a brief outline is given of the social ingredients which have played such an important part in its development. In earlier 'pre-television' days, more entertainment was sought outside the home, and close-knit families invariably produced one member at least who could exhibit a moderate degree of musical or theatrical skill. Sir Alan and Lady Cobham always considered it their duty to encourage and harness the talents latent within the workforce. Her show-business background meant that Lady Cobham was naturally suited for this task, and she became the 'driving force' behind many 'Company productions'. Although events had taken place at Ford and Malvern, it was during the first ten years at Tarrant Rushton, after Hugh Johnson and Company Secretary S. J. Pochin officially formed a Sports and Social Club on the communal site in January 1949, that the Company's involvement in social affairs undoubtedly reached its peak. Mary Lewis, then Assistant Secretary, vividly recalls that the Clubhouse resembled an aircrew mess during the time of the Berlin Airlift, but later assumed an international flavour with successive waves of American and Continental visitors enjoying its facilities. However, the Club was provided primarily for use by employees and their families, with separate sections catering for drama and music, and most sports, including flying.

The supply of local housing gradually improved throughout the Fifties, and as families moved away from the airfield, the Club fell into disuse. Sporting activities were then transferred to Merley, and this proved to be an advantage when FRL's staff eventually moved to Wimborne. In 1970, a group of employees approached the Company's management for its support in re-activating the Social Club, and, on 4th September 1971, a new Clubhouse was duly opened by Sir Alan. To describe the building as 'new' is perhaps a little inaccurate. At that time the

Sir Alan formally declares the new Sports and Social Club at Merley to be well and truly open, 4th September 1971.

local authorities could only approve extensions to buildings already on site, which resulted in a wartime Nissen Hut, used throughout the Sixties as a cricket pavilion, being converted into a skittle alley and other rooms gradually being grafted onto it. Despite progressive modifications the Nissen Hut still remains embedded in the Clubhouse used today, and could well achieve the distinction of becoming the longest surviving relic of W.W.II!

Although assisted financially by the Company, the Sports and Social Club owes its success to the many members who devoted considerable time and effort to creating and, initially, managing the facilities — particularly the nine-hole par 3 golf course, planned by ex-professional golfer and then Head of Works Police, Harry Hunt.

Childrens Day, organised each year by the Company's General Services, is an event that always

Childrens Day highlight. Mrs Michael Cobham exercises a firm hand during the 'cake cutting' ceremony, 1983.

Club Chairman David Cutler, receives a word of appreciation and a £5000 cheque from Michael Cobham to launch the new Sports and Social Club.

Sheila Scott, who received Sir Alan's patronage for her record flight around the world.

provides enormous pleasure for young and old alike. The first occasion, however, when a number of youngsters were taken to Bristol Zoo, was not without its problems, for the parents of one child picked up their offspring and left without informing the officials. The resulting panic over the child's disappearance, convinced all concerned that future events should be held on 'home ground'. Until the mid-Sixties, these took place on the airfield, and since then each summer has seen an army of employees' children descending on the playing field at Merley, where, with all the fun of the fair freely provided, Mrs. Michael Cobham conducts the annual ritual of 'cutting the cake'.

Two names – Dave Cutler and Mick Tanner – immediately spring to mind when social activities at FRL are discussed, and it would be hard to recall an entertainment event within the past twenty years in which they were not actively involved. Their joint organising skills were most evident at the Dinner Dances held annually since 1984 at Bournemouth's Pavilion ballroom, and at which Mr. and Mrs. Cobham presented awards to the Company's long-serving employees.

Whilst looking inwards towards its employees and their welfare, the Company heads, Sir Alan and Michael Cobham, have ensured that strong local philanthropic links have been forged and maintained. Sir Alan's patronage of the Bournemouth Symphony Orchestra throughout the post-war period until his

FRL's Managing Director, Robin Clark.

death is well documented. Perhaps less well known was the backing he gave to aviatrix Sheila Scott, when she encountered serious financial difficulties following her record-breaking round-the-world flight in 1966. Her plight had brought to mind his gratitude to Sir Charles Wakefield, and others, for the

support they gave him during his own early endeavours.

The Company has continued to sponsor worthwhile 'aviation causes' ever since, especially when youngsters on the threshold of their careers are involved. An example of this was the formal adoption in October 1978 of the local ATC squadron, thus allowing it to become No. 1069 (Flight Refuelling Wimborne) Squadron — and one of only three in the U.K. entitled to incorporate a company in its title.

Although Michael Cobham finds his primary relaxation in sailing, his extramural activities do include several associated with aviation. He is Honorary Life Vice-President of The Air League, a Trustee of the Fleet Air Arm Museum at Yeovilton, and President of the Christchurch Branch of the Royal Aeronautical Society — and it is most fitting that in the centenary of his father's birth, he has agreed to deliver the Christchurch Branch's prestigious Sir Alan Cobham Lecture to a distinguished audience.

It is appropriate to end this section with the words used by FRL's Managing Director, Robin Clark, when asked for his first impression of the Company. He said that it immediately struck him as 'a happy Company, whose history you could touch'. There cannot be many who would disagree!

PART TWO

FOURTEEN

A Force for the Future

In recognition of the Diamond Jubilee year, the main body of this book has been devoted to Sir Alan Cobham's early endeavours and the evolution of Flight Refuelling Limited. But no history of his founding Company would be complete without more detailed reference to the other operating companies which have in later years come together to now form Cobham plc.

This chapter therefore, charts the arrival and general progress of these companies, and provides an insight into the accompanying corporate expansion. In certain cases, particularly Alan Cobham Engineering and FR Aviation Ltd., the circumstances which led to their formation are inseparably linked to FRL's own story and have already been touched upon in the earlier chapters. The reader's indulgence is therefore requested when some repetition has been unavoidable in order to re-set the scene.

The formation of Flight Refuelling (Holdings) Ltd. followed directly upon the Cobham family's purchase, in 1954, of the publicly quoted Manitoba and North West Land Corporation. This then led to a two-tier arrangement in which FRL became Flight Refuelling (Holdings) Ltd's only asset, but for many years it was the Board of the subsidiary company, not the holding company, that effectively ran the business. However, this was merely a technicality as the membership of both Boards was identical. This situation existed comfortably until 1960 when Sir Alan decided to set up Alan Cobham Engineering to develop industrial versions of certain fuel system products then being produced by FRL. ACE's small but enthusiastic team, led by Eddie Knowelden, was then able to establish its own development priorities, and soon attained a reputation for reliable equipment and excellent customer service in a variety of industrial markets. The business continued to grow

and prosper when, in 1967, Arthur Watts took over from Knowelden as General Manager (later becoming a Director), and at the same time, 'Tiny' Thomas became the Managing Director.

Soon after its formation ACE became independent, and took on the responsibility for newly-acquired Broom Filters, which produced a range of vessels and filter elements which not only separated contaminants, but also coalesced the water out of aviation fuels. Before long the production of these units became the largest part of ACE's business, and was undertaken at Tarrant Rushton, although ACE's administration and design staff were by now occupying Eagle House, an attractive Georgian house in Blandford Forum, together with a number of buildings in the garden which became the company's workshops. By the end of the Seventies, with the closure of the airfield imminent and under increasing local pressure to move this industrial activity away from the centre of the historic market town, it became a matter of some urgency that new premises be found. Accordingly, when John Farnhill succeeded 'Tiny' Thomas as Managing Director, his first task was to locate a site and arrange for the construction of a new factory covering some 40,000 sq. ft. This was eventually carried out at nearby Blandford Heights, and work was completed in 1980.

At this time the company was supplying its products to all three Services, and in particular to the Royal Navy where 'Cobham' filters performed the vital task of coalescing the water from the Dieso fuel used in the ships' gas turbines. The Falklands War placed an unprecedented demand on ACE for these filters, and the effort made by the company's staff was such that after the conflict ended, the Controller of the Navy – Admiral Sir Lindsay Bryson – visited the factory to express official appreciation for an

Peter Hebard succeeded John Farnhill as Managing Director of Alan Cobham Engineering Ltd.

Giles Irwin joined Flight Refuelling (Holdings) Ltd as Financial Director in 1983.

outstanding performance. However, difficult waters lay ahead as many of its traditional products were supplied to the coal mining industry, and the miner's strike and subsequent contraction of the industry, severely affected sales of equipment. At the same time the market for military filters became ever more competitive and the situation was not helped by the moratorium imposed on defence spending in 1983. Faced with these adverse factors, the company turned its specialist skills in filtration and fluid handling to an entirely new application – the provision of complete ground fuelling systems for use in the 'hardened' shelters designed to protect aircraft from nuclear attack, then being constructed at RAF Leeming.

Complete fuel handling systems were also supplied for two Royal Fleet Auxiliaries during this period, together with a variety of test rigs to companies in the aerospace and oil industries. Peter Hebard eventually succeeded John Farnhill as Managing Director in 1990, and with an executive team that included Financial Director John Annis, and Sales and Marketing Director Ian Marcham, he set about concentrating the company's resources towards expanding the core business of fluid handling. Under the new management team, ACE was called upon to support the British Forces in the Gulf War, and, in 1991, its fine achievements were recognised with the well deserved award of a BEM to Production Controller, Alan Riggs.

Today, with its products in extensive use in the UK, Continental Europe and the Middle East, ACE is now well placed to establish a leading reputation for handling aviation and other fuels on the ground, that mirrors that of FRL for supplying high quality equipment for use in the air.

The acquisition of the Aviation Division of the Saunders Valve Co. in 1968, had no impact on Flight Refuelling (Holdings) Ltd.'s relationship with its two principal company assets, as it was not long before the Saunders Division was integrated into FRL's fuel system components business. This situation remained unchanged until the take over of Stanley Aviation in 1981, and Hymatic Engineering in 1983, dictated the need for an identifiable group structure, which was provided by Michael Cobham becoming Chairman and Chief Executive, with the three Managing Directors and the President of Stanley reporting directly to him. This small but effective headquarter's organisation was further strengthened in December 1983, when Giles Irwin became Financial Director of Flight Refuelling (Holdings) plc, and, with Mike Angel co-ordinating the insurance and pension schemes of the various companies, and the redoubtable Tom Brooke-Smith undertaking all public relations and exhibition activities, a strong cohesive team began to emerge. However, it was Michael Cobham's firm policy to delegate as much authority and responsibility as possible to the operating companies – each of which retained its own Board – and to keep the number of head-quarter's staff to the absolute minimum. A key feature of this structure was that Cobham became Chairman, and Irwin a Director of each of the companies – an arrangement which enabled both of them to monitor closely the performance and become actively involved with the management and major policy decision-making of those companies.

Although the Finance Directors of all four companies reported to their respective Managing Directors, they each had, in addition, a 'dotted line' reporting responsibility to Irwin in his capacity as Group Financial Director. Consolidation of the various companies' financial results became, under his direction, the responsibility of a Group Financial Controller, initially Peter Richardson before he became Financial Director of FR Aviation when it was formed in 1985. Also, although each operating company maintained its own current account, Flight Refuelling (Holdings) Ltd. carried out the treasury function and thus was responsible for major cash holdings and other investments. It was also a principle tenet of 'group' policy that the operating companies should retain their own identities and individuality, for it was Michael Cobham's firmly held belief that such an approach not only motivated the individual company management teams, but also generated loyalty and enthusiasm in the work-force at large.

Today, Cobham is convinced that the success of what, in 1985, became FR Group plc, and in 1994, Cobham plc, has in no small measure been due to the adoption and continued implementation of this policy.

As previously mentioned, the acquisition of Stanley Aviation was undertaken to provide an entry into the US market for FRL's range of aerospace components, but this company had for many years served as an American counterpart to Martin-Baker, specialising in the design and manufacture of ejection seats and crew escape systems.

Originally founded by Robert M. Stanley in 1948, the business began with the development of highly sensitive airborne seismometers for use in monitoring Russian atomic bomb tests, but it was not long before a contract was won to develop a standard downward-firing ejection seat and over an eleven year period some 2,800 seats of this type were produced for Boeing B-47 and B-52 bombers, as well as many other types of ejection seats for American combat aircraft. As aircraft speeds increased, the Corporation designed and produced highly sophisti-cated and exotic methods of crew escape, including the 'Bobsled Seat' which rotated backwards as it left the aircraft, so that it 'flew' with the streamlined bottom of the seat facing forward. There followed, in the late Sixties, a five year programme which produced an encapsulated aircrew escape system for the B-58 Hustler bomber – a venture successfully completed with the ejection at Mach 2 of a live bear (which, remarkably, survived without injury)!

This was followed by the 'YANKEE' escape sys-tem, a method which involved a man being pulled out of the cockpit by a rocket, rather than being pushed out in the more conventional manner, and which was instrumental in saving over eighty lives during the Vietnam war.

In 1964, the Stanley Corporation secured an 80 per cent controlling interest in the Gamah Corpora-tion, then based in Santa Monica, and five years later the remaining 20 per cent was purchased, allowing Gamah to become a wholly-owned subsidiary Divi-sion of Stanley. (The licensed production of Gamah couplings by FRL during this period has already been described in Part One).

At the start of the Seventies, although Stanley was still engaged in the production of 'YANKEE' escape systems for the Grumman EA-6B ECM aircraft, ex-cessive Navy demands resulted in the programme slipping hopelessly behind schedule, and running well over budget. This provoked the latest in what had been a series of confrontations with the Navy, and Stanley now found itself facing a battle over the Navy's intention to develop its own rocket escape system. However, although it appeared that Stan-ley's patent rights were being violated, a legal deci-sion was handed down in 1977 which mitigated against the Corporation. A further blow was suffered in July the same year with the death of Robert Stanley in an air crash. Jerome L. Ryan, his right-hand man since the firm was founded then be-came President, and the Corporation entered a re-grouping phase aimed at restoring the losses they had suffered due to excessive investment in the research and development of the 'YANKEE' system for helicopters and other aircraft. To this end, Stanley entered a ten-year agreement with Stencel Aero Engineering Corporation to manufacture and sell the systems under licence.

Ken Greene, President and Chief Executive of Stanley Aviation.

The Corporation also continued to manufacture escape systems until May 1988, when its Directors considered that it no longer had the expertise to compete in this market, and its interests in the 'YANKEE' system were sold to UPCO. Prior to this however, in June 1981, Stanley had become the first American company to join the Flight Refuelling (Holdings) Ltd. group, and in so doing became associated with a new and extended component product range. The Corporation also established a repair and stock facility for FRL products in the US, but this did not prove to be cost effective and was sold to Airborne Hydraulics in 1988. Along with its involvement with metal fabrication and metal seal coupling production, Stanley, under its President and Chief Executive Ken Greene, is now entering the field of aircraft ground support equipment manufacture, and to capture the market for the rapidly growing Pacific Rim area has set up a subsidiary company in Thailand.

The Hymatic Engineering Co. Ltd. (HECL) was formed in 1937 as an integral part of the Chloride Electrical Storage Group, specifically to produce a Swiss-designed compressor, as Chloride foresaw pneumatic systems soon challenging the established use of electrical systems for starting aero engines.

Joseph (later Sir Joseph) Hunt, who first headed-up the company, enjoyed telling the story about the five Hymatic employees who, soon after the formation of the company, visited the Air Ministry to negotiate contracts for the supply of compressors for the Spitfire. What the Ministry officials did not realise was that those five people constituted the total staff of the company at that time! The compressor was subsequently fitted to every Rolls-Royce Merlin engine produced, and the number required during the Second World War was so great that manufacture of the unit had to be subcontracted to other organisations throughout the country during the war years. In fact, Hymatic still supports the product to this day, albeit in very small numbers.

Following the end of hostilities in 1945, and particularly with the advent of the gas turbine engine, the immediate post-war years were difficult for the company. Progressively however, it applied its expertise to the design, development and manufacture of a range of fluid control components for aircraft fuel, cabin pressurisation and pneumatic systems, and by the mid-Fifties Hymatic was supplying components for practically every aircraft type then being produced in the UK.

In an attempt to become less dependent upon the aerospace business, there were several ventures in the 1950s into non-aerospace markets; one of the most successful of these was the development of the 'Hydrovane' compressor, which in 1969 became the core of another autonomous and very successful Chloride company – Hydrovane Limited.

The creation of Hydrovane as a separate company left a void which Hymatic attempted to fill by taking a licence from a US company to manufacture valves used in the petro-chemical industry. This proved to be a challenging project as it rapidly became apparent that the market-place for these products was vastly different from that to which Hymatic had previously been accustomed.

In 1971, in a continuing search for new products, Hymatic purchased the 'V'-clamp business of H.K.Porter, initially merely as a small additional product line, but, in the event, the business grew strongly, and in 1977 became Hymatic Clamps International Ltd.

There were many companies in the Chloride Group which, like Hymatic, and indeed Hydrovane, had no connection whatsoever with the battery business, and in 1972 Chloride took the decision to divest itself of its non-battery interests. In Hymatic's case, a management 'buy out' was arranged by a consortium consisting of the then current management team together with Sir Joseph Hunt, and two outside entrepreneurs, Peter Epstein and Rolf Schild, who had recently sold their business interests to E.M.I. and were looking for a new investment opportunity. Shortly thereafter, the consortium also acquired the Huntleigh Group, a small publicly quoted company, with a number of subsidiary operating companies. Thus Hymatic once again became part, albeit on this occasion, by far the largest part, of a public limited company.

Since as far back as 1958 the company had worked in the field of cryogenics when, under contract to the MoD, it developed its first cryogenic 'mini cooler'. That particular product was used in the 'Red Top' missile, but while production quantities were initially large they had reduced significantly by the early Sixties. Nevertheless the development of this product took the company into a new and, what proved to be a growing area of technology, namely that of infra-red detection. It soon became apparent that the development of this cryogenic technology gave rise to requirements for specialist valves, regulators and pressure vessels, together with a need for expertise in the production and handling of pure air — skills which Hymatic had certainly acquired over the years. The continued development of these products and the associated technology, despite the fact that, for many years, there were few production requirements of any substance, took considerable courage. Great credit is due to Derrick Higgs, who succeeded Sir Joseph Hunt as Managing Director in 1965, for his foresight and enthusiasm in continuing to pursue this policy, for it was not until the early Seventies that the true potential of these products became apparent. By 1978 however, substantial orders had been received, including those for the AIM9L 'Sidewinder' missile produced for the European market, and for new applications of the technology in the field of infra-red surveillance and night-vision equipment.

By the end of the Seventies the company had grown dramatically, and the premises it had occupied since 1937 cheek by jowl with the Chloride factory in Redditch, were rapidly becoming inadequate. The old buildings, which hardly projected a modern image, were a major obstacle to administrative and manufacturing efficiency, and in 1980, the decision was taken to relocate to its present purpose-built facility on what was then a new industrial development just outside Redditch. It was a big decision at the time, but one which was essential if the company was to grow.

In 1982 the management team met to discuss and formulate a future policy for the company, and reached the conclusion that the aerospace industry would inevitably have to rationalise into larger groups and that Hymatic would need to join such a group. Possible partners were discussed and a list compiled. By this time, incidentally, the business areas in which the Huntleigh Group operated were extremely diverse and there was little commonality of interests between Hymatic and other Huntleigh Group companies.

By 1983, Flight Refuelling (Holdings) Ltd., having in 1981 acquired Stanley Aviation Corporation, was looking for another acquisition — preferably in the UK — and when the Board learned that there was a possibility of acquiring Hymatic, it lost no time in pursuing the opportunity. The plan which was ultimately adopted was for Flight Refuelling (Holdings) Ltd. to acquire the share capital of Huntleigh on the basis of one Flight Refuelling share for one Huntleigh share, (which valued the business at some £29m) and then immediately to sell to Rolf Schild and his associates, for a consideration of £2m cash, all the companies in the Huntleigh Group other than Hymatic and Hymatic Clamps International.

The purchase of Hymatic was a major step as it was twice as large as any previous acquisition, and Hymatic itself was almost a third of the size of the rest of the Group. At the time Hymatic was headed-up by Brian Longbottom, who had succeeded Derrick Higgs as Managing Director in 1977, and he now became a Director of what had recently become the FR Group plc. Under his leadership the company continued to grow and prosper, and it came as a tremendous shock when in 1989 he died after a sudden heart attack. However, by 1988, several major contracts associated with cryogenic cooling and infra-red detection equipment were reaching completion, whilst at the same time forecasts were indicating a reduction in sales of the traditional Hymatic products. In these circumstances it was evident that Hymatic needed an additional product line if significant reductions in turnover and profitability were to be avoided. Fortuitously, early in 1990 the opportunity arose to acquire from British Aerospace (BAe) its 'Environmental Control Systems' (ECS) business, which appeared to be, and

Brian Longbottom, who joined the Flight Refuelling (Holdings) Ltd Board.

Alan Jan-Janin, Managing Director of Hymatic.

was, a natural outlet for Hymatic's expertise. Moving the ECS activities from two BAe sites to Redditch without inflicting severe damage to the business in the process, proved a complex and demanding task. That the operation was carried out so successfully was in great measure due to the efforts of Bob Twine, Director of Manufacturing, and members of

his staff, a number of whom actually moved into and set themselves up on the BAe sites. It is interesting to note that notwithstanding the detailed investigations relating to current sales and forecasts of potential business which had taken place in the course of the acquisition, the Hymatic team failed to detect, and was subsequently very surprised by, the size of the repair and overhaul activity associated with the ECS business. This activity has since become a significant, and organisationally separate, part of the company's operations.

Today, under Managing Director Alan Jan-Janin, Hymatic designs, develops and manufactures high technology systems, sub-systems and components in four main product areas. The first is environmental control systems both for aircrew and for sophisticated avionics; the second is cryogenic cooling systems associated primarily with infra-red detection devices, thirdly, lightweight high pressure stored gas systems, and finally, pneumatic and hydraulic valves for civil and military aircraft.

The unique circumstances which led to the formation of FR Aviation Ltd constitute an integral part of the 'FRL story' and as such have already been recalled in some detail in the earlier chapters. However, following the pioneering efforts of Ray Harris and Dennis Lewis to secure target-towing work under the all important 'Co-Co' arrangement with the Ministry, uncertainty existed regarding the best way to exploit and administer FRL's flying activities. As described earlier, after the transfer of FRL's Airfield Division from Tarrant Rushton to Hurn, it became the Aircraft Operating Division, and when the contract to operate in partnership with RCA at West Freugh was secured, FR (Services) was set up in 1982. However, it was Michael Cobham's decision to create an entirely separate company, FR Aviation Ltd, for the express purpose of providing contractorised flying services for the UK MoD, and he well recalls the strong feelings expressed by several members of the FRL Board when they told him that the 'severance' of this part of FRL's business would make them Directors of a smaller company!

It had become evident nevertheless that aircraft operations would not exist comfortably inside an organisation concerned predominantly with manufacturing, and with Colin Jones appointed Managing Director, FRA began an independent

Colin Jones OBE has spearheaded FR Aviation's spectacular success.

existence in January 1985.

Subsequently it has built upon uninterrupted success to become the fastest growing company within Cobham plc. The core of FRA's current business is the operation of twenty-two Falcon 20 aircraft which are mainly employed in providing an air defence training service for the Royal Navy. This operation, involving upwards of 13,000 flying hours per year, requires the Falcon fleet to work closely alongside FRADU's Hunters and Hawks, which, based at Yeovilton, are flown and maintained by FRA personnel under the terms of a Government-owned/Contractor-operated (GO-CO) arrangement. The Falcons are equipped to provide electronic warfare and threat simulation training, and they also supply a range of target-towing services that includes the Rushton low-level height-keeping target which emulates sea-skimming missiles.

This air defence training service has earned itself an enviable reputation for its professional standards, and its high levels of availability and flexibility; the latter quality being well demonstrated in the deployment of crews and aircraft to the Gulf in the run-up to Operation Desert Storm. Some 500 sorties were flown during the provision of valuable training for the Royal Navy's ships, and every aspect of target-towing, electronic warfare and threat simulation, including that posed by Exocet and Silkworm missiles, was exercised to the evident and expressed satisfaction of all – except of course the Iraqis! It was this excellent company performance that led to Colin Jones receiving the OBE from the Queen on 5th November 1991.

The employment of commercially-operated aircraft in military roles also brings into play the airworthiness authorities normally involved in regulating the civil sector of aviation. Their functions vary from country to country, but each is normally concerned with the certification of aircraft, the licencing of crews and the supervision of flying operations. No special mission aircraft, or any other, in point of fact, can fly without approval of the airframe, equipment, and any modifications necessary for the tasks to be carried out. The scrutiny is extremely thorough, and is based on the same precepts which apply to aircraft engaged in the carriage of fare-paying passengers. The training of aircrew and the procedures to which they operate also attract the same degree of vigilance, as does the aircraft maintenance and the financial viability of the operating company before it is awarded its Air Operator's Certificate. It is within this stringent framework that the company owns and operates 28 aircraft, and operates or maintains a further 114 aircraft of various types, owned by the MoD at a number of different airfields. Following the recent award of a contract to provide electronic warfare training for the RAF, a dedicated facility is now under construction at Teeside International Airport which, together with the Hurn base, will support the nine Falcon aircraft required to generate the 4,000 flying hours per year demanded by this new and important task. Over the years, the company has entered into joint ventures with overseas companies, and now teamed with Aviation Defence Service in France, and Aeroflight GmbH in Germany, provides air defence training for the French and German armed forces. FRA has consistently demonstrated that contractor-operated services are an efficient way of achieving lower operating costs without sacrificing availability or quality of service.

In the early Eighties the need for Economic Zone Surveillance took on greater importance. At that time, RAF Nimrods carried out 'shared' missions providing a degree of UK offshore surveillance for the Ministry of Agriculture, Fisheries and Food, but once again this proved to be a costly approach to a task that could be performed satisfactorily by a much less sophisticated aircraft. It is now a matter of history that the airborne element of the surveillance task, on behalf of the UK MAFF, is now performed by FRA, the company having been re-awarded this contract for the second time against stiff competition.

A special mission aircraft also undertakes surveillance duty on behalf of HM Customs and Excise, and over 4500 hours per year are flown on these two tasks in aircraft purchased, modified, certified and maintained by the company.

As part of its astonishing growth, extensive engineering design and workshop facilities have been established at FRA's Hurn base, but perhaps the most immediately visible addition is the hangar (129,480 cubic metres) which was built specifically to accommodate the RAF's VC10 C Mk.1s as they undergo tanker conversion. The construction of this impressive hangar was a huge undertaking in itself, and its successful completion in 1991 remains a fitting tribute to Ted Alsop who served as the company's project consultant until his final retirement in 1993 after forty-five years' service.

The Electronic Warfare engineering section has recently taken the lead in several research and development projects for the MoD, and in similar fashion, the Aerial Target section regularly conducts design, modification and flight clearance activities which are at the forefront of technology and task performance.

This then is FRA – and Michael Cobham makes no secret of the great personal satisfaction he derives from the success of a team which now numbers 1200, some 500 of whom are based at Hurn. A far cry indeed from the handful of people inherited by Colin Jones only ten short years or so previously, and a complete vindication of Cobham's controversial decision to 'split the promising offspring from its parent'!

———

In the USA, John Goodell and George Ord combined forces in 1957 and formed the Carleton Aviation Company to produce jet fuel igniters and pressure regulators for a range of military aircraft. This company later became Carleton Controls Corporation and achieved distinction not only as NASA's prime supplier of oxygen breathing regulators for the Mercury astronauts, but also as a manufacturer of pneumatic components for a wide variety of aerospace and defence applications. Since then, Carleton has been involved in every US manned space mission as a main supplier of environmental control and life support equipment. In 1977 Carleton Controls Corporation was acquired by Moog Incorporated, and operated as a wholly owned subsidiary until 1982, when it was integrated into the parent company, becoming the Carleton Group of Moog Inc. In the mid-Eighties, when Hymatic was seeking a licensee in the US for its cryogenic product line, one of the potential licensees was Carleton and following an impressive presentation, a licensing arrangement was reached. In October 1986, FR Group made overtures to Moog with regard to purchasing Carleton, but these were rejected until the following year when negotiations were re-opened.

Upon announcement of the sale, Carleton employees expressed considerable concern, especially when it was realised that control was passing into foreign hands. However, at the invitation of John Burgess, then in charge of the plant, Michael Cobham toured Carleton's plants in New York and Florida addressing employees and meeting as many as possible. The visit was highly successful, and with fears allayed, a smooth transfer of ownership took place on 10th August 1987 which allowed Carleton Technologies to become a main operating company within the FR Group, with John Burgess as its President.

One of the conditions of sale was that Carleton would vacate the premises it occupied in the Moog plant within two years, and work began immediately on a 93,000 square feet facility at Orchard Park, New York, which was formally opened on 8th August 1989. In 1993, in order to offset an overall decline in defence work, Carleton bought the assets of the Life Support Division of ARO, itself part of the Ingersoll-Rand organisation. The US operations of ARO have since been merged into Carleton's Orchard Park facility and a new Canadian subsidiary, Carleton Life Support Ltd. has now taken over responsibility for ARO's business in Canada.

In Tampa, Florida, Carleton produces special components for the US Navy's surface ships and submarines, but the main product line centres on closed circuit rebreathing diving equipment. The absence of air bubbles and extended diving time are key features of this equipment, which crucially enhances the effectiveness and range of Special Forces underwater operations.

John Burgess, President of Carleton Technologies.

Geoffrey Cooper, Managing Director of the Chelton organisation.

A common thread that runs through Carleton's impressive list of products is that of Life Support, and the company can proudly claim to be a leading supplier of such equipment for use in extreme environments, ranging from outer space to the depths of the oceans.

The most recent addition to the FR Group (as it then was) is Chelton, which started life in 1947 as the brainchild of three ex-RAF colleagues. As they all lived within the boundaries of CHELsea and KensingTON, the name of the company was somewhat naturally born. At this time their only product was a static wick which had been shown by the US Air Force during WWII to be capable of eliminating 'static noise' from aircraft radio transmissions. Chelton (Electrostatics) Ltd. was then set up to market an improved version called the 'Drywick Silent Discharger'. Essentially this consisted of cotton strands impregnated with a silver nitrate solution, and was produced in quantity until the late Sixties, initially, in Chelsea and, from 1949 onwards, at Marlow, which to this day remains the home of Chelton's headquarters.

By this time, the company was also developing and supplying High Frequency (HF) and Automatic Direction Finder (ADF) antennas to the UK aircraft industry. Also during the Sixties the use of plastic materials led to the creation of, firstly Chelton Mouldings Ltd. (which has long since ceased trading) and later, Chelton (Forming) Ltd. which specialised in the metal coating of plastics. Chelton (Forming) Ltd. remained independent until 1988 when it was purchased by the present Chelton group and is now absorbed within Cobham Composites, itself a company managed within the Chelton organisation. During the late Sixties and throughout the Seventies, Chelton expanded its range of aircraft aerials and became a major exporting company under Managing Director Charles Cooper, and his son Geoffrey who became Marketing Director in 1972. In 1983, the company was the subject of a management buy-out which allowed Geoffrey Cooper then to become Chairman and Managing Director.

During the Eighties, the company strengthened its market position by purchasing a competing product line from Shaw Aero Devices, and in addition to the production of antennas, (the new internationally accepted term for aerials) and static dischargers (the new term for wicks) it entered the electronic market,

Cobham plc's Chairman Michael Cobham (right) and Depty Chairman Air Chief Marshal Sir Michael Knight.

making airborne homing devices and emergency radios.

Michael Cobham had long been aware of Chelton and its capabilities, and in 1988 he and Geoffrey Cooper met with a view to FR Group acquiring the firm (which at that time was wholly owned by the management buy-out company Linborn Ltd.). Chelton did indeed become part of the FR Group the following year, and since that time its growth has been spectacular with income and turnover tripling over the five-year period. However, the greatest growth in recent years has taken place in the US, where, following the establishment of Dallas based Chelton Inc. in 1983, antennas are now supplied to virtually every major aircraft constructor.

Chelton has now become more actively involved in aircraft electronic and avionic systems, and, in 1991, acquired Northern Airborne Technology, a well established Canadian manufacturer of helicopter communication systems and radios. It has further enhanced its capability in the field of microwave systems, by taking over, in 1993, Complas Ltd., a company concerned with the design and production of high performance missile and aircraft radomes.

This, together with the assumption of control of Cobham Composites Ltd. in the same year, has completed Chelton's reinstatement as an advanced plastics technology leader.

The latest recruit to the Chelton organisation is Rayan SA, a French manufacturer providing all the communication and navigation antennas for the Airbus family of airliners. This acquisition convinces Chelton that it has truly attained the status of being the world's primary supplier of this specialist range of equipment, covering the entire spectrum of military and civil aircraft. The company regards today's success as a sound platform from which to seize tomorrow's opportunities in satellite-based global communication systems.

Of all the companies actively engaged in aviation during the inter-war period, only a handful of famous names remain — Short Brothers (now Canadian owned), Dowty, Martin-Baker, Slingsby, Marshall of Cambridge and Cobham's Flight Refuelling Ltd. All the others, at one time so instantly recognisable, have now either long since ceased trading or fallen victim to take-over by the conglomerates which now dominate the aerospace scene. Set against this, the fact that the Group's identity, both as Flight Refuelling (Holdings) plc and FR Group plc has not only remained intact, but has positively flourished over the intervening years, is clearly a most remarkable achievement. However, in order to represent more accurately the diverse range of highly-respected specialist companies now residing within the Group, the Directors have decided to adopt a more generic title, less closely associated with a single company and product. Accordingly 'Cobham plc' has been chosen as an appropriate and compelling title, suggesting as it does, reassuring continuity of management and control, and of course an unbroken association with the practical world of aviation.

As the turn of the century approaches, the group companies, under Chairman Michael Cobham and newly appointed Deputy Chairman Air Chief Marshal Sir Michael Knight, are now confidently poised to exploit their skills under a name that second to none, symbolises the very best in British industry — 'Cobham plc' — a true force for the future!

Appendices

APPENDIX I

THE 'LOOPED HOSE' METHOD OF REFUELLING

Sequence of operations for 'Ejector' or 'Looped Hose' method of refuelling in flight.

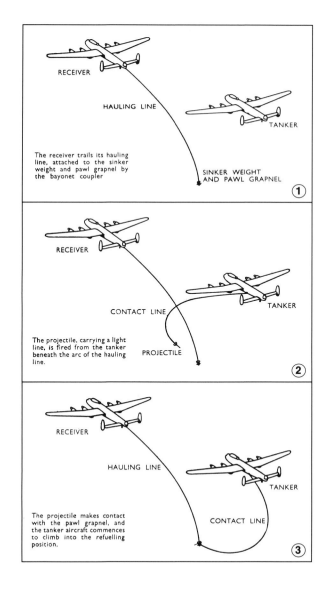

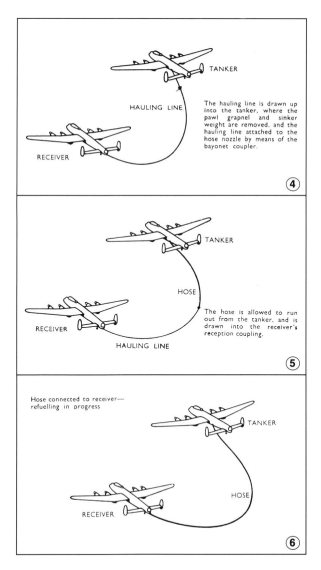

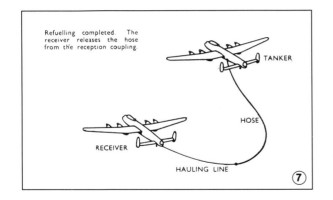

Refuelling completed. The receiver releases the hose from the reception coupling.

TANKER

HOSE

RECEIVER

HAULING LINE

(7)

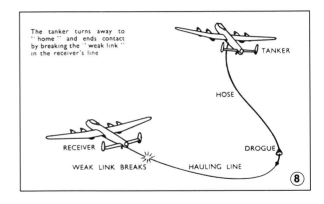

The tanker turns away to "home" and ends contact by breaking the "weak link" in the receiver's line

TANKER

HOSE

RECEIVER

DROGUE

WEAK LINK BREAKS

HAULING LINE

(8)

APPENDIX II

TWO 'HIGH SPEED' BOMBER PROPOSALS

Two 'high speed' bomber proposals, each capable of being refuelled in flight, were submitted for consideration by the Air Ministry.

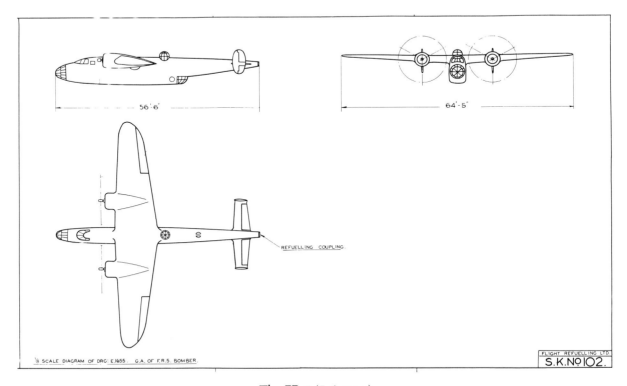

56'-6"

64'-5"

REFUELLING COUPLING

⅛ SCALE DIAGRAM OF DRG: E.1655.   G.A. OF F.R.5. BOMBER.

FLIGHT REFUELLING LTD.
S.K. No 102.

The FR 5 (5-6 crew)

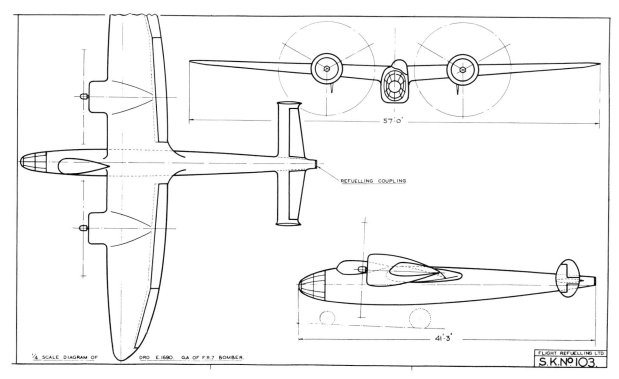

The FR 7 (2 crew)

Within the diagram:

¼ SCALE DIAGRAM OF   DRG. E.1690.   G.A. OF F.R.7 BOMBER.

57′·0″

41′·3″

REFUELLING COUPLING

FLIGHT REFUELLING LTD
S.K. N° 103.

APPENDIX III

PROPOSALS FOR AIRLINERS OPERATING OVER THE NORTH ATLANTIC

During the middle and late Forties, FRL produced several proposals for airliners capable of operating over the North Atlantic if refuelled in flight. The general arrangement drawings reproduced below were contained in contemporary reports issued to the Ministry of Civil Aviation.

TABLE 1

Data produced in November 1945 shows main particulars of flight-refuelled airliners proposed by FRL.

Type No.	F.R.10	F.R.11	F.R.12
Engines	4 R.R. Merlin, 14 sm	6 R.R. 14 sm	6 Bristol Centaurus 57
Passenger capacity –			
Sleeping	20	50	100
Seated	40	100	134
Component Weights, etc.			
Gross weight, lb	70,000	117,000	185,200
Passenger load, lb	3,500	8,750	17,000
Freight load, normal, lb	4,100	8.550	14,200
Total payload, lb	7,600 (10.85 per cent)	17,300 (14.96 per cent)	31,200 (16.84 per cent)
Structure weight, lb	21,430 (30.64 per cent)	34,800 (29.86 per cent)	63,285 (34.17 per cent)
Power plant weight, lb	13,400 (19.15 per cent)	22,650 (19.44 per cent)	30,760 (16.62 per cent)
Disposable weight, lb	25,849 (36.93 per cent	42,860 (36.80 per cent)	68,575 (37.03 per cent)
Fuel capacity, gallons	2,000	2,850	4,600
Main Dimensions.			
Span, ft	120	150	195
Length, ft	99	129	146
Wing area, sq ft	1,450	2,340	3,800
Aspect rates	10.0	9.62	10.0
Wing loading, lb/sq ft	48.25	50.0	49.0
Brief Performances.			
Maximum speed, m.p.h.	322	310	300
Cruising speed, m.p.h.	235	257	242
Landing speed m.p.h.	81	83	82
Maximum range, miles	2,400	2,400	2,320 at 242 m.p.h.
Take off to 50 yds	1,000	1,110	1,438
Power loading, lb/b.h.p.	10.5	11.7	12.25

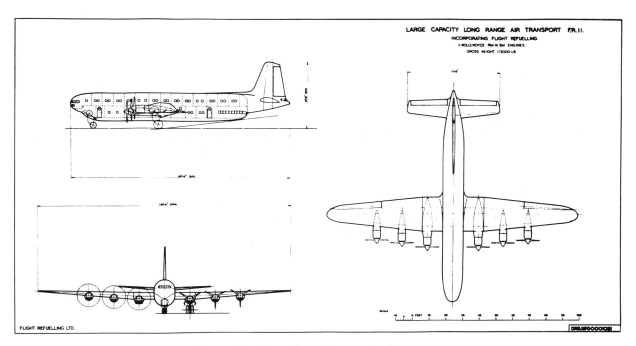

Fig. 1. The FR 11 Long Range Air Transport.

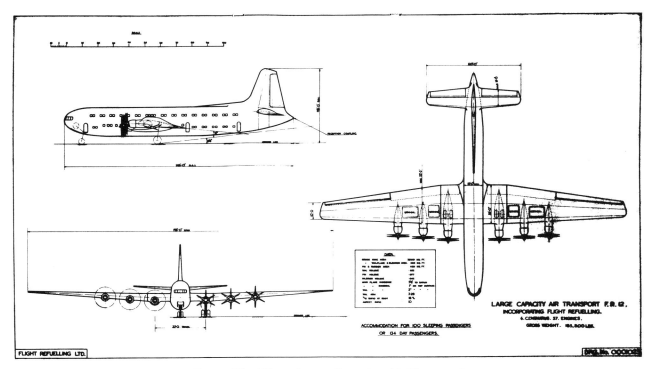

Fig. 2. The FR 12 Large Capacity Air Transport.

TABLE 2

Data produced in September 1948 shows salient features of a later series of flight-refuelled airliners.

	F.R. 13	F.R. 14	F.R. 15	F.R. 16
Max. all up weight	95,190 lb	101,450 lb	109,500 lb	94,000 lb
Weight empty	56,260 llb	55,600 lb	48,430 lb	58,110 lb
Equipped weight + crew	58,090 lb	57,430 lb	50,260 lb	59,980 lb
Max. fuel weight	22,000 lb	30,000 lb	45,895 lb	19,280 lb
Normal payload	13,300 lb	13,300 lb	13,300 lb	13,300 lb
Wing span	126 ft 4 in	126 ft 4 in	126 ft 4 in	126 ft 4 in
Length	105 ft	105 ft	105 ft	105 ft
Height to top of fin	34 ft 6 in	34 ft 6 in	32 ft 2 in	34 ft
Wing area	1,566 sq ft	1,566 sq ft	1,566 sq ft	1,566 sq ft
Max. wing loading	60.7 lb/sq ft	64.7 lb/sq ft	70 lb/sq ft	60 lb/sq ft
Engines	4 Bristol "Centaurus" 663	4 Gas turbines	4 Jet engines	4 Compound engines
T.O. power TOTAL	11,240 H.P.	13,520 E.B.H.P.	26,000 lb Thrust	12,480 E.B.H.P.
Max. speed at height	360 m.p.h. at 20,000 ft (W.M.)	430 m.p.h. at 25,000 ft (5 min) 390 m.p.h. at 25,000 ft	560 m.p.h. at 30,000 ft (approx)	418 m.p.h. at 25,000 ft
Const speed cruising	315 m.p.h. at 20,000 ft	365 m.p.h. at 25,000 ft	460 m.p.h. at 30,000 ft	316 m.p.h. at 25,000 ft
Range at const. speed	3,180 st.m.	3,340 st.m.	2,900 st.m.	3,450 st.m.

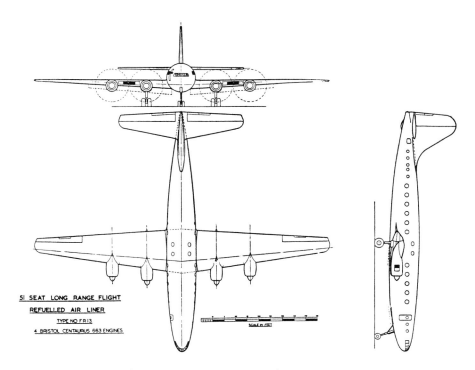

Fig. 3. The FR 13 Long Range Airliner – 4 Piston Engines.

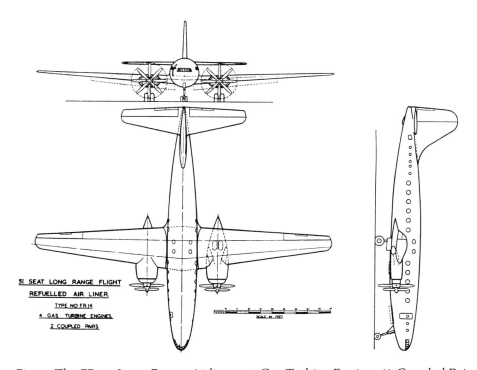

Fig. 4. The FR 14 Long Range Airliner – 4 Gas Turbine Engines (2 Coupled Pairs).

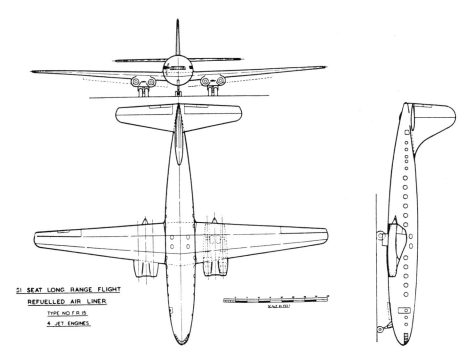

Fig. 5. The FR 15 Long Range Airliner – 4 Jet Engines.

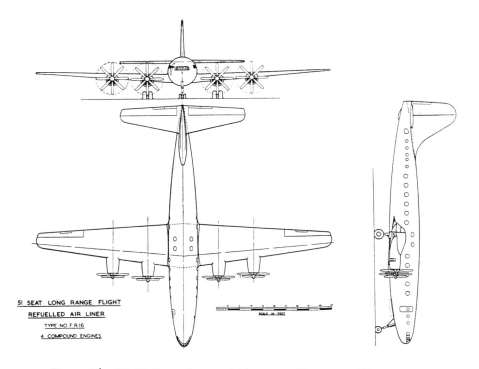

Fig. 6. The FR 16 Long Range Airliner – 4 Compound Engines.

APPENDIX IV

THE BERLIN AIRLIFT

Flight Refuelling Ltd's performance during the Berlin Airlift, 27th July 1948 to 10th August 1949.

1. Total amount of fuel carried, 6,975,021 gallons
2. Total flight time, 11,627.21 hours
3. Total distance flown ,1,714,596 statute miles (equivalent to sixty-nine times around the world)
4. Maximum number of staff retained to meet peak commitment, including 32 complete aircrews: 652 at Tarrant Rushton, 205 at Hamburg, plus 30 German nationals.
5. Peak Utilization Factor per Aircraft Day was 4.15 sorties, which was the highest recorded for any type, British or American.

TYPE	REGISTRATION	SORTIES	HOURS	TONNAGE	REMARKS
Lancaster	G-AGWL	361	881.25	2,422.6	
Lancaster	G-AHJU	438	1,175.59	2,429.1	
Lancaster	G-AHJW	40	130.20	221.0	Crashed near Andover 22.11.48
Lancastrian	G-AGWI	226	597.14	1,381.0	
Lancastrian	G-AHVN	279	657.28	1,586.1	
Lancastrian	G-AKDO	431	1,141.02	2,683.0	
Lancastrian	G-AKDP	378	1,053.53	2,216.9	Force-landed Russian Zone 10.5.49
Lancastrian	G-AKDR	526	1,472.04	3,070.1	
Lancastrian	G-AKDS	480	1,305.31	2,784.5	
Lancastrian	G-AKFF	449	1,129.14	3,022.5	
Lancastrian	G-AKFG	439	1,099.38	2,943.0	
Lancastrian	G-AKTB	391	985.33	2,354.8	
	TOTALS	4,438	11,627.21	27,114.6	

APPENDIX V

CORRESPONDENCE CONCERNING TARRANT RUSHTON AIRFIELD

This amusing correspondence relating to the accuracy of published data concerning
Tarrant Rushton Airfield took place in 1953.

<u>COPY</u>

G.R.

From:- No. 1 A.I.D. Unit, Royal Air Force, Ruislip.

To:- The S.A.T.C.O. Air Traffic Control, Tarrant Rushton.

Date:- 28th April, 1953.

Ref:- AID/1010/45/EAV

<u>APPROACH AND LANDING CHARTS:- ELEVATION</u>

It has been brought to our notice by Air Ministry,
Works 8, who operate in conjunction with Ministry of
Civil Aviation that during a recent survey the elevation
of Tarrant Rushton differs from the one printed in
pilots Handbook.

The elevation as printed is 300, whilst that of
the Survey Team is 301ft.

It is therefore requested that you confirm one or
the other of these elevations, and inform this unit
accordingly.

(Sgd.) C.D. HALLETT P/O
for Squadron Leader, Commanding,
No. 1 A.I.D. Unit, Ruislip.

From:- Royal Air Force, Tarrant Rushton.

To:- No. 1 A.I.D. Unit, Royal Air Force, Ruislip.

Date:- 15th May, 1953.

Ref:- GRM/55/Air

APPROACH AND LANDING CHARTS – ELEVATION OF TARRANT RUSHTON AIRFIELD

1.   Reference is made to your AID/1010/345/NAV dated 28th April, 1953, requesting confirmation of one of the alternatives, 300 or 301 feet as the correct elevation of the above-mentioned airfield.

2.   It is pointed out that, owing to the sinusoidal characteristics of the runways, temperature changes throughout the year cause the elevation of the touch-down points to vary from their mean values roughly in accordance with the equation

$$d = \pm \, 6'' \cos 2 \pi t$$

where 'd' is the vertical displacement from the mean position in inches and 't' is the epoch in fractions of a year measured from the average date of maximum displacement due to low temperature.   This date is fixed as 14th February.   The plus or minus sign depends on whether the touch-down position is above or below the mean elevation on that date.   (Owing to the thermal inertia of runways, diurnal variations are tentatively considered negligible.)

3.   It will be seen from the above equation that the total range of elevation of the runways is one foot, neglecting very slow secular changes consequential upon Weber's Theory of Continental Drift, and it is advanced that this difference possibly accounts for the ambiguity in the elevations recorded.

4.   The operational aspect, however, must not be ignored and attention is directed to the following facts regarding the use of the current standard height reference instrument of the Royal Air Force: viz, the Mark XIV Sensitive Altimeter:-

   (a) This instrument is calibrated to an average atmosphere (the I.C.A.N. atmosphere) and prevailing weather conditions can, and in fact often do, cause departures from the standard which, in turn, causes the true altitude to differ from that indicated by more than one foot.

   (b) Furthermore, the face of this instrument is not graduated to read so small an interval as one foot.

(c) Finally, even if the above two points were eliminated as factors in the case - a most unlikely contingency - there is no pilot who can fly an aircraft within a height band of a thickness of one foot.

5.   In addition, your attention is directed to the 1:500,000 scale map of Southern England and Wales, G.S.G.S. 4072, first edition, with air information as at May, 1951, supplied by the Ministry of Defence, J.I.B.5, wherein it is written that the height of Tarrant Rushton airfield is 255 feet.

6.   In view of the foregoing, therefore, and the fact that there is in any event a variation of 60 feet between the highest and lowest points on the airfield, it is humbly and yet quite confidently submitted that not even the most pernickety of pilots, either service or civilian, would be unduly concerned over a possible error of 12 inches in the advertised height of Tarrant Rushton Aerodrome.

7.   If however it is maintained that an error of 12 inches in the published height of the airfield constitutes a hazard to the safe operation of aircraft from Tarrant Rushton, it is recommended, in order to save the taxpayer the cost of a further and more comprehensive survey, that the greater height i.e. 301 feet be accepted as standard.

(Sgd.) D.F. HYLAND-SMITH.
Wing Commander,
for Officer Commanding,
Royal Air Force, Tarrant Rushton.

Bibliography

Blake, J. and Hooks, M. *40 Years of Farnborough* (1990)
Bramson, A. and Birch, N. *The Tiger Moth Story* (1964)
Chant, C. *B29 Superfortress Super Profile* (1983)
Cobham, A. *A Time to Fly* (1978)
Dawson, L. *Wings Over Dorset* (1983)
de Havilland, G. *Sky Fever*
Delve, K., Green, P. and Clemons, J. *English Electric Canberra* (1992)
Gardner, B. *Skytanker: The Story of Air-to-Air Refuelling* 1985)
Gardner, B. *Wartime Refuelling Projects* (1984)
Gardner, B. *Air Refuelling in the RAF* (1986)
Hesketh, J. *No. 55 Squadron History* (1993)
Hesketh, J. *No. 55 Squadron and the history of the Victor* (1993)
Hobson, C. *75 Years of Excellence – No. 101 Squadron* (1992)
Langley, M. *Refuelling In Flight* (1939)
Latimer-Needham, C. *The Flight Refuelled Bomber* (1950)
Querzani, J. *Royal Air Force – Lyneham* (1993)
Ransom, S. and Fairclough, R. *English Electric Aircraft* (1987)
Rippon, P. and Mottram, G. *Yeovilton* (1990)
Rodrigo, R. *The Berlin Airlift* (1960)
Tanner, R. *Seventy Years of Aerial Refuelling* (to be published 1995)

Selected Index

Notes

1. The section devoted to aircraft has been kept as simple as possible, and only takes account of basic type designations to cover the many variants referred to in the main text, eg KB-29T is included under the broad heading of B-29. Certain types have also been listed under the original constructor's name, eg Buccaneer appears under 'Blackburn', not 'Hawker Siddeley' or 'BAe'.

2. Sir Alan Cobham, Michael Cobham, and Flight Refuelling Ltd appear so frequently throughout the text that individual index references have purposely been omitted.

3. The author expresses his grateful thanks to Cobham plc's PR team, Roger Smart, Alison Dean and, especially, Carole Hewitson for the welcome and timely assistance given in compiling this index.

PERSONNEL

COMPANIES AND ESTABLISHMENTS

AIRCRAFT – MISSILES – TARGETS